CHARLES WILLIAMS

SELECTED WRITINGS

CHARLES WILLIAMS

SELECTED WRITINGS

CHOSEN BY

ANNE RIDLER

LONDON
OXFORD UNIVERSITY PRESS
1961

Oxford University Press, Amen House, London E.C.4

GLASGOW NEW YORK TORONTO MELBOURNE WELLINGTON
BOMBAY CALCUTTA MADRAS KARACHI KUALA LUMPUR
CAPE TOWN IBADAN NAIROBI ACCRA

FIRST ISSUED IN OXFORD PAPERBACKS 1961

PRINTED IN GREAT BRITAIN

PREFACE

THIS selection from the writings of Charles Williams (1886–1945) is intended as an introduction to his work, and therefore tries to represent him at his best and most characteristic in all the forms in which he wrote except that of fiction. He was a writer of most varied talents, and since every part of his work illuminates the rest, it follows that the more you read him, the better you understand him. But it is not necessary to understand his thought fully in order to catch fire from it, and it can be approached equally well through his religious or his literary writings.

The criticism in this selection is taken from *The English Poetic Mind*, first published in 1932 and now out of print. For reasons of length it was only possible to include the chapters on Milton and on Wordsworth, and the editor much regrets the omission of the long chapter on 'The Cycle of Shakespeare'.

Seed of Adam was chosen to represent Williams's drama, rather than the full-length *Thomas Cranmer of Canterbury*, which is already available in a cheap edition.[1] *Seed of Adam* is described as a Nativity Play, but the reader who approaches it with his memory stored with Christmas tableaux, night-gowned angels, and hirsute Josephs, is in for a surprise.

The religious essays, which were not collected together in Williams's lifetime, are taken from *The Image of the City*, published in 1958. They contain Williams's teaching on the Incarnation of Christ, on the relationship of men to each other and to God, and on the Atonement. The splendid essay on the Cross has been found by many people to contain the heart of all his teaching, and 'The Way of Exchange' explains the doctrine which he described as 'substituted love', and of which he wrote in his novel *Descent into Hell*.

Last, the poems. These are all taken from the cycle on the Arthurian myths,[2] published towards the end of Williams's life, although his earlier poems—especially those in the

[1] *Four Modern Verse Plays*, introduced and edited by E. Martin Browne (Penguin Books).

[2] *Taliessin Through Logres*, O.U.P.

volume called *Windows of Night*—are well worth study. The poems chosen are those which are related to the central themes, but it is to be hoped that the reader who first meets them here will go on to read the whole cycle so far as it was completed. The selection has this advantage, that it is prefaced by Williams's own commentary on his re-creation of the myth—fragmentary, but still the most helpful introduction we can have. The first piece is taken from his unfinished prose book on the Arthurian legends, which was edited by Professor C. S. Lewis after Williams's death with the title of *Arthurian Torso*. The second piece is an article contributed to the *Dublin Review* and reprinted, with other prose writings on the subject of Arthur, in *The Image of the City*. After certain preliminaries, it takes up the discussion at the point (the tournament of Lonazep) where the *Torso* ended, so that the two pieces can be read as one commentary. The reader who has followed this account can begin to see the myth through Williams's eyes, and if he then goes on to the poems, attentive to receive their intellectual power and beauty rather than worried by what is obscure to him, he is made free of a rich world, a world that is strange but not remote, because it has much to tell him of his own condition.

ANNE RIDLER

ACKNOWLEDGEMENTS

Acknowledgements are due to the proprietors of *Theology*, the *Dublin Review*, and *St. Martin's Review*.

CONTENTS

CRITICISM

I

A NOTE ON GREAT POETRY[1]

THE word 'poetry' is generally used in one of two senses. It either means the whole mass of amusing and delightful stuff written in verse, or it is restricted to those greater lines, stanzas, or poems which are comparatively rare even in the work of the great poets. There is no certain method of deciding on these last, except by personal experience (which is not quite reliable) or by authority—the judgement of sensitive readers over many years. There is no way of discovering how the thing is done, nor exactly how a great line produces its effect. But it is to some extent possible to see what the difference is between the lesser kind of verse and the greater.

Wordsworth in the *Prelude* (I. 149–57), defines three things as necessary for the writing of poetry. They are (i) 'the vital soul', (ii) 'general truths', (iii) 'external things—Forms, images'. With these possessions in himself he feels prepared for his own 'arduous work'. The distinction exists for the reader as well. The third necessity ('aids Of less regard') is an obvious part of most poetry: it includes metaphors, similes, comparisons; even the story, and the persons in narrative or dramatic verse or the hypothetical speaker, the individual poet, in lyric. These things are 'needful to build up a poet's praise', and at their most exquisite they play an important part in the whole. But the greatest poetry can exist without them. 'A rose-red city, half as old as Time' is a lovely line. It stops at being that.

'General truths'—'subordinate helpers of the living mind' —on the other hand, though more important, are less reliable aids: for they have a way of pretending to be the living mind, the 'vital soul' itself. Some of the poets—Longfellow, Tenny-

[1] This and the following three chapters are taken from *The English Poetic Mind*, first published in 1932. [A. R.]

son, Wordsworth himself—appear occasionally to have thought they were writing poetry when they were merely communicating general truths, or what appeared to them to be so. The *Excursion*, as opposed to the *Prelude*, gives examples of this; although even the *Excursion*, if a reader will only accept the conditions it postulates, as he is ready to accept the plot of *King Lear*, may turn out to be a better poem than is often supposed. Perhaps, however, such a couplet as Hamlet's yields the best example of general truths, which, adequately expressed, delight us almost as much by rational as by poetic strength—

> Imperious Caesar, dead and turned to clay,
> Might stop a hole to keep the wind away.

But what then is the 'vital soul', without which the forms and images and general truths lack something? It is 'genius'; it is 'poetry'. But that takes us no farther. It cannot be merely the relation of labials and gutturals, or the play of stresses and pauses. These are, in another shape, the 'forms and images'. It cannot be the diction—however exact or unexpected; that is but a general truth. All such things are 'subordinate helpers of the living mind', which must itself use them for its own purpose. What does that mind do in *Hyperion* which it does not do in *Horatius*? Why is Pope a greater poet than Prior or Praed?

Poetry, one way or another, is 'about' human experience; there is nothing else that it can be about. But to whatever particular human experience it alludes, it is not that experience. Love poetry is poetry, not love; patriotic poetry is poetry, not patriotism; religious poetry is poetry, not religion. But good poetry does something more than allude to its subject; it is related to it, and it relates us to it.

> Through the sad heart of Ruth when, sick for home,
> She stood in tears amid the alien corn:

those lines relate us to an experience of exile. They awake in us a sense of exile; more accurately, a realization of our own capacity for enduring exile.

> Let this immortal life, where'er it comes,
> Walk in a cloud of loves and martyrdoms;

that awakes in us—not certainly love and sacrifice, or love and sacrifice would be easier things than they seem to be. But it does awake a sense that we are capable of love and sacrifice. It reminds us of a certain experience, and by its style it awakes a certain faculty for that experience. We are told of a thing; we are made to feel as if that thing were possible to us; and we are so made to feel it—whatever the thing may be, joy or despair or what not—that our knowledge is an intense satisfaction to us; and this knowledge and this satisfaction are for some period of time complete and final; and this knowledge, satisfaction, and finality are all conveyed through the medium of words, the concord of which is itself a delight to the senses. This sensuous apprehension of our satisfied capacities for some experience or other is poetry of the finest kind.

Lesser verse does not do so much. It may remind us that we have some capacity or other, but it does not communicate a delighted sense of it, nor therefore can it join that sense to the equally delighted sense of words. *The Armada* is, in its way, an exciting and pleasing piece of writing. But it does not arouse in us a sense of our capacity for staunch patriotism; it excites by reminding us that there is a capacity for staunch patriotism.

Bolingbroke in *Richard II* talks very beautifully about exile. But we are much more inclined to think as we read, 'That is how I should like to talk if I were ever exiled'; we are reminded of our capacity for beautifully expressing our grief at exile rather than of our capacity for suffering exile—that is with Ruth more than with Bolingbroke. Horatius confronting Lars Porsena, FitzJames confronting Roderick Dhu, do not convey a sense of man's capacity for heroism; they at most remind us that man has a capacity for heroism.

> Round turned he, as not deigning
> Those heathen ranks to see;
> Naught spake he to Lars Porsena,
> To Sextus naught spake he.

How jolly to behave like that! The pretence of such behaviour is agreeably invoked by those admirable lines. For they are, in their degree, admirable; it is another, and a moral, question how far we allow them to deceive us: they do not try to. They thrill us, and thrills are good, only one cannot live by thrills. But

> So spake the Seraph Abdiel, faithful found,
> Among the faithless faithful only he;
> Among innumerable false unmoved,
> Unshaken, unseduced, unterrified.

It would not be so easy to behave like *that*. Our capacity for heroism is stirred—or at least our desire for, our recognition of, that capacity. But can we desire or recognize something of which we are *entirely* incapable? 'Hadst thou not found me, thou couldst not be seeking me', said Christ to one of the mystics; and the same thing is true of the faculties awakened by poetry.

Certainly this awakening, this communication, is rather a result than a motive. Tolstoy declared that art existed wherever there was a conscious communication of emotion. Tolstoy was a great man and a great novelist; but we must not stress that admirable definition as if the poet primarily, in the very definition of his work, demanded an audience. If it is so, then our sensation that the great things of poetry exist purely and simply in their own right, and independently of man, is false. It may be; sensations are doubtful things and prove nothing unless we choose that they shall. But, putting that choice aside, it is surely true that the chief impulse of a poet is, not to communicate a thing to others, but to shape a thing, to make an immortality for its own sake. He often writes from other motives, no doubt; Pope probably wished to communicate his emotions about Addison, and Shelley his about the death of Keats. But did Keats really want first of all to communicate his emotions about a Nightingale? or Shakespeare his about Macbeth? Did Shakespeare primarily want to make *us* feel what a murderer's heart was like? It is inconceivable; he primarily wanted that heart to be.

Certainly if no one, no one *ever*, reads a poet, if no one cares for him, he may leave off writing. But that is the weakness of his nature, as Milton said. Fame is 'the last infirmity of noble mind'. Infirmity. But a poet might be content to communicate anonymously? Even so, he wants his work to produce a social effect. Does the poet, *qua* poet, care whether his work has a social effect? *Incredibile; nec crediderim nisi Tolstoy*—and not even then.

But, leaving this dispute and returning to the nature of poetry, we come to a further division. If it is true that the minor poets describe heroism or love or exile or what not, and the major poets arouse in us an actual sense of our own faculties for heroism and love and exile, what of the greatest? If the Marlowes are greater than the Macaulays, why are the Miltons greater still? What is it that makes us instinctively introduce the idea of relative values?

In so far as the poets can be hierarchized, it can only be done by two classifications (i) quantity, (ii) quality. The smallest poet who has written one good line—say, Dean Burgon, with his 'rose-red city'—is, so far, equal to any other poet who has written a good line—even Shakespeare. He arouses in us a capacity of enjoying a particular picture, by placing a picture before us which we do actually enjoy. It is delightful to have such a thing in our minds—and that is that. We are obliged—deeply obliged—by the Dean, but if he can only provide us with one picture whereas some other poet can provide us with twenty, we must regard the second poet as more important for us; unless we have a peculiar passion for rose-red cities.

But quality is more important, and the question of quality very soon becomes a question of complexity. Of the development of that poetic complexity this book is meant to be a small consideration, and there is no need to forestall it here. The rose-red city becomes inhabited by human emotions, and its poetry disappears under the stress of theirs. In turn the single poignant utterances give place to lines which sum up states of involved experience. Such lines may in themselves appear to draw nearer to or to pass farther from the complexity which they describe. But either way they are aware of it, whether in increase or decrease. The decrease is a decrease from something that has been. Neither increase nor decrease is better than the other; they are merely two poetic methods of dealing with very profound and almost universal apprehensions of our faculties of experience. 'Absent thee from felicity awhile' is a very great and complex line; it has two worlds of experience in it; it calls up the whole idea of, the whole of our capacity for, felicity only to meet it with our capacity for rejection, and it unifies, it prolongs, both ideas in the 'awhile'. If Hamlet had been asking Horatio to reject felicity for ever, if he had wanted him to be quite final about it, we should have had a very different line, and one which implied a decrease of complexity. 'Life is a tale . . . signifying nothing' tends towards a decrease of complexity. But it must be allowed also that it implies the complexity it leaves behind; the word 'signifying' with its multitudinous associations does that. Compare the words 'awhile' and 'nothing' and you have the two different states towards which the greatest poetry tends. Satan in *Paradise Lost* remains a highly charged and complex figure. But Lear is becoming a transmuted and simple figure.

Our capacities then for some sort of general experience of the world are awakened by the greater masters. As far as poetry is concerned it does not matter what that capacity is: Macbeth is as poetically effective as Samson. Both express our sense of a faculty for taking in many experiences as a whole, for knowing and enjoying them, for knowing and enjoying them in the exquisite sensuous delight of words. Anybody who can cause us to do that is a great poet.

II

'THE GROWTH OF A POET'S MIND'

THERE is in English poetry only one long study of the poetic mind. That study is the *Prelude or the Growth of a Poet's Mind*. 'A Poet' to most readers means Wordsworth; to Wordsworth himself it would certainly have meant Wordsworth. But in the course of that account he describes at least one crisis which has been treated, in a very different way, both by Shakespeare and Milton, which has been approached by other poets and avoided by yet others. It seems worthwhile, therefore, to note once more, very briefly, the chief points in that growth and development, in order that its most important moment may be kept clearly in mind. Most of the books upon the *Prelude* consider it in relation to Wordsworth, and Wordsworth too often in relation to Nature, the sensationalist philosophy, Godwinism, and mysticism. He is comparatively rarely considered as a poet whose value lies in, and only in, the poems he writes—not in what he means by them. The *Prelude* has yet to be fully considered in relation to general poetry, and that would probably best be done by an edition of the poem annotated for that purpose with parallel passages from other poets. The present quotations are rather reminders of themselves than evidence of any theory. Wordsworth wrote the *Prelude* as a prelude, an account of his own preparation for what he was about to do; it was to invigorate him, to 'fix the wavering balance' of his mind, to 'spur' him on. It is therefore largely an account of his own experiences, and those experiences were for him 'Nature' and Man. He was inclined to stress the necessity of 'Nature' for poets; he sympathizes with Coleridge for not having had his own advantages, for being 'debarred from Nature's living images', and regrets that his influence had not soothed Coleridge's youthful unhappiness. But the times at which Wordsworth's own personal opinions enter into the *Prelude* are fairly clear, and we need not take those periods too seriously. The authority of poetry is only present when great poetry is present; poetry in the *Prelude* is never far away, but it is not always active.

It is Wordsworth's personal opinion—he offers it as his 'best conjecture'—that the poetic spirit is natural to every man. The passage in the 1805–6 version is more metaphysical than in the 1850. There it is explained that the Babe, gathering 'passion from his Mother's eye', is eager to combine 'in one appearance' all the apparently detached elements and parts of 'the same object'. The baby, one gathers, having vaguely realized that his mother is unity, is anxious to recognize unity in every object. This 'conjecture' Wordsworth afterwards removed, but it remains of interest for it suggests how the sensational apprehension of completeness in one being excites the poetic mind to see such a completeness in other separate objects. Each one is separate, yet each is complete, each is a whole. This is the first small result of that power which works afterwards to create in poetry 'Composure and ennobling Harmony'.

Secondly, from its sense of its mother, from its 'most apprehensive habitude', and from the 'sensations which have been derived' from its knowledge of its mother—from all these the baby derives 'a virtue which irradiates and exalts' all other objects. Its mind already works 'in alliance' with the works which it beholds; it is at once creator and receiver. It is these two characteristics which mark the small poet—(*a*) its passion for unifying, (*b*) its powers and quickness to co-operate with 'the active universe'. But this 'first poetic spirit' is, in most, afterwards 'abated or suppressed'; in some it is 'pre-eminent till death'. These last presumably are the poets —the poets and the poetry to whom Wordsworth so often applies the words 'Powers' and 'Power'. For example: of books and their writers (v. 218)

> speak of them as Powers
> For ever to be hallowed;

Of words in tuneful order (v. 556),

> sweet
> For their own sake, a passion, and a power;

Of the shell that was poetry (v. 107),

> The other that was a god, yea, many gods,
> Had voices more than all the winds, with power;

and so also (v. 595):

> Visionary power
> Attends the motions of the viewless winds,
> Embodied in the mystery of words.

Of imagination (vi. 592)

> here the Power so called,
> Through sad incompetence of human speech,
> That awful Power, rose from the mind's abyss:

and there are other instances.

This Power, Wordsworth held, was of the first importance to man. He left the statement unaltered, or, if anything, slightly enforced, through all the modifications of the *Prelude*. Some things he unsaid, but *that* he never unsaid. In Book V is the vision of the Arab, carrying geometry and poetry, escaping on a camel from the deluge and the floods that are to destroy mankind; and to this vision Wordsworth says that he often deliberately returned, consciously changing the Arab to a 'gentle dweller in the desert', seized with a noble madness; consciously regarding him and his quest of salvation for poetry with reverence, and identifying himself with him. In such a madness, such a dream, is reason. There are enough people on earth to take in charge

> Their wives, their children, and their virgin loves,
> Or whatsoever else the heart holds dear.

Wordsworth himself, in such a catastrophe will, with his own dreamed fanatic, abandon everything else to save poetry.

This, for the solemn, the conventional, Wordsworth is pretty good going; and might make us wonder whether we have not overmuch subdued that violent young poet who wrote 'we murder to dissect'. But it fits in very well with the continual use of the word 'power'. It is in that power which is poetry that 'darkness makes abode'; it is in poetry that 'forms and substances'

> through the turnings intricate of verse
> Present themselves as objects recognized,
> In flashes, and with glory not their own.

In the first version he had written 'scarce their own'; he gave to poetry in the last version a complete dominion. 'Woods and rills', 'fountains, meadows, hills and groves', are not to speak to us in poetry with their own authority. Wordsworth in fact was not ever writing a child's primer of Nature-mysticism; he left that to his commentators. He was himself concerned with the Nature 'that exists in works of mighty poets', with glory not its own.

It is then to such a future that the baby (already

> powerful in all sentiments of grief
> Of exultation, fear and joy)

is introduced. In certain fortunate cases, in the poets, this 'sensibility' is augmented and sustained, and the two great fostering virtues are 'beauty and fear'. These two themes run all through the *Prelude*, though for beauty is more often substituted the word joy. But it is a joy which is caused by beauty. And fear is, in Wordsworth, an emotion absolutely necessary to the poet's development: he stresses it continually. When he is speaking of the modern child, whom he did not like, he complains that

> natural or supernatural fear,
> Unless it leap upon him in a dream,
> Touches him not.

It is not a mere physical fear; it is indeed something which precludes this lesser terror. The example which he gives is his own experience, at the age of eight, when he saw the body of a dead man drawn up from Esthwaite Lake, 'a spectre shape Of terror'. But he, whose 'inner eye' had often seen such things before, in fairy-tales and romances, was unsubdued, and beheld it patterned and harmonized, decorated with 'ideal grace', and dignified as if already in poetry.

The kind of fear which he believed the young mind ought to undergo, and from which he thought modern education was separating it by over-anxious vigilance, protection, and instruction, is described in the two most famous passages of the First Book. The one tells how, after he had stolen a trapped bird from someone else's snare, he heard

> Low breathings coming after me, and sounds
> Of undistinguishable motion, steps
> Almost as silent as the turf they trod.

The second is when he had (again!) stolen someone else's boat, rowed out on the lake, and seen the huge peak, 'as if with voluntary power instinct'.

> After I had seen
> That spectacle, for many days, my brain
> Worked with a dim and undetermined sense
> Of unknown modes of being; o'er my thoughts
> There hung a darkness, call it solitude
> Or blank desertion. No familiar shapes
> Remained, no pleasant images of trees,
> Of sea or sky, no colours of green fields;
> But huge and mighty forms, that do not live
> Like living men, moved slowly through the mind
> By day, and were a trouble to my dreams.

The second passage is an enlargement of the first, and they are both great poetry. The poetic mind is aware of 'low breathings', 'sounds of undistinguishable motion', 'unknown modes of being', 'huge and mighty forms'. It is the pressure of the genius on the outer consciousness; this also perhaps is common to men.

But the poets are not content to leave it at that, as the rest of us largely have to do. An undetermined sense of unknown modes of being may be with them at their commencement, as with all of us. The difference in our developments is between those who lose that sense altogether (this is probably what is called 'losing one's early illusions'), those who keep it but cannot of themselves deal with it (among these are perhaps most of the readers of poetry), and those who are able to do something about it—and these are the poets. For their business is to discover and express, more and more exactly, more and more powerfully, those unknown modes of being. They work towards 'the two great ends of Liberty and Power'. Between those two passages are lines which may well have a secondary relation to the growing poetic genius.

> Dust as we are, the immortal spirit grows
> Like harmony in music; there is a dark
> Inscrutable workmanship that reconciles
> Discordant elements, makes them cling together
> In one society.

This is precisely the achievement of the great poets; in each of them discordant elements are united in one society by the inscrutable workmanship of their genius, and the society is the style.

But in the earlier period this unison is not yet consciously present. All things have the character 'of danger or desire'.

> The surface of the universal earth
> With triumph and delight, with hope and fear,

works 'like a sea'. For Wordsworth it was 'the Presence of Nature' which brought this about, but it need not be only his kind of Nature to which such a disturbance is due; cities and men may produce it also.

There ensues on this a kind of personal determination by the poet. He encourages himself; he subjects himself at every opportunity to the experiences in which he discerns this power; in effect, he takes care that his soul 'is unsubdued' by the world. Wordsworth described himself as becoming attentive to the details of the things he observed, their 'transitory qualities'. But also he breathed in moods 'by form Or image unprofaned', moods in which 'visionary power' came to him. Visionary power here is identified with 'shadowy exultation'. Such moods are of use to the soul—to the poetic genius—because the memories of them teach it *how* it felt; they provide it with a sense of possible sublimity

> whereto
> With growing faculties she doth aspire,
> With faculties still growing, feeling still
> That whatsoever point they gain, they yet
> Have something to pursue.

This is the labour of poetry; this is the very sense which attends on the writing of poetry. This 'something to pursue' is the something which lures and provokes the great poets into their greatness. The 'sublimity' of their experiences is the height to which they desire their analysing and synthesizing poetry to reach, and the infinite by which they measure their achievements.

But the poetic sense is still very much under the domination of the poet's personal enjoyments. The subjects of his contemplation receive part of their effect from his own mind. Wordsworth says

> What I saw
> Appeared like something in myself, a dream,
> A prospect in the mind.

The mind in fact imposes its own enjoyment on outer things; the sun, the birds, the wind, the fountain, the storm, appeared much more like themselves because Wordsworth willed them to be, and he derived increased transport from this knowledge. He coerced 'all things into sympathy'. Unless, intoxicated by his own feelings, he could feel 'the sentiment of Being spread o'er all', he was not perfectly contented. The young romantic poet, the young and violent Wordsworth, insisted on sending 'the fleshly ear' to sleep. It was natural; it was romantic. Even Milton had his *L'Allegro* and *Il Penseroso*—and everything in each of those great poetic gardens was lovely.

In the Third Book this process continues. The poetic mind is still imposing its own world on the world.

> I had a world about me—'twas my own;
> I made it, for it only lived to me,
> And to the God who sees into the heart.

But with this imposed unity went a no less strong sense of observed diversity. The strongest workings of his genius at that time were 'searching out the lines of difference'. It is at this point that Wordsworth exclaims in awe at the youthful might of 'souls'. He again attributes this power to every man: all do things 'within themselves' while earth is new. This is the 'genuine prowess' communicated from the point within the mind where each is single, from the poetic centre.

Nevertheless, in the new world of Cambridge this

imagination for a while rests, except in its concern with mythology. It seeks the apprehension of antiquity and the powers of antiquity—Newton, Chaucer, Spenser, Milton; and by a natural but regrettable transition Wordsworth for some time leaves off talking of the creative soul and goes on to talk of William Wordsworth, Universities, Presidents, and Deans. It is not till he (symbolically) returns to 'his native hills' that he begins again to be interesting. The Fourth Book contains the famous dedication episode, but it is led up to by a warning of a change in apprehension. Something opens which Wordsworth calls 'human-heartedness'. Objects which have hitherto been 'the absolute wealth of his own private being' now cause other thoughts 'of change, congratulation, or regret'. Poetry is feeling the first faint stirrings of universal mortality as opposed to the attributed universalism of the poet's young emotions. The order of progress, he tells us, was from fear to delight and hope ('love enthusiastic'), and thence to this new thing. Poetry is beginning to write more about things, and less about what the poet felt about things.

Here Wordsworth knew of a difficulty which he was honest enough to admit. It would have been better to concentrate on solitary study, meditative peace. He *ought* to have done this. Yes, only—only the sense of his real dedication came to him *not* at such a concentration, but after a night of music and dancing and laughter and 'shocks of young love-liking' —presumably with the 'frank-hearted maids of rocky Cumberland'. Shakespeare perhaps would not have been surprised.

Book VI (*Cambridge and the Alps*) underlines another state of young genius. He is now dedicated; the poetic genius is conscious of its capacity, and looking forward (as Milton did) to doing lasting work. He is aware (1) of the more fanciful side of poetry, Spenserian visions; but also he is concerned with (2) abstractions—especially geometric; and (3) with indulgent moods of sadness. There is emphasized a consciousness of the difference between the youthful poetic apprehension and the mature. Even geometry is still 'a toy

To sense embodied'; it is not yet a world 'created out of pure intelligence'. When, writing the *Prelude*, he looked back, he was conscious of his idleness at that time; perhaps because he was aware of the greater poetic material he might then have gathered. But he could not regret it, for all this time poetry itself was collecting itself in increasing power. It is still in an 'unripe state of intellect and heart', and later on (in Book VIII) we are told how Wordsworth always, at this time, attempted to decorate mere facts: an elder-tree growing by a mortuary must have a dismal look; a yew must have a ghost by it; a widow who has once visited the grave of her husband must do it every night. 'Dejection taken up for pleasure's sake' is a line which might describe her as well as Wordsworth. But the best description of the poet approaching poetry, of the great poet at work, occurs in those noble lines (VI. 592–616) which follow the crossing of the Alps.

Their immediate application is to Wordsworth's consciousness of the nature of man. But their secondary application is only less important.

> Imagination—here the Power so called
> Through sad incompetence of human speech,
> That awful Power rose from the mind's abyss
> Like an unfathered vapour that enwraps,
> At once, some lonely traveller. I was lost;
> Halted without an effort to break through;
> But to my conscious soul I now can say—
> 'I recognise thy glory:' in such strength
> Of usurpation, when the light of sense
> Goes out, but with a flash that has revealed
> The invisible world, doth greatness make abode,
> There harbours; whether we be young or old,
> Our destiny, our being's heart and home,
> Is with infinitude, and only there;
> With hope it is, hope that can never die,
> Effort, and expectation, and desire,
> And something evermore about to be.
> Under such banners militant, the soul
> Seeks for no trophies, struggles for no spoils
> That may attest her prowess, blest in thoughts

> That are their own perfection and reward,
> Strong in herself and in beatitude
> That hides her.

Anyone who has ever written verse, will recognize the justice of

> hope that can never die,
> Effort, and expectation, and desire,
> And something evermore about to be.

The difference between the satisfactory and the unsatisfactory poet is in the last line. The good poet has patience and power to wait till that 'something about to be' has been brought about, however many minutes, hours, or years he may spend in effort and expectation and desire. Unsatisfactory poetry happens when, through incapacity or ignorance or impatience or poverty or kindness to others, the poet is content to write something down before the extreme moment of expectation has been reached, before the line has formed itself. That formation comes in a state in which the thought of spoils and prowess, of reward or fame, is equally blotted out, for nothing but poetry matters. In the great poets it is probably true—for Wordsworth said so—that the coming of the 'perfection and reward' is beatitude.

But also this passage is significant of the difference between the false imagination of the monotonous nightly visits of the widow to the yew, and the true imagination of sorrow, the difference between 'all the sad etcetera of the wrong' and the knowledge of the

> impersonated thought,
> The idea, or abstraction of this kind.

This consciousness of poetry—of imagination—breaks out again later, as he enters London on the top of a stage-coach. 'A weight of ages' descends on him—'weight and power'—'power growing under weight'. He spoke of Imagination as 'the Power so-called', and in London he continues to feel it thus. London provides him with 'strong sensations' of past and present; and he is craving for the power which such sensations provide. 'Influxes of power' come to him.

At the conclusion of the first part of the *Prelude* then we have the poet intensely aware of the presence of this power. The unknown modes of being—of which he had been aware years before—are beginning to shape themselves. All that he saw while he was in London moved him passionately, but not beyond the suburbs of the mind; the distinction is Wordsworth's, and he goes on to compare this movement with the movement of which he was conscious after he had been reading Shakespeare (VII. 477–85).

realities of act and mien,
The incarnation of the spirits that move
In harmony amid the Poet's world,
Rose to ideal grandeur, or, called forth
By power of contrast, made me recognise,
As at a glance, the things which I had shaped,
And yet not shaped, had seen and scarcely seen,
When, having closed the mighty Shakspeare's page,
I mused, and thought, and felt, in solitude.

It seems that Shakespeare's poetry was still affecting him rather as that mountain of his youth had done; he was left with 'an undetermined sense', and yet sufficiently determined to enable him to recognize 'realities of act and mien', the 'incarnation of the spirits that' moved, necessarily, in his own world of poetry. His genius was recognizing its own power. He gives one example—that of a blind beggar wearing a placard describing his story; Wordsworth saw it as if that scrawled label was all that we could know of ourselves and the universe—the beggar loomed on him, a supernatural apparition, one of those mysterious solitaries who crossed and recrossed his own solitary and awful path.

Poetry is on the very verge of greatness. The poet is aware both of the diversity and unity of things. He feels, and he knows he feels, the power of Imagination moving within him.

This is the end of the Seventh Book; the Eighth is Retrospect. The Ninth opens with quite a different note, and so far as poets in general are concerned, the rest of the tale is short —'Oh, how much unlike the past!'

Everyone knows it. The Revolution broke out and all

emotions and thoughts were swept into a unity of delight and wonder. The unknown modes of being were taking on the shape of a renewed world. Wordsworth himself did not much feel this new world in the abstract idea of freedom—he tells us how he picked up a stone from the ruins of the Bastille, 'affecting more emotion than I felt'. But this was a part of a danger he notes several times, the tendency to provoke the false emotion instead of the real, the lingering habit of encouraging the widow to come every night. The poet experiences 'real fervour', but also that 'less genuine and wrought up within myself'. It is when he sees men and women—the 'hunger-bitten girl', Beaupuy, and the people,

> from the depth
> Of shameful imbecility uprisen,

that his spirit is really stirred.

> Bliss was it in that dawn to be alive,
> But to be young was very heaven.

Power from the mountains and lakes of Westmorland, from London strangers, from Shakespeare; power from the Revolution, from the work of honour France was doing—

> from all doubt
> Or trepidation for the end of things
> Far was I, far as angels are from guilt.

There was no doubt; there might be distress, but the great movement accordant with all his past prophesied its august end. And then the English Government declared war on the Revolution.

Wordsworth, in his account of the matter, has been blamed for admitting, in the later version of the *Prelude*, a little gush of patriotism just previous to his account of this crisis. It is not very good poetry certainly, but Wordsworth may have had a reason for letting it in. He may have wished to accentuate the fact that he had a quick sense of England as well as of France. He did feel that the 'sacred ground' of 'Albion' had given way under him; the mountains of England were at war with the plains of France, and he was ravaged by the fact of that conflict. Change, injustice, evil, could then *be*.

Not in my single self alone I found,
But in the minds of all ingenuous youth,
Change and subversion from that hour. No shock
Given to my moral nature had I known
Down to that very moment; neither lapse
Nor turn of sentiment that might be named
A revolution, save at this one time;
All else was progress on the self-same path
On which, with a diversity of pace,
I had been travelling: this a stride at once
Into another region.

There fell upon him 'a conflict of sensations without name'. Things were changed 'into their contraries'. In the poets, the poetic mind is the most intense and enduring thing for good or evil, and they must feel such a conflict, such a revolution and subversion, in their genius. That genius is their soul; the wound is dealt to their soul. Wordsworth was wounded there, and never recovered. It is not the smallest count against the government of England of that day. 'Power' had been within him; it was changed into its contrary. There was with him in his dreams

a sense
Death-like, of treacherous desertion, felt
In the last place of refuge—my own soul.

From the point of view of poetry there are no more important lines in the *Prelude*, and few as important. For the result of that desertion is given later:

The days gone by
Return upon me almost from the dawn
Of life; the hiding-places of man's power
Open; I would approach them, but they close.

In those lines Wordsworth, ostensibly looking back towards his childhood and seeking to recall the moments by which his mind had been 'nourished and invisibly repaired', did more than that. He recalls—to the submissive reader, if not to himself—the 'unknown modes of being'; he asserts what his genius meant, and was meant, to do; he declares the failure of his genius to do it. Wordsworth is our third greatest poet, but even Wordsworth was never the poet he should have been. It is with a sense of profound irony that the reader finds him speaking of the dream which

> entangled me
> In long orations, which I strove to plead
> Before unjust tribunals.

The dream did but prophesy his doom; from then till now much of Wordsworth's verse has been regarded precisely as his genius entangled in long orations before our unjust tribunals. Unjust, at least, if there is the smallest kind of patronage. It is not merely iniquitous, it is imbecile, to patronize Wordsworth—only a little more iniquitous and imbecile than to patronize Coleridge; it is cutting our initials in Westminster Abbey or the Parthenon. It will be time enough to patronize or pardon the great ones when we can also do things that are 'felt in the blood and felt along the heart'.

This was Wordsworth's personal experience. But that is not the immediate point. An experience *of that kind* is here the subject of the poetry—it happens to be his own, which is interesting to the biographer but unimportant for poetry. His poetry is here concerned to discover, to express, to define, a particular state of being. We are no longer in the presence of low breathings and silent steps; nor even of some huge and mighty form that is a trouble to our dreams. On the contrary we are shown a form which is a trouble not to its own or our dreams, but to its own and our life. Poetry is here awakening in us our sense of our capacity for 'change and subversion'—for 'a conflict of sensations without name'. Wordsworth happens to be the writer of the verse, but the Wordsworth who is the subject is that almost mythical figure who sits in the village church, silent, revengeful, solitary; the figure whose soul is only aware of a mystical desertion, the figure thrown 'out of the pale of love'.

The *Prelude* is an account of Wordsworth's mind up to the writing of *Lyrical Ballads*. But it is something else too; it is an account of the developing powers of poetry up to the time when poetry imagines to itself a crisis of utter overthrow and desolation. At the beginning of the work of all the poets is an undetermined sense of unknown modes of being; the aim of all poets is to approach the hiding-places of man's power, to discover the impersonated thought. Even of the poets there have not been many who do this; Wordsworth himself did so only in a limited sense. The remainder of the *Prelude* does not carry the history of the poetic mind in general much farther, though it is full of illuminating phrases on poetry, and though it tells us of the immediate future of Wordsworth's own mind. But in doing so it continually looks back; it recovers sight of its awful sources but hardly contact with them. The close of the *Prelude* is one of the noblest passages in English verse. But the subject of that close is the poet doing something; it awakens our capacity to learn, to believe, to know. Wordsworth promises to indoctrinate us; his poetry, rising to a marvellous lucidity, flashes on us the consciousness of the mind of man

> above this frame of things . . .
> In beauty exalted, as it is itself
> Of quality and fabric more divine.

'Clear as crystal . . . descending out of heaven', wrote another poet. It is poetry declaring its own salvation. But Wordsworth's personal intention was to instruct man; he is concerned more with our belief than with that divine fabric.[1]

[1] Before considering Wordsworth's own achievement, Charles Williams continues with a chapter entitled *The Cycle of Shakespeare* and a chapter on Milton, 'to see what other parallels to that "change and subversion" exist in English verse'. The chapter on Shakespeare is here omitted. [A. R.]

III

MILTON

I

THROUGHOUT Milton, from the first poem in his first book to the last choruses of his last, one subject continually recurs, and that is War. A very few poems leave this subject for others. *L'Allegro*, *Il Penseroso*, a few of the sonnets—these indulge themselves with quieter things, delighting in circumstances or occupations which for a little are not disturbed by armed champions. The landscapes of the early poems are comparable with those in the *Faerie Queene* or *A Midsummer Night's Dream*, but the travellers are of another sort from romantic wizards or townsmen or fairy kings. A severe and bright virtue—a young virginity of righteousness—a beautiful but stern justice—comes shining through those Miltonic brakes and glades. Of such a kind are the 'bright-harness'd angels' who sit round the stable of the Nativity; of such the Lady and her brothers in *Comus*, and Sabrina. The richness of the land seems more luxurious around them, just as the magnificent speech in which Comus urges on the Lady not merely her folly but her injustice in refusing the bounties of earth comes with increased force against her beautiful austerity. The disappearance of these virginal figures is one of the most marked results of Milton's developing genius; they recur for the last time when Ithuriel and Zephon search Paradise for 'some infernal spirit'. After that we are not shown again 'Virtue in her shape how lovely'. How necessary, how desirable, how final perhaps; but not again 'how lovely'. Christ in *Paradise Regained* hardly makes us feel *that*.

It is then in this double sense that the young genius of

Milton sets out to enjoy itself—by an intense rendering of sensuous satisfactions and of chastity rejecting them. He—and we—enjoy Comus's palace as much as we enjoy the Lady's refusal. It is delightful to receive the double enlargement of

> No goblin or swart faery of the mine
> Hath hurtful power o'er true virginity.

It is delightful to hear of 'the thousand liveried Angels' that lackey the chaste soul; but it is no less delightful to hear of the evil thing

> that walks by night
> In fog, or fire, by lake, or moorish fen,
> Blue meagre hag, or stubborn unlaid ghost,
> That breaks his magic chains at curfew time.

The poetic union of these two groups of wonders lies in the refusal by the one of the other. This refusal, or its failure, is the subject of practically all Milton's verse.

But with Milton we have neither an account, as with Wordsworth, of the growth of his genius, nor, as with Shakespeare, a mass of poetry covering all his working life. There is in the centre a long suspension, covered, no doubt, to some extent by his prose. But we are not concerned with his prose; only with what his poetry did, and the witness it bore in itself to the place where ' 'twas nourisht'. The two groups of which that poetry consists are therefore unconnected. But they are undoubtedly connected by their theme, and the theme at the end as at the beginning is war. The crash of the Philistine theatre on Dagon's feast concludes a battle which 'the helmed Cherubim and sworded Seraphim' had long before begun. The only question that can be asked would seem to be—is it the same battle?

In one sense, of course, it is; it is the battle between (what Milton thought was) good and (what Milton thought was) evil. It is even a battle, at the very end as at the very beginning, between God—the word throughout this essay means the God of Milton's poetry and nothing else—and false gods. Dagon had had a scornful line in the *Nativity Hymn*: 'with that twice-battered god of Palestine', and the poetry returns

—twenty-six years afterwards—to describe something very much like a third battering. During those years the war had been carried on in many places. In the *Nativity Ode* it is in the stable at Bethlehem, a foreseen spiritual conflict. In *Comus* it is between indulgence—especially gluttony and drunkenness—and a severe temperance; and the place is in a romantic English landscape. In *Lycidas* it is between selfishness and duty, and the place is in the churches and public heights of England. In the *Sonnets* it is in the Vaudois or the literary world of London, or it is part of the Civil War (or rather, the Civil War is a part of it). In *Paradise Lost* it is enlarged or restored to its original greatness, to include the whole time and space of the created universe. In *Paradise Regained* it is localized to a particular intellectual duel between the protagonist on either side in a special time and place. In *Samson* it is reduced again to its human aspect in Philistia centuries before Christ.

As a result of this continued concern with an everlasting struggle, Milton has been accused of dualism, and no doubt this, in a semi-philosophical sense, is true enough. It may very well be that English poetry will never be quite happy until its thought has retrieved a unity which Milton seriously harmed. Since Milton philosophical poetry has not been altogether successful in returning towards that unity. Pope was a very fine poet; but his pathetic repetition of 'Whatever is, is right' is silly. Wordsworth was prevented from justly fulfilling what perhaps he alone could have fulfilled. *The Ring and the Book*, great poem though it is, fails on the metaphysical side. *The Dynasts* merely denies both sides. Somehow we may have to get back to pre-Miltonic ideas—in fact, to Shakespeare. But that is only as regards our more or less conscious philosophical business. In Milton's own poetry the division has its own union; for the war is the reconciling thing. If the Lady had said to Comus, 'I have my own views, but I don't say they're right for you'; if God had given Satan a little bit of void to play with, it might have been becoming in them, but there would have been no poetry. The war brings them into touch.

But what is the war about? To answer that question is to follow the curve of Milton's genius, from its undetermined modes of being to the hiding-places of its power. But these phrases mean something different in him from what they did in Wordsworth or Shakespeare; and the first difference is in the fact that he was much more deliberately an artist. He 'arranged' much more than those other poets did. He arranged *Lycidas* as he arranged *Samson*, and *Paradise Lost* as much as either. Consider how *Lycidas* turns and returns on itself both in sound and sense; it ascends in spirals. It can even be plotted, as follows:

Introduction 1–5; lament 6–24; pastoral note 25–49; first questioning 50–63; first parenthesis 64–90; second questioning 91–102; second parenthesis 103–31; pastoral note 132–53; lament 154–64; conclusion 165–85; epilogue 186–93.

Comus indeed may be said to be full of undetermined modes of being, being full of magical detail. Comus himself is the child of Bacchus and Circe, and is what he is by his mere nature, without any question of choice. He casts spells into the air to deceive the Lady; against him the Brothers are protected by the herb Haemony; the Lady cannot be released except by the use of Comus's wand to reverse his spells, or by the miraculous intervention of Sabrina. Even the extreme loveliness of the speeches on chastity, with their revealed transmutation of all the senses into immortal being, leaves a mystery in the virtue of which they speak.

The magical detail, the nature of Comus, the half-esoteric doctrine of virginity—these are the undiscovered secrets of Comus; undiscovered to us because undiscovered by Milton's poetry. The poem acts by magic; it touches us with 'chaste palms, moist and cold'.

Lycidas, if it does not explore farther, does definitely point to other places of exploration. It is, in some sense, a prelude to *Paradise Lost*. 'Fresh woods and pastures new'—but that is the language and place of Milton's past occupation. It is in those other lines that the prophecy is heard, in their sound and in their statement.

> For so to interpose a little ease
> Let our frail thoughts dally with false surmise.
> Ay me! Whilst thee the shores, and sounding seas
> Wash far away, where'er thy bones are hurled,
> Whether beyond the stormy Hebrides
> Where thou perhaps under the whelming tide
> Visit'st the bottom of the monstrous world;
> Or whether thou to our moist vows denied
> Sleep'st by the fable of Bellerus old,
> Where the great vision of the guarded Mount
> Looks toward Namancos and Bayona's hold,
> Look homeward, Angel, now.

The Angel of Lycidas might; the Angel of Milton's verse could not. 'The guarded Mount' faces, far off, that other Mount in heaven around which the 'Thrones, Dominations, Princedoms, Virtues, Powers' displayed themselves. And 'the bottom of the monstrous world' has already in it a sense of metaphysical prophecy: 'bottomless perdition' is to be found there,

> Where all life dies, death lives, and nature breeds,
> Perverse, all monstrous, all prodigious things,
> Abominable, inutterable, and worse
> Than fables yet have feigned, or fear conceived,
> Gorgons and Hydras and Chimaeras dire.

Even the God is changing. Jove in *Comus* was no doubt supreme, but he and his servants are only concerned with those mortals who 'aspire'; 'but for such' even the Attendant spirit 'would not soil these pure ambrosial weeds'. They are all away beyond the starry threshold. But 'all-judging Jove' in *Lycidas* is—all-judging. He pronounces on each deed; he is (one feels) in relation to St. Peter and the two-handed engine. He is still solemn, beautiful, credible, but a little aged, a little more concerned with rewards and punishments, a little more driven to make use of mortal weapons: in short, a little nearer the Deity of *Paradise Lost*.

Lycidas is a lament for Edward King. But it is also a calling to remembrance of Milton's young poetry, a lament, a farewell. No wonder it hesitates by Amaryllis and Neaera; the laborious days it foresees are of a different kind to those which virtuously enjoyed themselves contemplating virtue in *Comus*. No wonder it interposes 'a little ease'; *Paradise Lost* would have no room for faint thoughts or false surmise.

Lycidas is a lament, and great authority has declared that it is not a quite sincere lament. What is more certain is that it is a conscious, a self-conscious, lament. Such a self-consciousness had been in Milton's verse from the beginning. The *Nativity* poem inquired of itself whether it had no gift for Christ—many such poems by other poets had similarly inquired and been themselves dispatched in answer. But Milton's was ceremonial, and it was ceremonial because it was self-conscious. One of the advantages of ceremony, rightly used, is that it gives a place to self-consciousness, and a means whereby self-consciousness may be lost in the consciousness of the office filled or the ritual carried out. The art of Milton's poetry is its self-consciousness absorbed in ceremony. *L'Allegro* and *Il Penseroso* also had been conscious—though in their respective ways less ceremonial—the Lady and the Brothers are self-conscious. In one of the sonnets his poetry is already rebuking itself for its unfruitfulness, and pledging itself to that same lot 'Toward which Time leads me, and the will of Heav'n'. A less solemn self-consciousness appears in the Sonnet to the Captain or Colonel or Knight at Arms. The whole of Milton's early poetry—or almost the whole—had this element in it, and this element, being a natural and inevitable part of it, proceeded on into *Paradise Lost*. But there it did more, for there it was not only an element in the poetry, but it became the subject of the poetry. The war in *Paradise Lost* is a real war, but it is also the means to something else, it is the method by which this self-consciousness is fully explored and revealed.

It is sometimes forgotten that Milton did not say he was going to justify the ways of God to man—not like that. He said

> That to the heighth of this great argument
> I may assert Eternal Providence,
> And justify the ways of God to men.

He said it in poetry; that is, his poetry said it; and what poetry says depends on what poetry is being *at that time*, and on nothing else. For what poetry says *is* the poetry. It is not and cannot be concerned with anything but itself. Nor shall we, reading those lines, expect this poetry to fulfil its own desire after any style but its own. We shall not expect intellectual justification—though our intellects must not be offended. Nor moral, though whatever scheme of morality be implied, whether our own or not, must be of a high and enduring sort. We shall, in fact, require only that those three lines shall prelude a sufficiently satisfactory sequence; in short, that the poem shall justify itself. Doing that, it will come as near justifying the ways of God to man as anything can.

This poetry, then, was to assert, to sound, Eternal Providence. But, as nature-poetry is not nature, and love-poetry is not love, so religious poetry is not religion. It may convey religious teaching; it may express our religious emotions; it may make us religious. But in itself, like all poetry, it is the result of a process which Milton, at the beginning of *Paradise Lost*, attributed to the Spirit of God at the creation. The genius of a poet

> [sits] brooding on the vast abyss
> And [makes] it pregnant.

This is what Milton's genius proposed to do; the abyss was to be pregnant with justification.

But though war is the narrative subject of *Paradise Lost*, and justification is the poetic subject, the intellectual subject is Free Will. 'Of man's first disobedience', what moved our parents 'to transgress his will'—this is stated to be the theme. The words 'free will' recur continuously through the poem. But to express what moved our parents to transgress, it is necessary to express how our parents could be moved to transgress—what are the very springs of action. If this is so, then, at the opening of *Paradise Lost*, we are in a similar state of poetic effort to that in which Shakespeare was when his genius was trying to discover, by expressing it, the cause and the manner of the action of men. Only the poetry of Milton knows and asserts what it is about; the poetry of Shakespeare —formally—does not. Nobody knows whether Shakespeare himself knew or not. But his great figures express each a state of being; Milton's figures express their own conscious knowledge of their states of being. They have, in fact, no other subject of conversation; which is perhaps why they do not converse. They do not even argue. They tell one another, but that is not quite the same thing. There are orations, proclamations, prayers, challenges, taunts, inquiries, expositions, defiances, judgements. There is, in fact, everything except conversation. What does God talk about? Himself. What does Satan talk about? Himself. Adam? Himself, as far as possible, but, as he has neither omnipotence nor experience, he is driven back on talking about himself in relation to Omnipotence, until after the Fall. After the Fall he has something more to say about himself, for something more has happened to him, and he says it. And all this talk revolves round two centres—Satan's choice and Adam's choice, the double exercise of free will. Given the narrative-subject of the poem, there could be no other philosophical subject.

By several necessities, then, Milton's poetry comes before us as a self-conscious poetry. It is epic and not dramatic; it is doctrinally epic; it insists, by its arrangement and by the august art of its verse, on its own attention to itself; its chief characters make long and involved speeches about themselves; its chief subject is an understanding of free will which involves an understanding of the nature possessing free will. But the myth of the story involved two chief characters having free will (the subordinate devils may be regarded as typified in Satan, and the good angels do not add much to the exploration; except in one marvellous phrase of Raphael's which will come in later). One of them had all the advantages. He had, when the story opens, experience; he had complexity. And his exercise of will was the primary cause of the exercise of will in the other. Inevitably, therefore, Satan took the chief place.

When Shakespeare was seeking the cause and manner of man's action and had not yet succeeded he made *Hamlet* out of the pother. When Milton was seeking the centre of man's knowledge of himself (in will and action) he made Satan. Of course, Satan is not Milton; Hamlet is not Shakespeare. Milton need no more have approved Satan's character than Shakespeare need have approved Hamlet's. But certainly it is Satan in whom the farthest determination of hitherto 'unknown modes of being' is carried out, and 'the hiding-places of man's power' are so far known.

This determination was carried out in blank verse, and Miltonic blank verse at that. The importance of this fact—sometimes overlooked—is that there is carried into the very form of the poem something which corresponds to the described Omnipotence of God. Everything exists within that dual control. All happens under the Eternal Eye, but all happens also within the bounds of that great decasyllabic progress. Satan is a rebel against God; but he is in some sense a rebel against the blank verse also. It is true he talks it; that is theologically accurate. Satan can only rebel in virtue of the strength that God has given him. 'Immutable, immortal, infinite', that overwhelming style rolls on. It is at times almost impossible to leave off reading it; the verse drags after it the protesting weakness of the reader's mind.

The first hundred lines of the poem present and sustain their subject. For *Paradise Lost* opens with the presentation of the most terrific 'change and subversion' in English verse; terrific in the fact described, terrific in the language used.

> Him the Almighty Power
> Hurled headlong flaming from th' ethereal sky
> With hideous ruin and combustion, down
> To bottomless perdition, there to dwell
> In adamantine chains and penal fire,
> Who durst defy th' Omnipotent to arms.

Not only has this united the verse with the idea—or (to put it more exactly) not only has the poetry discovered itself in its strength of domination, but it has also raised the problem which it has to solve. 'Who durst defy th' Omnipotent'—

compared to this Adam's later effort to dodge the Omnipotent is pathetic. But, sooner or later, it is impossible to avoid asking Milton *why* the myth should be thus; isn't it stupid? Who could, who would, defy Omnipotence? Milton cannot, of course, escape by saying, 'Well, that's an old story'; he must make that old story convincing.

His logical answer is given in the Fifth Book (ll. 856–63). The rebel angels imagine themselves 'self-begot',

> the birth mature
> Of this our native Heaven, ethereal sons,

and they imagine God to be of the same nature, only more powerful. Exactly how much more powerful they may reasonably proceed to try and find out. But though this is rational, it is by an irrationality that Satan is shown us. Omnipotence is engaged upon something to which Satan is with his whole being antagonistic. Reason bids him submit—God and Raphael both point this out: even after his fall from Heaven he considers the possibility. To do that, however, would be precisely to lose *himself*; he would be something other than he is. He must act from what he is, and he expresses this in a minor contradiction. When he is addressing his followers he points out that none of them will envy him his throne; no one will want 'the greatest share of endless pain'. Reasonable enough, true enough; only it is precisely this which he himself must demand. 'Better to reign in Hell than serve in Heaven.' This contradiction is not deliberate deceit; it is the irrational strength of his nature, which his own inner force has precisely 'made supreme Above his equals'. His various speeches on this are united in his soliloquy on Niphates. There the deliberate acquiescence in a divided consciousness is made, and it is made because 'he can no other'. Submission itself would produce no other result than a repetition of the past revolt. Both he and God know this; there is between them no smallest possibility of agreement. It is expressed in the poem by his knowledge that a new world has come into existence in his place—

> behold, instead
> Of us out-cast, exiled, his new delight.

It is a phrase which Troilus, could he have talked Milton, might have used of Diomed. No circumstances could be more different; no essential agony could be more alike. Troilus rushes to arms against Diomed; Othello—more fully expressed—murders Desdemona; Satan makes war on God and man.

> It is the cause, it is the cause, my soul.

It is a state too well known to man. The skies and the abysses, the archangels and chaotic powers of this poem are not necessary to our recognition of it; nor by them is our capacity for a similar choice awakened. The corner of a suburban road, a metropolitan doorway, are equally adequate surroundings; were those others necessary *Paradise Lost* would be more spectacular and less essential poetry. Milton stresses the moral choice in the contradiction, the choice which so many men have made, the preference for the existence of their own will as the final and absolute thing as against the knowledge (whatever that may be) of some 'great commanded Good'. The only choice which a man can make in such a crisis is between submitting to that good or refusing to submit to it, and if he refuses to submit he does so precisely because so, and so only, he can hold 'divided empire with heaven's king'. Every bold bad baronet in the old stories did the same thing. He cannot get rid of the good, he cannot destroy it. He can only know, and refuse, and hate it, and be equivalent to it.

So Satan accepts the contradiction within him, with no hope of its resolution and no fear of its agony.

> So farewell, Hope, and with hope, farewell Fear;
> Farewell, Remorse; all good to me is lost;
> Evil, be thou my good; by thee at least
> Divided empire with heaven's king I hold.

The divided empire means double consciousness within him for ever. His own self-consciousness accepts and includes that.

Compared to Troilus, Othello, and Lear, this is a self-conscious state, and involves a moral choice from which those distracted figures are free, for to them, as they are presented, the moral choice is not offered. The question of their duty is not raised: at least, I suppose no one seriously blames either Troilus or Othello (justified and unjustified as they respectively are) for not following some lovelier course of action. Nor Lear. Shakespeare is intent on tracking out the paths by which human nature wanders in 'the dark unbottomed infinite abyss'. Milton reflects also the intense consciousness of himself that takes him there. But Shakespeare's explorations took him to the imagination of a dual and rapturous knowledge, and after that to new life. Milton's went at once farther and less far.

This, at any rate, after the long suspension, was the changed capacity of Milton's verse in its reissuing. Comus had had no such complexity, nor any such self-consciousness and self-decision. There had been shown in him no possibility of choice, and even the Attendant Spirit was bound to admit that his followers did, as a matter of fact, 'roll with pleasure in a sensual sty'. But this being the common desire of humanity, and Milton's own verse having at least walked with pleasure in a sensuous palace, the two opposite states of being are contemplated as opposite persons. In Satan they are one.

But if this created complexity is one greatness of the poem, there is another in the rapture that proclaims its doom. Satan accepts both evil done and evil suffered, rebellion and pain, not merely the evil of his own will but the evil which that will involves. It is in his choice of both that he holds the divided empire, and is (so long as his vital spirit lasts) something God cannot be; he is as unique as God. But this 'evil' then must be expressed in its fullness. Satan would not be the figure he is if the poetry failed here. The poem would not be the poem it is if its poetry did not discover, as it were, God's consciousness of Satan as well as Satan's consciousness of God. And this can be done even better by the narrative than by the Omnipotent Victor. A self-conscious Omnipotence, a self-conscious and victorious Omnipotence, is a figure which poetry itself can hardly make attractive. And even Milton appears to have been aware that God ought, sometimes, to be attractive.

The narrative therefore gathers itself into intense verse to overthrow the intensity which proclaimed itself within it. To 'Evil, be thou my good' it answers 'be *thou* my evil'.

> Him the Almighty Power
> Hurled headlong flaming from th' ethereal sky.
>
> So spake the Son, and into terror changed
> His countenance, too severe to be beheld,
> And full of wrath bent on his enemies.
>
> Hell heard th' unsufferable noise, Hell saw
> Heaven ruining from heaven.[1]
> Hell at last
> Yawning received them whole, and on them closed,
> Hell, their fit habitation, fraught with fire
> Unquenchable, the house of woe and pain.

The spirit which inflicts, the spirit which endures, have both accepted the 'thing inseparate'. Between God and Satan, divided 'wider than the sky and earth', yet there is no orifice. This is the conclusion on that subject of *Paradise Lost*.

But in what sense, then, can there be justification in this poetry? The verse has been raised to its height to deny something which the tremendous power of the verse continually expresses. Chaos itself never came nearer discovery than in the description of Satan's awful journey through it. But the poem itself tempts

> with wandering feet
> The dark unbottomed infinite abyss.

[1] It is not in the meaning of the verse except by accident; but it is precisely 'heaven ruining from heaven' which describes the crisis involved. Compare Troilus again—

> Instance, O instance! strong as Pluto's gates;
> Cressid is mine, tied with the bonds of heaven:
> Instance, O instance! strong as heaven itself;
> The bonds of heaven are slipp'd, dissolv'd, and loos'd.

and Othello:

> If she be false O then heaven mocks itself.

How can it

> like a weather-beaten vessel hold
> Gladly the port, though shrouds and tackle torn?

The answer is that its port is threefold: (1) the other militant solitaries, (2) Eden in Books VII and VIII, (3) *Samson Agonistes*.

Having created Satan, Milton's poetry had to do something else. It had—if there was going to be any more of it—to discover some other way of existing, but (inevitably) some related way. It had also to deal with Adam who was the ostensible subject. By the end of the Fourth Book, Satan had been sufficiently achieved; indeed the episode of the 'back-chat' between him and Gabriel at the close of that book is, in a sense, a luxury. It recapitulates, condenses, and emphasizes all that has gone before—defiance, selfhood, and compulsion by superior power.

> [Satan] fled
> Murmuring, and with him fled the shades of night.

And now what was going to happen?

The end of Book V answers with an exact parallel—the Seraph Abdiel turning his back

> On those proud towers to swift destruction doomed.

Satan chooses evil—Abdiel chooses good; and Milton conscientiously (and quite unsatisfactorily, for the first four books had done their work so well that only Milton's strength of imagination could have invented this episode) allows Abdiel later on to overcome Satan in single conflict. But the trouble is that though this choice and heavenly defiance is a marvellous piece of work, though the 'Unshaken, unseduced, unterrified' has become one of our most glorious possessions; though the corresponding line 'All night the dreadless Angel unpursued' has immeasurable distance in it, and is a brief—and yet infinite—parallel to Satan's own journey through Chaos—yet the poetry has not discovered anything different. *Plus ça change, plus c'est la même chose*—only rather less profound. For the choice is not as effective as Satan's. Obviously not, since Abdiel's choice, however difficult at the moment, will involve nothing like the acceptance of 'infinite wrath and infinite despair'. Milton therefore cannot let himself go over it. It and he are circumscribed by the heavenly host. And even Milton hardly succeeded in making the heavenly host—or the hymns of the heavenly host—interesting. If one *could* skip in Milton it would be occasionally one of the choric odes to God. Abdiel, like the Lady in *Comus* before him, has to be one of the lesser defiances that surround, in Milton's work, the figure of Satan.

But there is, if not another solitary, at least the prophecy of another solitude in the foretold solitude of Christ. From the beginning this solitude is set in opposition to Satan's. The silence of Pandemonium is the counterpart of the silence in heaven.

> All sat mute,
> Pondering the danger with deep thoughts;
> . . . none among the choice and prime
> Of those Heaven-warring champions could be found
> So hardy as to proffer or accept
> Alone the dreadful voyage, till at last
> Satan, . . .

> All the heavenly quire stood mute
> And silence was in heaven: on man's behalf
> Patron or intercessor none appeared,
> Much less that durst upon his own head draw
> The deadly forfeiture . . .
> . . . had not the Son of God.

In spite of this equivalence of virtue it remains true that the choice of Christ is not to the reader of the same imaginative greatness as the choice of Satan. Yet the likeness between Christ and Satan, so expressed, is more than a comparison in mere narration; it is more even than a moral comparison. It is, or it contains within it at certain moments, a psychological comparison. At the end of the Sixth Book, where the Son, riding in 'the chariot of Paternal Deity', casts the rebel angels out of heaven, the description of their overthrow imagines not merely a mythical but an individual defeat. The spirit that rejects the Good is tormented by the Good that it rejects—the shaking of its whole being (all but the 'Throne itself' of that Good)—the infixed plagues—the tempestuous arrows—the glaring eyes—the collapse of all energy, leaving it 'exhausted, spiritless, afflicted, fallen'. Fear and pain and arrows of desire and the strong sense of being a spectacle of mockery and impotent affliction—it is not necessary to turn to legendary battles to recognize those signs. *Paradise Lost* is in its two themes a contrapuntal harmony. The story of the rebels turns back on itself: it opens in hell after their fall, describes Satan's exploration of chaos, and his arrival in Eden, goes back to recount their revolt and expulsion, and then concludes with their local victory and transformation into hissing serpents. But the psychological presentation is continuous; the spirit which in the opening magnificently rejects is itself overwhelmed by the rejected, and after that greater failure boasts of its lesser triumph, before it finds even in that only 'hatefullest disrelish'. The figure of Satan himself, however, is not specifically mentioned in the overthrow; whenever he is defeated it is as a demigod should be; and when he becomes a serpent he is 'still greatest'—

> his power no less he seemed
> Above the rest still to retain; they all
> Him followed.

Milton may have disapproved of Satan but he certainly had an artistic—if no other—tenderness for the 'archangel ruined'.

Attracted by this artistic tenderness the rest of us have rather neglected to attend to the lines which describe—which discover and express—Christ. 'The grand foe' has lured us after him poetically, partly no doubt because our own natures are much more like his complexity than Christ's singleness. But also because he is the most successful example, in *Paradise Lost*, of 'the impersonated thought', which Wordsworth formulated as a maxim. In him the impersonation and the thought are equal. But in God and in Christ the impersonation is much weaker than the thought. They are indeed almost abstractions, and perhaps *Paradise Lost* would be easier to read if we frankly accepted them as abstractions.

God would be more comprehensible, even more probable, if we took Him to be but a mode of the Good; Christ would be more comprehensible—even as the Sole-Begotten Son—if we regarded Him simply as a mode of the Will accepting the Good. In that way, though He would remain less thrilling than Satan, He would be equally important and exalted, even poetically. We need not deny Satan his extra impersonalization, so long as we allow to Christ His full place as 'an idea or abstraction of his kind'. The poem demands so much; it provides so much. It is for us to recognize that it provides what it demands. Thus the relationship of the Son to the Father becomes credible and beautiful; the great lines which utter that relationship, of the Will perfectly free accepting the Perfect Good, expand within us into something like their power of full communication:

> He said, and on his Son with rays direct
> Shone full, he all his Father full exprest
> Ineffably into his face received,
> And thus the filial Godhead answering spake.
> O Father, O Supreme of heavenly Thrones,
> First, Highest, Holiest, Best, thou always seek'st
> To glorify thy Son, I always thee,
> As is most just; this I my glory account,
> My exaltation, and my whole delight,
> That thou in me well pleased declar'st thy will
> Fulfilled, which to fulfil is all my bliss.

We have tended to repeat other lines rather than those; we have tended to concentrate on the devil rather than the God. But then in *Paradise Lost* the devil is a lonely figure and the God is not, until the devil succeeds. It seems as if there were in the triumph in Eden something which, while leaving Satan's character as effective as ever, yet opens up the possibility of other defiances. You cannot, it seems, win a victory without running the risk of a rebellion; or only if that victory is the secret desire of the overthrown power—and this perhaps is the difference between man and Satan. But I think that is not in Milton, nor perhaps even in Shakespeare. The journey of Satan from Hell through Chaos to Earth is paralleled by the departure of Adam and Eve from Paradise through Eden to their future, and their future is Christ. Satan's determination is manifested in action, but the action must have a result, and the result is still to be explored. Thomas Ellwood has been blamed often enough for his question, 'What hast thou to say of Paradise Regained?' But, in so far as the conflict of contradiction in the consciousness of Satan, of Adam, is not resolved, but remains as a final accepted choice, Ellwood was perfectly right. Christ is to solve it; he is aware of his own future acts; he is aware that he will do so. But he is not aware of himself in the immediate knowledge of union as Satan was aware of himself in the immediate knowledge of contradiction.

In effect, and in Milton, he never was. But in *Paradise Lost* he is a place of prophecy, a hiding-place of man's power.

The second answer is Eden. Between the first arrival of Satan in Paradise (Book IV) and the Fall (Book IX) there is a pause. Books V and VI, however, are largely taken up by Raphael's account of the war in heaven, and therefore, effectively, the pause is postponed to the Seventh Book where he recounts the Creation, and the Eighth where Adam describes his own waking and meeting with Eve. But they are preceded by the lovely appearance of the Archangel and his first talk with Adam, and the war is told by him and not directly by Milton; so that even that strife is a little removed. It is all around Eden, but it is not within. Satan and the agonizing double consciousness are postponed. In so far as Milton's poetry could be tender and gentle and at peace—and that was much more than is often admitted—it is so here. Here is Adam's great speech on Eve—though Raphael does a little grudge it him; here is Raphael's own definition of free will—'We freely love'. He says it, and for a moment a sudden new universe hovers in *Paradise Lost*; he says it, and goes on to speak of the war. Nothing like it happened again in Milton—except (almost) when Adam ate the fruit that he might not be parted from Eve, and (quite) when Eve offered herself as a just victim for Adam's fault as well as hers.

'We freely love.' Perhaps 'the affable Archangel' did not notice the high perfection of the phrase. It—and it alone—is the complete and final answer to Satan's spoken taunts and Adam's perplexities; the following books are a kind of descant on it. But it was not to be explored, and, unexplored, it is not sufficiently related to the greatness and complexity of Satan to be a progress from him. And when we come to the Fall and what follows, we find that we are returning towards a variation on the earlier theme of union in division.

The duplication of this state in Adam occupies, with its results, the last part of *Paradise Lost*. But there is a difference: in Satan his past and future are subordinated by the manner of the poetry to his own intense immediate being; in Adam the immediate being is subordinated to his past and future. Adam is largely concerned with what will happen to him and to his sons, unrealized as yet, whereas Satan seems to have realized and accepted his future. Adam's looming future, both of despair and grace, is a great poetic fact, but it is a fact of inquiry, uncertainty, and dread, not of finality. Besides which, Adam argues, and when a poet's character argues it is always possible to disagree. With the speech in which Adam proves to his own satisfaction that he must not regard God as responsible it is not only possible but necessary to disagree. This however passes, and there follows the vision of the future which occupies Books XI and XII. Passages of this, and the art of Milton through the whole of it, one can enjoy; but as a vision it is perhaps something of an anti-climax. Even Milton seems to have tired. He had formerly used all sorts of phrases to describe an Angel speaking—'the Angelic Virtue answered mild', 'Raphael . . . benevolent and facile thus replied', 'So spake the godlike power', 'Thus he in scorn', 'which Gabriel spying thus bespake', and so on. He now used 'To whom thus Michael' (or 'the Archangel') eleven times, and for the rest only 'said' or 'answered Michael': indeed at one point, when the two are discussing

> Convulsions, epilepsies, fierce catarrhs,
> Intestine stone and ulcer, colic pangs,
> Dropsies, and asthmas, and joint-racking rheums

(and how dreadful the threat of the verse is!), and Adam asks if there is any escape—at this point Milton for a moment seems to give up the effort—

> There is, said Michael, if thou well observe
> The rule of not too much.

But he recovered himself for the serene and terrible close. Amid vision and prophecy, amid suggested capacities of good and evil, amid counsels meant to direct prolonged life, *Paradise Lost* ends; it ends in suspense, in banishment, in journeying, in expectation, in hope. It ends with the departure from that gate 'with dreadful faces thronged and fiery arms' of 'our lingering parents'; but not the least of those dreadful faces was the one which Milton's genius had sealed with the knowledge of unutterable division and the union of immortal and irreconcilable states; not the least of the angelic voices was that which uttered

> Hail, horrors, hail,
> Infernal world, and thou, profoundest hell,
> Receive thy new possessor.

II

The third answer is *Samson*, but another poem came between. *Paradise Regained*, by general consent, is not so great a poem as *Paradise Lost*. The general consent may partly be due to the fact that an argument is less interesting than a story, especially a story where the exciting parts are as exciting as Milton made them. In the first poem Milton improved to such an extent on the few hints which the Bible gave him that we have all attributed Biblical authority to his work ever since, so final has it seemed. But the Temptation of Christ is much more exciting in the Bible than it is in Milton. The short anecdote which opens with the apocalyptic figure of the newly baptized God 'driven up by the Spirit into the wilderness to be tempted of the devil' has a concentrated force which is dispelled even by such a stately loveliness as

> So spake our Morning Star, then in his rise

and which is not recovered till we come to

> To whom thus Jesus: Also it is written,
> Tempt not the Lord thy God, he said and stood,
> But Satan smitten with amazement fell.

We have, of course, to remember that Satan is not merely trying to tempt God; he is trying to find out whether it is God whom he is tempting, and the temptation itself is the only means of doing so. 'Who this is we must learn.' It is this inquiry which he pursues throughout up to that sudden great moment at which he at last discovers in his opponent's nature, not in his words, the actual truth:

> As that Theban monster that proposed
> Her riddle, and him, who solved it not, devoured;
> That once found out and solved, for grief and spite
> Cast herself headlong from th' Ismenian steep,
> So strook with dread and anguish fell the fiend.

All his arguments have meant just this, and Christ's answers are adequate—not perhaps always to the argument but—to the purpose behind the argument. He says, in effect, 'Find out what I am if you can; it is not my business to tell you. I shall answer precisely what you ask, and we shall see how much farther on you are.'

It is this underlying conflict which prevents the dispute from being a purely philosophical discussion, this conflict between Satan's burning anxiety to know, and Christ's contented patience.

> What concerns my knowledge God reveals.

It is otherwise a discussion on values. It has a likeness to the discussion of values by the Trojan princes, to Wordsworth's concern with

> the ground
> Of obligation, what the rule and whence
> The sanction.

Shakespeare abandoned his discussion; Wordsworth abandoned his ('yielded up moral questions in despair'); Milton, closing his in a stately decency, nevertheless abandoned it also. Christ, in a sudden burst of energetic poetry, stands; the devil falls in 'amazement'. Something new has entered the discussion and destroyed it. The style of that discussion is—with reverence be it spoken—less compelling than that of *Paradise Lost*; i.e. it is possible, almost anywhere, to stop reading *Paradise Regained* whereas it is almost impossible to stop reading *Paradise Lost*, once one has begun. This may be why comparatively few people begin.

Whether as a result of this changed concern or not, it is to be noticed that the characters of the later *Paradise* are diminished from their former augustitude. Satan is less, but also Christ is less. The most unfortunate personage, however, is Belial, who was thus originally described:

> Belial, in act more graceful and humane;
> A fairer person lost not heaven; he seemed
> For dignity composed and high exploit.

It is true 'all was false and hollow', for 'his thoughts were low': still—but he has now become

> Belial the dissolutest spirit that fell,
> The sensuallest, and after Asmodai
> The fleshliest incubus.

'A fairer person'—'the fleshliest incubus'. But, of course, he appears in the second *Paradise ad hoc*. He is there merely to propose tempting Christ by women

> Skill'd . . . to draw
> Hearts after them tangled in amorous nets.

His proposal is scornfully rejected, and the entire omission of that temptation (remarkable even in the original, except on the orthodox hypothesis of the Nature of Christ) explained.[1] The 'Filial Godhead' and 'the archangel ruined' are both of smaller appearance and less lonely kind. As there are no great defiances so there are no great solitaries. Christ had been more lonely in heaven than He is on earth, among the angelic choirs than in the wilderness. He is here—if not

[1] It is perhaps worth remarking that one of our greatest difficulties in the scheme of *Paradise Lost* is to understand why the rebel angels, except Satan, were ever in heaven at all. Moloch, Mammon, and Belial, are quite unsuitable to it, and we are not told that their natures were changed by their fall. However, it is part of the story and must be accepted as such.

comfortable—at least not much more than uncomfortable. He had such thoughts

> as well might recommend
> Such solitude before choicest society.

The Lady in *Comus* perhaps had them also. But hardly Satan or Abdiel or the later Samson. Their thoughts might *drive* them to solitude, but that is not the same thing.

Is then *Paradise Regained* a kind of active pause between *Paradise Lost* and *Samson*? It would hardly please Milton to say so, and indeed (though it has a hint of Milton at his lordly ease about it) it is something more. What more may be found by asking another question—Why the Temptation? Paradise was never regained, according to any Christian dogma or even according to *Paradise Lost*, until the Passion and Resurrection of Christ. Yet Milton proposes to sing

> Recover'd Paradise to all mankind,
> By one man's firm obedience.

Intellectually, theologically, the answer is that the 'firm obedience' of Christ to the Father's will can be presented as well by the Temptation as by the Passion; and it is in such obedience that the virtue of Christ's human will lay. This being so, and the Temptation being (to that extent) a proper subject, it follows (1) that it was in Christ's human will that Milton was interested, (2) that an argument was much more suited to the Temptation than the Passion, (3) that the Passion might easily have involved Milton in a problem far too much like that of Satan in *Paradise Lost* to be desirable.

Properly to discuss the first of these would involve theology. It may be sufficient to say that Milton's aristocratic and hierarchic mind had hardly ever succeeded—except in a descriptive line or two—in identifying the Person of Christ with the Equal Godhead of the Son. The Son is begotten in time by the will of the Father; and throughout the whole first poem he is entirely subordinate. He is the impersonization of the Will accepting the Good, not necessary to the Good. *Paradise Lost* and the Athanasian Creed (which is also a very fine poem) are entirely opposed. Long before, at the time of the Ode on the Nativity, it had been a serious and conscious poem which Milton sent to a serious and conscious Child. A thousand carols had sung of the innocence, the helplessness, of the incarnate Godhead. But Milton, it seems, was incapable of seeing Omnipotence helpless and an infant; it had to be something other than Omnipotence. Could the blank verse which is the sound of that Omnipotence break into the nervous singleness of 'I sing of a Lady'? There could only be Omnipotence, and therefore Christ must be something other. It is his subordinated, his human, will in which we are to be interested.

Besides this, it seems that Milton was going to write a discussion. It is not very likely, whatever his ostensible subject had been, that he would have done anything else, since that is what he *did* do. He could, obviously, have treated the Temptation in an entirely different way; he need not have made it an argument. Since he did, it must be assumed that he would have made any subject into an argument, and his genius saved him from a less suitable subject. Christ is something of a public character. He recounts (I. 202) how in his childhood all his mind

> was set
> Serious to learn and know, and thence to do
> What might be public good; myself I thought
> Born to that end.

He abandons this idea, but still the poem never convincingly expresses salvation. What, in effect, we have is something rather like a devout and aristocratic statesman being interviewed, at the request of the Government, by an atheistical and ungentlemanly newspaper-correspondent, who goes even beyond his limits in recommending policies and means to policies. Now, whatever the figure of the Crucifixion may have been, it was not that of a devout aristocratic statesman. It was a figure in some respects (as Blake saw) much more like the figure of Satan in *Paradise Lost*.

> All is not lost; the unconquerable will,
> And study of revenge, immortal hate,
> And courage never to submit or yield,
> And what is else not to be overcome.

Of those four lines only one is Satan's peculiarly; the others are equally Christ's. Indeed, on the Christian, on Milton's theory, the last is Christ's *only*; for there can be nothing which cannot be overcome except Christ. And God.

'Milton', said Blake, 'was of the devil's party without knowing it.' If this meant that Milton admired his devil more than his Christ it would be silly. But if it means that he had given the whole great striving with the contradiction in things, all the force it has in itself, and all the strength necessary to meet and bear it without yielding to it—that he had given all this to Satan, and could not therefore repeat it with Christ, then Blake was quite right. A poem on the Crucifixion would have been altogether too much like the self-knowledge of the earlier power which dared

> Through all the coasts of dark destruction seek
> Deliverance for us all.

In the Temptation Milton was able to present Christ as submissive; the Crucifixion would have shown him defiant—and not an aristocratic defiance at that, but a much more desperate one, a defiance (so to speak) of the universe by the universe. When the Image of Godhead demanded of Godhead 'Why hast Thou forsaken me?'—what did Milton propose to do about that? Nothing; he did a wiser thing—he waited, and then took a mortal figure, as much less in kind than Satan as Christ would have been more, and gave to Samson defiance and submission, entreaty and protest, before he touched on the mystery of the reconciled self-consciousness of man.

Meanwhile, in *Paradise Regained*, he did two things. (1) He enjoyed himself with a long discussion between a Miltonic intellect and a coarser—say, King Charles II's or the Bishop of London's. (2) He used this to suggest the impossibility of the lesser nature understanding—not merely what the greater one is doing, but what the greater one is. There had been in *Paradise Lost*—amid all the battles and judgements and talk about free will—that marvellous moment when Raphael uttered three words: 'we freely love'.

It is no use for anyone—angel or mortal—trying to find that out except by doing it. *Paradise Regained* is the effort of Milton's aristocratic intellect to explain to the devil the nature of love and freedom. Milton may make mistakes sometimes in the argument. But that is its basis.

'Do this', Satan suggests, 'that I may know what you are.' 'If I did that,' Christ answers, 'I should be you and not myself.' 'But why won't you do that?' Satan presses. 'Precisely because I am myself and not you,' Christ answers again. 'I don't understand you,' Satan exclaims, 'I think you are an obstinate fool, and I am afraid you are God.' To which Christ can only add that the devil never could, and never did, understand God. Farther, Milton could not go; the human will of Christ was undivided and unagonized. It disputed, and triumphed, but it left on one side the 'conflict of sensations without name'.

The solemn opening of *Samson* does but renew the movement which had closed *Paradise Lost*. It was undesirable in discussing that, to have forced its last two lines into an allusion to the poetry itself; but in *Samson* it is another matter. Of the fifteen thousand or so lines which made up Milton's work there remained but something under two thousand: seven-eighths of his journey had been covered. And now, after that discussion which was *Paradise Regained*, the movement recommences.

> They hand in hand, with wandring steps and slow,
> Through Eden took their solitary way.
>
> A little onward lend thy guiding hand
> To these dark steps, a little further on.

The first of those couplets is narrative; the second dramatic. It was by God knows what artistic accident that Milton turned to drama at the end, but it was of the most profound use; and perhaps the power of his genius alone dictated it. For in *Samson* almost for the first time, certainly only for the second time—it depends on whether we reckon *Comus* as drama—his poetry chose a form in which its business was, to an extent, to conceal his art. In the *Paradises* he had displayed it; the high invocations, the personal irruptions, had all contributed to make us aware of the self-consciousness which was part of the poem. Poetry was never more self-conscious than in the *Paradises*, and its self-consciousness is, in a certain sense, one with its subject. But, as far as he could—he could not very far—this self-consciousness was withdrawn in *Samson*; where it was not withdrawn it was formally conventionalized; and where it could be neither withdrawn or conventionalized it was intensified into human emotion. An example of the first method is to be seen in a comparison between the two laments over blindness. The first is in *Paradise Lost* at the opening of the Third Book: those noble fifty lines of which the concluding passage begins—

Thus with the year
Seasons return, but not to me returns—

Compare with that Samson's

O dark, dark, dark, amid the blaze of noon,

and what follows. Neither is more moving than the other; but the one awakes in us a knowledge of our capacity for realizing that we are blind; the other a knowledge of our capacity for blindness. The second method is the introduction of the Chorus. Now the Chorus are come

To visit or bewail thee, or if better,
Counsel or consolation we may bring,
Salve to thy sores.

They form the recording, the commenting, the exhorting or encouraging faculty of the mind; they are self-awareness personified. It is this which 'bears witness' to Samson's patriotism, warns him to 'advise how to receive' Manoah, remembers old stories and applies them, universalizes Samson's, and sums up the moral of the whole. A great deal of what the Chorus says might be uttered by Samson himself. The rest is that general expansion of self-consciousness beyond his own, into man's, that is, poetry's, which in the end concludes and consummates the progress of Milton's genius. Had *Samson* been a narrative poem the part of the Chorus would have been divided between the protagonist and the poet: self-arguments (as with Satan), or adjectives, descriptions, and comments (as from Milton) would have taken its place. But the dramatic form enabled this element to be withdrawn from both sources and united in one utterance.

Of course, Samson in himself remains self-conscious; he does not lose in realism because this other means of speech had been used. The necessity which perhaps dictated it was the need for some comment upon the whole of Samson's experience. But Samson was to die, and even if he had survived still the self-conscious poetry of Milton must discover its own finality—something larger than the hero's.

It is perhaps fanciful to see in the irregular metre of *Samson* a variation on that blank verse of the *Paradise Lost* which was so intensely significant of its Deity. Yet the later rhythms —not more subtle nor more beautiful—are less triumphantly controlling everything. They pause; they hesitate; they change. But so does the earlier blank verse? Yes, but never without a much more immediate reference to the norm; in *Samson* we are passing as far as possible from a universal norm. Indeed in some places the norm is only reached again with difficulty, if at all. I leave the discussion to the prosodists; only adding that the variations of rhythm combine with the sharpness of direct human experience in the poem to remove us from the verbal reflection of the ruling Will. The modulation is not merely stylistic or dramatic; it is also metaphysical and poetic.

Samson is a solitary figure like the Lady, Satan, Abdiel, and Christ: the poem is in this sense a repetition of the earlier poems. But there are three differences:

(1) Samson's own state of being;
(2) the thrice-recurring dispute with God;
(3) the allusion to 'dire necessity'.

The poetry is not here expressing a spirit capable of sustaining division and contradiction: it has gone beyond that. Satan's vital energy kept him from perishing. But Samson's vital energy is already perishing. He is perhaps a less tremendous figure than Satan. But he is in a state of defeat which Satan never was. The poetry awakens our knowledge of a more extreme collapse—a collapse as extreme as a great solitary can consciously suffer and yet consciously still exist. The sense of being overwhelmed by Omnipotence is in both Satan and Samson. Satan's answer is 'Evil, be thou my good': his defeat shall be his life. If he must know himself so, he will 'enjoy' that sole method of knowing himself. But Samson is expecting to cease to know himself. Against the earlier 'unconquerable will' we have a conquered will—or rather a conquered *being*, a 'double darkness'.

> Nature within me seems
> In all her functions weary of herself;
> My race of glory run,

glory of Satan or glory of Christ

> and race of shame,
> And I shall shortly be with them that rest.
>
> Nor am I in the list of them that hope;
> Hopeless are all my evils, all remediless;
> This one prayer yet remains, might I be heard,
> No long petition, speedy death,
> The close of all my miseries, and the balm.

Adam had thought that this might be the best for all mankind; here is mankind asking for it. But there is a difference. Adam had, so to speak, taken all the blame. Samson once, Manoah once, the Chorus once, question the actions of God. They do it with all reserves; they stop one another doing it; but they do do it. Personal suffering, contemplation of another's suffering, contemplation of the general state of man, all begin to cry out. Man's self-consciousness is bound to admit his common fate—

> Just or unjust, alike seem miserable,
> For oft alike, both come to evil end.

And the poetry itself? What but this poetry which had set

out to 'justify the ways of God'—now come to a point where it is rebuking God—exclaims

> So deal not with this once thy glorious Champion,
> The Image of thy strength, and mighty Minister.
> What do I beg? how hast thou dealt already?
> Behold him in this state calamitous, and turn
> His labours, for thou canst, to peaceful end.

'The Image of thy strength, and mighty Minister'—is there a better description of Milton's work? 'State calamitous'—is it not when this image of the good man 'blinded in Gaza at the mill with slaves' is the best result of justification? Here is the good man demanding justification. 'Yet why?' says Samson, even in the midst of blaming himself. God can 'with his own laws best dispense'; it is he who prompted Samson 'to seek in marriage that fallacious Bride'. Again similarly Manoah protests

> Alas methinks whom God hath chosen once
> . . . He should not so o'erwhelm.

> Immeasurable strength they might behold
> In me, of wisdom nothing more than mean;
> This with the other should at least have paired,
> These two proportioned ill drove me transverse.

Similarly the Chorus—in a passage too long to quote in full (667–704).

It is this bewilderment, even more than any exterior likeness between Milton and Samson, which makes that great line applicable to this last poem. The poetry that was to see and tell 'of things invisible to mortal sight' was itself blinded; it was in Gaza at the mill with slaves. But there it found its confession; in a poem unrelieved by any but mortal defiance of mortals Milton's poetic mind used a phrase which *Paradise Lost* would have had to explain away. Samson dies; the Chorus, contemplating that death, exclaim that he is victorious

> Among thy slain self-killed
> Not willingly, but tangled in the fold

> Of dire necessity, whose law in death conjoined
> Thee with thy slaughtered foes in number more
> Than all thy life had slain before.

The words refer directly to the death, but they carry with them a larger implication; they admit at long last something which Milton had excluded till now. Necessity has brought Samson to an unforeseen end. And what is necessity but God dispensing with his own laws, and ill-proportioned strength and wisdom, and all against which protests have been entered? Victory now is in defeat; defeat in victory; the champion and the enemies of God are alike overwhelmed. There is, so far forth, no thought of Samson in any future life; the Chorus and Manoah are concerned with two things: (1) Samson's secular fame, (2) their own awareness of his death. There flashes into the verse—for the last time—one of those reminiscences of Shakespeare which had occasionally occurred in Milton: curiously in an allusion to the phœnix, to a new life rising from an old, to a transmutation of beauty and power.[1] And then we come to the separate awareness which Manoah and the Chorus have of the death of Samson. Manoah is concerned with it as a noble fact. 'Nothing is here for tears'—he will gather the body and build over it a (very Miltonic) monument. Samson will have his place in the history and fame of the world, his acts enrolled in poetry,

> Copious legend or sweet lyric song.

His memory will awake in others the consciousness of great deeds; it is the business (some hold) of poetry.

But the Chorus, not denying this, have, however short their speech, something else to say. They too are aware that a great reconciliation has taken place; they have their own knowledge; their knowledge is Milton; and that knowledge is peace.

[1] It is obvious, in fact, as modern criticism does not yet seem boldly to have said, that these lines are by Shakespeare; it is therefore obvious that Shakespeare had a hand in *Samson*; and therefore that Milton was not composing a poem of his own but revising an old one. An edition of *Samson* assigning the different parts to the probable authors is much to be desired. Bacon may easily have had a hand in the political parts and perhaps Jonson in the classical allusions. Perhaps only the Delilah speech is Milton's.

Poetry in *Paradise Lost* had consisted of the narrator and the narrative; in *Samson* these are dramatized into the Chorus and the actors. But *Paradise Lost* had ended with the emphasis on the narrative; *Samson* ends with the emphasis on the Chorus. It is they who are aware of their own alteration.

> His servants he with new acquist
> Of true experience from this great event,
> With peace and consolation hath dismist,
> And calm of mind all passion spent.

The mind knowing things had always been an ostensible part of Milton as it had never ostensibly been of Shakespeare. It is of the mind knowing things that these words are spoken. Yet—that allowed—perhaps this conclusion is not so far from the close of Shakespeare's own verse. It was after many ways of dealing with life had been discovered by poetry that the 'great globe itself' vanished, and the music of Ariel was heard. It is that vanishing which, in another manner, the more conscious Milton calls 'all passion spent'.

Milton's genius remained conscious of itself. It could not become other, as Shakespeare's did in the end. It is not possible for Shakespeare's genius to *know* it is being pardon or Ariel; pardon that knows itself is not pardon, Ariel self-conscious of his non-humanity could not be Ariel. Self-consciousness can only be calm.

He had, in the young brightness of the Attendant Spirit, sung long ago

> —If Virtue feeble were,
> Heaven itself would stoop to her.

But not as quickly as all that. Virtue—poetry—had to go elsewhere—

> To-morrow to fresh woods and pastures new.

And still farther after the thing inseparate had been known in Satan—after change, solitude, and action—

> They hand in hand, with wandring steps and slow
> Through Eden took their solitary way.

It prophesied its own secret return to a reconciled knowledge:

> he unobserved
> Home to his mother's house private returned;

and at last to

> calm of mind, all passion spent.

Heaven had stooped to virtue in a very different way from that which the Attendant Spirit may be supposed to have expected. The justification of the ways of God to man had spread as a final calm through the consciousness in which war had ceased by mutual destruction.

The end of *Paradise Lost* in one sense returns to the beginning. Our first parents issue into a world where experiences already impersonated in the poetic figure of Satan await them. Adam's vision has shown them so much. Their solitary way is, as Milton's moral imagination presented it, either Satan's journey through chaos or Abdiel's through a veiled heaven. It leads to Troilus and Othello, to Lear on the heath and Wordsworth in the church. It leads also to *Samson*; where, as Shakespeare had set the concord of two opposites against the discord of two opposites, so Milton set the quiet of the conscious mind beholding a somewhat similar simultaneous defeat and victory. Shakespeare's subject had been things being so—even their knowing themselves had been part of their being. But Milton divided the spirit of man; and so was able to take, in a sense, an even more extreme moment. Poetry in Shakespeare had imagined at one moment death and life. But poetry in Milton imagined that moment as having been and it was composed in itself—'all passion spent'.

The phrase is the self-awareness of that state in which Shakespeare produced the last plays.

IV

WORDSWORTH

'FROM Milton,' said Landor, 'one must descend, whichever road one takes.' Even to find Shakespeare or find Wordsworth, though then in order to reascend; and of Shakespeare and Wordsworth it is true also. There are other poets of almost equal height, but they are only peaks compared with those three great ranges. There are other ranges, but they are not so high and they are made up of many poets.

To ascend Wordsworth is to ascend a mountain around which there clings a perpetual mist. Often that mist disappears or is blown apart, and then landscapes open below us, landscapes comparable to those we see from Milton or Shakespeare, landscapes of the mind of men. And then the mist gathers again and we are for awhile lost in it. It is this uncertainty gathering over the certainty, this intermission of sight, which is unique in Wordsworth among the three greatest poets. He possesses a power as great in its opening maturity as Milton's, yet that maturity never itself matures; the greatness of his poetry suffers no diminution even when compared with that other sublime sound; yet it moves to no final state of resolution. At its greatest his poetry is as far beyond the capacity of the human voice to utter as either Milton's or Shakespeare's. 'She should have died hereafter' cannot be spoken; it means more than our voice can carry: so does

> Jehovah, who in one night when he passed
> From Egypt, marching.

Our tongues cannot echo that divine exodus; we feel it as the soldiers felt the music when the god left the palaces of Alexandria. So with the finest things of Wordsworth—

> In beauty exalted as it is itself
> In quality and fabric more divine.

Mighty poets in their misery dead.

Diversity of strength
Attends us, if but once we have been strong.

And O ye Fountains, Meadows, Hills, and Groves,
Forebode not any severing of our Loves;
I only have relinquished one delight
To live beneath your more habitual sway.

The solemn sincerity of such lines is beyond the compass of our voices. The manner in which Shakespeare, Milton, and Wordsworth respectively defeat us would form the subject for another inquiry. Roughly, it may be suggested that Shakespeare does it by a unison of many implied if not expressed (but usually expressed) intellectual as well as emotional intensities; Milton does it by arousing a sense of the awful spiritual importance of a particular intensity; Wordsworth by arousing a sense of the unity of individual life with universal life. The shell of his verse 'murmurs of the ocean whence it came'; something more than us, more than Wordsworth, more than the poetry of Wordsworth, seems to open up and expand in the sound, as afterwards it withdraws and closes itself in the more expected, but still noble, verse to which it returns. Those central successes in all poets dispose themselves through the rest of the verse, which approaches or recedes from them, and is affected by them. But Wordsworth's style is more dangerous than Milton's. Milton's includes everything in its godlike capacity; if we protest and rebel, we are hurled headlong from that ethereal sky. But Wordsworth's is natural and has the dangers of nature. It is diffused; we do not escape from it—or from nature—so easily as we think. A page even of the worst part of the *Excursion* has often something attractive about it. The details Wordsworth inserts are there because they were there or would be there in nature, and Wordsworth is reluctant to leave anything out. But we are more easily tired.

At its greatest, this is his poetry. But there is, not merely the rest of it but, the depressing rest of it. Of course, he wrote badly sometimes; that is nothing. Shakespeare did it so often that we have—some of us—almost had to rob him of most of his work. Milton did it sometimes; a personal confession may admit that a few lines at the end of *Samson* (of all places in poetry!) appear almost funny:

> His lot unfortunate in nuptial choice,
> From whence captivity and loss of eyes.

Even the 'tame villatic fowl', just previously? I do not myself find the explanation of angelic digestion funny, and the use of artillery seems just an intellectual mistake, like the temporal begetting of the Son. But however this may be, even Milton occasionally lost hold. These poetic failures do not count. We can excuse, we can even enjoy, such a break as

> 'Impute it not to impatience, if', exclaimed
> The Wanderer, 'I infer that he was healed
> By perseverance in the course prescribed'.

It should never be imputed to our impatience that we over-zealously protested against such things; nor against 'Spade! with which Wilkinson hath tilled his land', or 'then cheered by short refreshment, sallied forth'. But what generations of readers have protested against is the appearance of something in Wordsworth which sounds like poetry and is not poetry, of something neither richly good nor richly bad; in two words, of dull verbiage.

> And shall the venerable halls ye fill
> Refuse to echo the sublime decree?

Who cares? 'Life', Wordsworth had told us, 'is energy of love'; what we need is the corresponding poetic energy.

That he wrote so much when that energy was lacking suggests that he did not recognize his want of it. On the other hand, he never completed the philosophical poem which he purposed, which the *Prelude* was to have preluded, of which the *Excursion* was to have been the second part, and the *Recluse* an extract from the first. The *Excursion* itself is a poem from which poetic energy can be sensibly understood to depart. There are great and noble things in it, as there were scattered through all Wordsworth's later life; and it has a right to demand—what it is not always allowed—that it should be a poem of its own kind and not of ours. But when we have done our best, it remains true that though the *Excursion* has nobler poetry in it than *Don Juan* has, yet *Don Juan* is a better poem and more homogeneous poetry than the *Excursion*. It would be a saint, a 'holy fool' of poetry, who would consent to keep the *Excursion* and lose *Don Juan*. And his sanctity and his folly would be equal.

This mass of unsuccessful stuff, this slow change in the *Excursion*, this abandonment of the great poem which Wordsworth had intended—to what cause are they due? to what cause in his poetry, not in his personal life (with which this essay is not concerned)? The answer is that his poetry could not sufficiently trust itself.[1]

Wordsworth had one poetic habit in common with Milton—the habit of introducing solitary figures. But there is a difference between them: Milton's are active, Wordsworth's are passive. Milton's are in revolt; Wordsworth's are in—what are they in? They are not in revolt; they are not entirely in acceptance, at least they are not in willing and exalted acceptance. They express—or some of them do—a trust in God. But this is secondary, even where it occurs, and it does not always occur. They communicate a strange sensation of semi-mystical fear; they rise before us in that verse, as shapes partly of terror, partly of sympathy, wholly of mystery. Examples are the soldier at the end of Book IV of the *Prelude*; the beggar in Book VII (ll. 635–49); the girl in Book XII (ll. 248–61); 'the single sheep, and the one blasted tree' also in Book XII (ll. 292–302, 317–23); the Leech-Gatherer; Margaret (in the *Affliction of Margaret*—though here the solitary figure speaks); the old Cumberland Beggar; the Solitary Reaper. These are the most striking among many

[1] To say that Wordsworth did not trust it is hardly sufficient. A man cannot write poetry by willing it. Besides which, we have no right to dogmatize about Wordsworth's personal mind. And besides which again, the very fact that he wrote so much suggests that he meant to trust, and thought he was trusting, in it. It was his genius that misled him, not he who miscompelled his genius. But, of course, that misleading was partly due to mortal things. I prefer myself to think that his genius was right in the account which it gave of the whole matter itself. For these reasons I have not discussed Annette.

solitudes; there are many others of less apparent significance —Lucy Gray is one—whose ghost

> sings a solitary song
> That whistles in the wind;

Margaret in the First Book of the *Excursion*, and other figures scattered through that poem; the Shepherd at the end of *Michael*; Leonard in the *Brothers*; the Forsaken Indian Woman; Ruth—all these, and more, sing their own solitary songs or preserve their solitary silences. And around them is that third circle which is only by accident solitary—the flowers and birds whom Wordsworth names singly, the Sky-lark, the Daisy, the Lesser Celandine, the Swan on still Saint Mary's lake, the Linnet, the Butterfly. Add the solitude of Lucy and the recurrent solitude of Wordsworth himself, and the groups will be sufficiently presented. Now among these there are, of course, many human solitaries, many who have been made lonely by their own actions or those of others, and this the poems tell us, arousing in us a sense of our own capacity for solitude and endurance. It is such things as those that make part of Wordsworth's greatness, confirming his instinctive claim to be part of our philosophic mind. Michael by the sheepfold, and Leonard and the Indian Woman, and Wordsworth, are all presentations of humanity. But that first group are not in fact presentations of humanity at all; they are something vaster and stranger.

Of the London beggar Wordsworth says that his own 'mind turned round as with the might of waters',

> And on the shape of that unmoving man,
> His steadfast face and sightless eyes, I gazed
> As if admonished from another world.

Of the soldier—or just before—he says, speaking of Solitude, that by night

> the soul of that great Power is met,
> Sometimes embodied on a public road,

and it is only after 'subduing my heart's specious cowardice' that he dares speak to that appearance

—Companionless
No dog attending, by no staff sustained,
He stood

his form
Kept the same awful steadiness—at his feet
His shadow lay, and moved not.

These are unnerving apparitions—at least, they almost unnerved Wordsworth; they came to him like the incarnations of the otherness he had in childhood known more vaguely in the 'low breathings', or the peak which called up

huge and mighty forms that do not live
Like living men.

And greater than beggar or soldier is the Leech-Gatherer. Wordsworth gave that poem a second title—'Resolution and Independence'. It is very proper that we should read it as, apparently, he meant us to; it is proper that we should realize what a great and moving poem it is. But it is permissible also that we should derive from it all that it contains; and one of the things it does contain is a sense that the Leech-Gatherer is the impersonated thought of some other state of being, which the acceptance of the noble doctrine it teaches leaves in itself unexplored.

He seems 'the oldest man . . . that ever wore grey hairs'; he was like 'a huge stone . . . on the bald top of an eminence', that seems 'a thing endowed with sense'; again he was like a

sea-beast, that on a shelf
Of rock or sand reposeth, there to sun itself.

He is 'motionless as a cloud that heareth not the loud winds'. He speaks 'in solemn order'—'a lofty utterance'.

His voice to me was like a stream
Scarce heard; nor word from word could I divide.
And the whole body of the man did seem
Like one whom I had met with in a dream.

His shape, his speech, 'the lonely place', all trouble Wordsworth.

In my mind's eye I seemed to see him pace
About the weary moors continually,
Wandering about alone and silently.

Confronted with this great experience Wordsworth might have done one of two things—in doing the very thing he did do. He asked him, out of the midst of his own bother about his future income—and God, He knows how real and urgent that bother can be; we shall never understand the poets if we pretend that money is not of high importance—he asked him, 'How is it that you live, and what is it you do?' And—as if 'sent To give me human strength'—the Leech-Gatherer told him, and Wordsworth listened and admired and believed and went away comforted. Nevertheless, that question might have been asked with another meaning—with the desire for some knowledge similar to that which caused Jacob to wrestle with the Angel: 'What is thy *name*?' It might have been asked not for strength and comfort, but for discovery and increase of poetic wisdom.

What *is* this apparition—this stone—this sea-beast—this cloud—this dream-like body—this undivided stream of lofty utterance? What is it in itself? Never mind what it means to our lives, what moral or message it has for us, or let that be secondary; 'what is thy *name*?' He belongs to that strange world from which the woman came, who bore a pitcher on her head and walked leaning against the wind, and the beggar who wore a label that seemed

> to typify the utmost we can know
> Both of ourselves and of the universe;

and the soldier who was an embodiment of the power of Solitude; and the Highland Reaper who sang 'the melancholy song', 'the plaintive numbers', of which Wordsworth knew that they might be 'of old unhappy far-off things'.

Lear on the heath, Satan on Niphates—if these had not been forced by the poets to speak, and speaking, to explain their being, would not they too have seemed to belong to that terrifying world?

In effect they do. Wordsworth drew from figures looming as Lear and Satan loomed, as Othello, and the Ghost of Caesar, and Samson in Gaza, a high and lofty doctrine. But it was a doctrine: his poetry ceased to inquire into them; perhaps therefore inevitably his poetry ceased. For it was a doctrine that concerned itself more with the way men should live than with poetry itself.

But so did Milton? *Nego*; at least not before his poetry had done all it could with Satan. Milton trusted poetry absolutely —Satan is the proof—and he was justified. Shakespeare trusted poetry absolutely—Lear and Macbeth are the proofs —and he was justified. But Wordsworth did not, could not, quite do that; therefore his poetry left his philosophy to get on as best it could, and his philosophy could not get on. The great philosophical poem was never written.

I do not suggest that either Milton or Shakespeare put it like that to themselves. But it is clear that both of them did wholly what they had to do, and left the rest to the Muse. It was, after all, *Milton* who dared the sublime defiance of 'Evil, be thou my good'; he himself must have trusted poetry profoundly before he could believe that his poem would get over that. He did not refuse it because his intelligence told him that it might prove harmful or shocking or wrong, just as he did not do it because it was harmful or shocking or wrong. It was Satan. Now there is a sense in which Wordsworth was compelled to avoid his own Solitaries. It is a sense so rare that, though he did it, Wordsworth remains our third greatest poet. But it is a sense so definite that he came near to thinking that good intentions would write poetry for him. It is a sense so unimportant that what he did is still 'felt in the blood and felt along the heart'. But it is a sense so important that what he did is thought to be good for the young and is consistently misapprehended and disliked by the young.[1]

And yet Wordsworth was a very great poet; if he had not been we should not even have known that he missed the final wrestling. It is not to any slackness on his part that we dare attribute this last—this very last—lack. It is to be attributed, little though they knew it, to Pitt and all those who declared

[1] There are no doubt exceptions. But anyone who has spoken of Wordsworth to the young will know how dull they suppose him to be. Well, of course, as long as we send them to him to discover moral impulses—and at that probably our own—in vernal woods, what can we expect? Bliss is it in *that* dawn to be alive?

war on the Revolution. Or so his poetry states, and what his poetry dared not or did not state must be left to students of his individual life.

The crisis of Troilus and the crisis of Satan is related to the crisis which fell on Wordsworth: at least as he discovers and expresses it in the *Prelude*. There is not only the account itself—'pity and shame', 'change and subversion', a shock 'to my moral nature', 'a revolution, at this one time', 'a stride Into another region', 'from that pleasant station torn And tossed about in whirlwind', 'a conflict of sensations without name'. These are the direct phrases—I do not see how they could be stronger. But there is more—he exulted when Englishmen were defeated, killed, and put to flight. And there follows the picture of Wordsworth, who loved the village and its people, and its people in the church at common prayer, himself sitting in the church, 'like an uninvited guest', silent, feeding 'on the day of vengeance yet to come'. The last line has to be fully felt before the depth of this part of Wordsworth's poetry can be realized. If anyone had asked him what England had done to 'soil our mothers' he might have answered, exactly in Troilus's words, 'nothing at all, unless that this were she'.

But *Troilus* was written half-way through Shakespeare's poetic life; so was *Paradise Lost* in Milton's. It was the poetic immaturity of Wordsworth's *Evening Walk* and *Descriptive Sketches* which suffered subversion. In 1792 Wordsworth all but became a leader of the Girondins; in 1793 he received this shock; in 1795–6 he wrote the *Borderers*; in 1797–8 he wrote the *Lyrical Ballads*, the *Recluse*, *Peter Bell*; in 1799 he began the *Prelude*, and ended it in 1805. It covered the second half of his great ten years; somewhere about the 1803–6 period he wrote also the *Ode on the Intimations of Immortality*, and in 1805–6 the *Happy Warrior*. The important point is that his personal experiences preceded nearly all his poetry; his poetry followed his personal experiences. No wonder he talked about emotion recollected in tranquillity! And how unwise of us to apply the phrase to anyone but Wordsworth.

For from these dates it is clear that when that crisis of

destiny fell on Wordsworth he could not attempt to explore it in high poetry, because he did not, till afterwards, reach high poetry.

It is, of course, just possible, in the abstract, that he might, in that state of outraged being, have destroyed all the unpublished poetry he had up to then written. It is just possible that as Othello struck at Desdemona, so Wordsworth struck at what was dearest to him. Poetry was not guilty as Othello supposed Desdemona to be. But if the universe had played him false, he might, for a few moments, have loved and hated what the universe and England had given him, and in that insanity destroyed it. 'Evil, be thou my good.' It is not likely, but it would be possible with any poet, and it is barely possible with Wordsworth. But it is likely that there would have been some trace of it in Dorothy's journals or elsewhere, and it may fairly safely be assumed that he did not. Besides, there is *Guilt and Sorrow*—but he might have left *that*.

His poetry therefore reflected his life up to then; his concern with Nature, and with man, his consciousness of that dreadful separation of the thing inseparate, and the means by which he was healed. But his healing, his recovery, was on the hither side of that divided universe, not on the yonder. His poetic genius therefore remained on the hither side. It knew there was another; it knew there was some greater resolution of the strife in man's heart. But it never had the strength to go there.

The abdication of the pure poetic authority in his verse in favour of some other authority is because it was by some other authority than the purely poetic that he was revived. 'Imagination and Taste,' is the title of the last two books of the *Prelude*, 'how impaired and restored.' They were restored; they were no more than restored—except for the operative faculty of discovering themselves in poetry. The comparison of certain lines in the *Prelude* with the discussion between the Trojan princes in *Troilus* is too marked to be neglected. 'What is aught but as 'tis valued?' What is value?

What the rule and whence
The sanction?

Hector had broken off the discussion, by Shakespeare's choice, either designedly or accidentally, long before that point had been reached. The end of the argument there is not decision, but Hector. The farther search was carried on not by the working of intellect but by the writing of poetry. It is true that Wordsworth's great subject was not men acting and suffering; these serve only as illustrations. His subject was the mind of man in relation to men, to the universe, and to God. He was—or would have been—a philosophical and not a dramatic poet. But poetry is all one; its glory equal, its majesty co-eternal. It uses doctrines; it does not obey them. It discovers ways through chaos; it does not follow them. It sits brooding on the vast abyss; it does not wait till the abyss has been delimited—even by Nature and Dorothy.

It could not do this at that time for Wordsworth, and for that single reason—he was a poet and he was not writing poetry. His soul relied on other authorities. His poetry, therefore, when it came to be, did not sufficiently distinguish between its own authority and that of other traditions. Towards the end of the *Excursion*, Wordsworth really does seem to think that to mention 'the voice of wisdom whispering Scripture texts' or Baptism was enough; he thought those things themselves had authority in themselves. So they may have, but not in poetry. If poetry is to refer to 'Scripture texts' it must make of them a poetic experience; if poetry is to thrill us with Baptism, it must make Baptism part of its own mythology. Wordsworth assumed that merely to mention seduction would make us disapprove of it; but in poetry this is not so, we must be urged by the poetic force. Poetry has to do all its own work; in return it has all its own authority.

Yet for ten years, and at intervals thereafter, how close to that central subject his poetry lay! how near it seems to be to holding in itself the great awareness of the divided consciousness, and presenting some new resolution of it! It has its doctrine for us, and it has more—it has the continual approach of something greater. There is in it the knowledge of something it cannot quite discover. 'We feel that we are greater than we know', 'Thoughts that lie . . . too deep for tears', 'we will teach them how', 'high instincts', the label on the beggar, the 'brightness' of the Happy Warrior. There are strange and solitary forms appearing, on lonely roads, on moors, in cities; and somehow—as in certain antique legends—the poet never asks quite the right question. Wordsworth took part with Coleridge in the *Lyrical Ballads*, and it is not always noticed that the actual themes of their verse are sometimes close. The Ancient Mariner is kindred to those other apparitions; only *they* could not speak of themselves, but must be challenged. The verse which Coleridge added to the *Ancient Mariner*—and blamed himself for adding—is a Wordsworthian verse translated into Coleridgian. 'He prayeth best who lovest best. . . .' But Coleridge was right; it ought not to be there. The *Ancient Mariner* is a tale of a similar crisis—of accident, doom, death, and life-in-death—but it flies between Wordsworth and Shakespeare. It has no reference either to man's enduring mind as Wordsworth has, nor to the hiding-places of the new power as Shakespeare has. It is faerie, and therefore the Mariner is compelled to tell the unrelated story. Had it been human, his embodied power would have had to wait to be challenged. Could that figure which was like a sea-beast sunning itself have held Wordsworth as the Mariner held the Wedding Guest . . . but alas, it was not to be.

Nevertheless, what came to be was a great thing. From the *Borderers* to the *Excursion* there is communicated a sense of the human spirit that does everything but what only Shakespeare did. The earliest long poem after the recovery was the *Borderers*. The *Borderers* is precisely an attempt to present a similar crisis to that through which Wordsworth passed—

> There was a plot,
> A hideous plot against the soul of man.
>
> A man by pain and thought compelled to live,
> Yet loathing life.
>
> Suffering is permanent, obscure, and dark,
> And shares the nature of infinity.

> The mind of man, upturned,
> Is in all natures a strange spectacle,
> In some a hideous one.

But there is no suggestion of a resolution. Then there came the many noble poems 'on man, on nature, and on human life', in which the authority of poetry is everywhere present. Among them are the solitaries who are significant of other things, but also those who awake our own knowledge of mighty endurance.

> The gods approve
> The depth and not the tumult of the soul;

the depth of the soul is shown here in the repose which had been restored to Wordsworth, and which he now searched out. Everywhere it is that to which his genius returns, with counsel, with wisdom, with exalted hope. He explores that state of being, even if he leaves others undetermined. The noblest expression of it—outside the *Prelude*—is the *Intimations of Immortality*. It is a platitude to say that it is not about immortality; it is about his own poetry. It is that which 'hath kept watch o'er man's mortality', which feels the 'fallings from us, vanishings', which in certain rare encounters trembles 'like a guilty thing surprised'. It is this which, after the 'hour Of splendour in the grass, of glory in the flower' has disappeared, is to find 'strength in what remains behind'. But strength in what remains behind is not the strength of Imogen, of Perdita, of Pericles, or of Ariel, nor the knowledge of the Chorus in *Samson*.

In the *Excursion* Wordsworth made an effort—a final effort—to gather everything in. He succeeded in manufacturing four eidola of himself: the Wanderer, who is Wordsworth's idea of the incarnation of his own poetic mind; the Solitary, who is Wordsworth's idea of himself gone wrong; the Vicar, who is Wordsworth's idea of himself ordained, and the narrator, who is just Wordsworth. After the first book or two it is almost impossible to be greatly interested. Yet even there poetry breaks out—of the same kind and concern—

> poor humanity's afflicted will
> Struggling in vain with ruthless destiny.
>
> The intellectual power, through words and things,
> Went sounding on, a dim and perilous way.

It is the very description of poetry making itself; it is a description of Shakespeare and Milton. It is a way, nevertheless, which Wordsworth's genius did not wholly take: it paused almost at the exact point at which he used the lines. For it was humanity's afflicted will struggling *in vain* of which his poetry was most intensely aware. He shaped the image of man repulsed by destiny, and made it into an everlasting nobility. The *Happy Warrior* is a single poem's vision of something else; but it is the *Ode to Duty*, the end of the *Immortality* Ode, the *Elegiac Stanzas*, and other poems of the kind, including parts of the *Prelude* and the *Excursion*, which do the work. This unique presentation we owe to Wordsworth and to Wordsworth alone. The depressing, the uninteresting, verse is a necessary accident of that achievement; we may not read it, but we ought to realize that it is a condition of what we have and do read, and no more to be regarded in itself than the plot of *Cymbeline* is to be solemnly discussed apart from Imogen and the Dirge. That Wordsworth wrote it is due to the same cause that shaped the particular burden of his great poetry—the fact that he, whose subject was his own experience, did not write poetry while he was undergoing that experience. He could not explore his own crisis by meeting it in poetry. He had to deal with his crisis as it had been resolved by other aids, and those aids and their result his poetry never fully assumed. But if we could be allowed to attribute will and intention to the English Muse, it might seem that she deliberately refrained from visiting her son until his central experience was ended, in order that we might have for our delight that great song of solemn endurance and hope. It is a music which might have accompanied Adam and Eve as they passed from Eden at the close of *Paradise Lost*.

DRAMA

SEED OF ADAM

A NATIVITY PLAY

CHARACTERS

THE TSAR OF CAUCASIA (*King of Gold*)
HIS CHORUS
THE SULTAN OF BAGDAD (*King of Frankincense*)
HIS CHORUS
ADAM
EVE
JOSEPH
MARY
THE ARCHANGEL
TWO ROMAN SOLDIERS
THE THIRD KING (*King of Myrrh*), a Negro
MOTHER MYRRH (*Hell*), a Negress

The scene is before the house of Adam; to the right of it are the stables; on the left, at the front, the stump of a tree or a high stone

SEED OF ADAM

The TSAR *enters with some of the* CHORUS

CERTAIN VOICES. Juggle, sir; throw up the golden slivers.
OTHER VOICES. Sir, no; show rather the rivers,
molten and golden streams; fertilizing, barricading,
cities and nations, from stations of earth-edging Esquimaux
to the hanging gardens of tropical sense:
and there the high ships sailing, the deep ships unlading.
FIRST VOICES. Necklaces, bracelets, ear-rings; gaudies and gew-gaws!
OTHER VOICES. Purse rather and pocket of outer commerce; mind
finding after kind, and all traffic its own.
THE TSAR. I am Gaspar,[1] Tsar of Caucasia;
I sprang from our father Adam's loins
in a bright emission of coins; Eve's need
of gilded adornment nourished me to dig and dive.
Pearls I brought up; springs I let forth: who
will be beautiful now? who profitable then?
Men thrive and I take my fee.
Tricked out in riches half the world follow me;
who fall, crawl or are kicked into dry ditches.

[*The* SULTAN *enters, with the rest of the* CHORUS

CERTAIN VOICES. Sir, play; throw up the notes of gold,
or stir into silver smoke the rich incense.
OTHER VOICES. Sir, no; our old throats are tired.
Show rather the philosophical plan,
chess-playing, brick-laying, sooth-saying;
the design of line, point, and curve.
FIRST VOICES. Titillate the brain by ear and eye!
OTHER VOICES. Build the austere academies to show why.

[1] Traditionally, Melchior is the King whose gift is gold. C. W. has reversed Melchior and Gaspar, here and in an early poem. [A. R.]

THE SULTAN. I am Melchior, Sultan of Bagdad.
Adam my father and Eve my mother
construed me aloof from sister and brother
through a post-paradisal afternoon.
I build my mosques under a philosophical moon;
I ride on the body's curves through spirals of air
to the bare and rare domes of Bagdad my see.
I give to whoever serves with me
gnomic patterns of diagrammatic thrills.
Half the world live in my train;
who refrain, bereft of brain, are left to common ills.

SEMI-CHORUS. Give us the golden matter,

SEMI-CHORUS. and the golden chatter,

THE CHORUS. for to-morrow everything begins again.

[*They gather about the* KINGS, *some sitting or lying*

ADAM [*coming out of the house*]. Dullards of darkness, light's lazy-bones,
poor primitives of our natural bareness,
where's your awareness ? will moans and groans
for gold of brawn or brain regain
the way to the entry of Paradise ? up!
shut your eyes, will you ? or make a play
for your leisure, and a treasure of your idleness ? You,
have you nothing better to do
in our world but play hide and seek with oblivion ?
Say, say something, say
who are you ? I will tell you, tell you what you knew,
I am Adam.

SEMI-CHORUS. Father Adam, the pasture is thin,
the sheep and the hogs are thin, our coats
button thinly about our throats
thrawn with wind and thirsty for wine.
Exchanges—his and mine—help us
to bear with the bitterness of having nothing.
What should *we* do, feeling for Paradise ?
Better to suck at the heel of the Tsar.

SEMI-CHORUS. Father Adam, if we go looking and snooping round corners,

we see terrible shapes trooping,
things eagle-beaked, giants with scimitars.
In Eden you found them friendly; here
what should we do but hide while they stride and deride
the bitterness of our having nothing?
Have you seen us slinking from those neighbourly taunts?
Better to go drinking the rhythms of the Sultan.

ADAM. If you found Paradise, you would find everything.

THE CHORUS. Call with the old bluster to muster by masses, and seek!

SOLO. Speak civilly, father!
Where
shall we go? climb invisible cords into the air?
for road, river, and lane
are searched; it is not to be found.

THE CHORUS. And to-morrow everything begins again!

SOLO. What is this way? behind what sight or sound?

SOLO. He lost it, and he cannot say.

SOLO. There is not any.

SOLO. Yes; it is bought for a penny
and slept off.

SOLO. No; wise men have recognized
it is only our mothers' forms rationalized.

SOLO. The Tsar declares it is hope learning to grope.

SOLO. The Sultan says it is sensation living in negation.

SOLO. It is the loss of the one thing prized
masochistically advertized;

SOLO. or adolescence flushed with immature sense.

ADAM. Babies!

THE CHORUS. Who lost it?

ADAM. I. What do you know,
children, of what living on this earth is like then?

THE SULTAN. Father, you must not think you are everyone.

THE TSAR. Your children are men and women, and not you.

THE SULTAN. Individualized essence of you, perhaps;

THE TSAR. with each his particular Paradise in a nutshell.

THE SULTAN [*touching his lyre*]. Nuts! nuts!

THE TSAR [*throwing gold pieces*]. Nuts! nuts!

BOTH. Nuts for the men-monkeys!
Monkey-nuts! follow, follow, monkey-nuts!
scratch and snatch for a portion of monkey-nuts!
grab and grizzle for a ration of monkey-nuts!
houp-la!

[*The* CHORUS, *chattering and fighting, run about like monkeys. They gradually become involved in a general fierce battle and drift off, following the* KINGS, *with high shrieks*]

ADAM. I must set my law upon them; one thing first.

[*He turns, meeting* EVE, *who has come out of the house at the noise*]

EVE. Are they fighting again?

ADAM. What else?
They have not the pain that in us stops us fighting.

EVE. Have they found anything?

ADAM. Nothing, my Eve.
They cannot find the centre, the core of the fruit
where the root of return is. I dropped it; it is gone.
Where is Mary?

EVE. Mary has gone to the fair.

ADAM. Under the Mercy! . . . what is she doing there?

EVE. Watching mountebanks, laughing at clowns,
applauding jugglers and tightrope walkers,
listening to talkers, admiring lovers,
riding with children on the roundabout,
everywhere in the middle of the rout,
being, by her nature, all things to all men.

ADAM. Will she never discover any preference? any partial
liking for this where or that when?
Will she never care to marshal phenomena?
Cows, clowns, and crowns are alike to her—
has she not a trick of nursing the sick,
and as agile through all as the honey-plucking bee,
catching as much sweet there as from booths at the fair?
She must follow now another mind than mine.
I am set. Call Joseph; they shall be married.

EVE. Married! Mary? but why? and why Joseph?

ADAM. Lest I should die. She shall be wedded
lest our youngest born should be a prey
in her simplicity to her sisters and brothers.
I will not have her a scullion and a scorn
in the huts of Caucasia or the harems of Bagdad.
Joseph is a warlike and dutiful lad.
Call him.

EVE. What is he, where is he, now?

ADAM. Lieutenant-general of the Sultan's horse,
an Islamite, a genius in cavalry tactics!
To see swung whole squadrons in the charge,
and—in a wild clatter of words breaking—flung
down the speaking of a poem, when the matter is sprung
to the flashing and slashing of a steel line
at the throat's blood. Hafiz taught him
and Omar; he outgenerals them; call him.

EVE. Will Mary have him?

ADAM. As soon as any.
O pest on her for a zany of goodwill!

EVE. Husband!

ADAM. Be easy. I am petulant. My want
worries at my throat, while she wants nothing,
nor ever sighs for nor even denies Paradise.

EVE. Paradise perhaps is hers and here.

ADAM. Among the sick or at the fair?—
Look, there she comes: call Joseph, I say.
He is in Bagdad's train. I must go again
to quieten their brawls. I will give them peace.
I will show them if I am Adam for nothing.

[JOSEPH *and* MARY *enter*

ADAM. Joseph, am I your lord?

JOSEPH. In all things, sir,
under the justice of God.

ADAM. Your father, Mary?

MARY. Sir, by the Direction.

ADAM. It is well; hear me.
I do and undo; I am Adam. Paradise
shuts its last mouth upon us, and I am afraid.

It may be, after I have conquered yonder apes,
and shaped them to placabilities, that I shall find
by counting them some form unguessed,
some archangel disguised, some person or place
where is the grace of the Return. If, well;
if not, the thing this world must soon become
catches us up. Whether this be or not
I am determined you two shall be married.
A heart of purity and a mind of justice
to be integrity. What say you?

JOSEPH. Sir,
I am of no more worth to the princess Mary
than the fly-flick of her mule's tail.

MARY. But as much, Joseph, indeed.

JOSEPH. You hear, my lord?

ADAM. Never mind her.
Since she loves all, she loves you. What of you?

JOSEPH. She is the manifest measurement of God's glory
correcting time.

ADAM [*motioning them before him*]. You are both my best of
children.

[JOSEPH *and* MARY *kneel;* ADAM *raises his right arm*

By the single indecipherable Name
I swear you, Joseph and Mary, to betrothal.

[JOSEPH *and* MARY *rise and face each other. The up-raised palms of their right hands touch. They turn to face* ADAM]

When I return from conquering the world, be ready,
as then shall be, in time and space, convenient.
Come, Eve. [ADAM *and* EVE *go out*

JOSEPH. Am I appointed for your husband? . . .
Answer, princess . . . no? no then, do not speak,
do not break through such an outgoing stress of light,
as is the sovereign blessedness of the world,
there indivisible, all ways else divisible.
Do not with descent, O altitude, even of mercy,
sweeten the enhancèd glance of those still eyes
which to my lord's house, and to me the least,

illumine earth with heaven, our only mortal
imagination of eternity,
and the glory of the protonotary Gabriel.

[MARY *stretches out her hand to him; he kneels and kisses it*]

MARY [*murmuring the name*]. Gabriel, Gabriel: well spoken is the name.
As I came from the fair I looked back; there
I saw it all in a sheath and a shape of flame,
having an eagle's head that turned each way
as if it were guarding something and looking for something.
Its eyes burned at me; the noise
of the hurly-burlies and the hurdy-gurdies,
the ball-spinners, the silk-sellers, the rum-peddlers,
the swings, and the songs, rose to a whirring voice,
the air was a hum of sound; I heard it come
as if the fair all rose in the air and flew
on eagle's wings after me; I ran
through the fear and the laughter and the great joys.
I came by the vineyards to my father's roof;
there it held aloof a little.
I saw you; I gave you my hand, Joseph,
at my father's will. It has still power,
this hand of Adam's daughter, on all creatures of heaven.

JOSEPH [*as he kneels*]. O princess,
your hand is the fact of God's compact of light.

MARY. I have heard such talk among the lovers at the fair.
Bless you for telling me, Joseph.

[*He releases her hand. The* ARCHANGEL *appears at the back, as it were casting sleep towards* JOSEPH, *who sinks slowly forward, and lies still*]

MARY. Joseph! [*A pause*
Joseph! [*She sees him lying*

THE ANGELIC CHORUS [*without*]. Adonai Elohim! Adonai Elohim![1]

[1] The Hebrew is written phonetically, as for the Sephardi pronunciation (vowel sounds as in Italian, all *r*'s distinctly sounded, *ch* as in *loch*). The Ashkenazi pronunciation can be used if desired.

THE ARCHANGEL [*standing behind* MARY]. Adonai hu ha-elohim!

THE CHORUS [*as the angelic army without*]. Shalom lach eschet-chen, Adonai immach beruchah at bannashim.
Al-tiri Miryam ki-matsat chen lifne ha-elohim.
Vehinnach harah veyoladt ben vekaret et-shemo Yeshua.

MARY. How shall these things be, seeing I know not a man?

THE CHORUS. Ruach hakkodesh tavo alayieh ugevurat elyon tatsel alayich: al ken Kadosh yeamer layyillod ben-ha-elohim.

MARY. Behold the handmaid of the Lord; be it unto me
according to thy word.

[*The* ARCHANGEL *passes round and enters the stables.* MARY *remains rapt*]

JOSEPH [*he rises to his knees, as before, and wakes*]. Under the Protection! Mary . . . Mary . . .

MARY. Yes, Joseph?

JOSEPH. Mary, you are changed; you are in love.

MARY. Yes, Joseph.

JOSEPH [*starting up*]. Ah, ah! but who . . . ?

MARY. No one, Joseph.
Only in love.

JOSEPH. It must be then with someone.

MARY. Dearest, you did not hear: we said *in love.*
Why must, how can, one be in love with someone?

JOSEPH. Because . . . but that is what *in love* means;
one is, and can only be, in love with someone.

MARY. Dearest, to be in love is to be in love,
no more, no less. Love is only itself,
everywhere, at all times, and to all objects.
My soul has magnified that lord; my spirit
rejoiced in God my saviour; he has regarded
the nothingness of his handmaid. He has thrust
into this matter his pattern of bones, as Eve's
towers of cheeks and arrogant torches of eyes
edify red earth into a pattern of manhood.

JOSEPH. But it must be at some time and in some place.

MARY. When you look at me, dear Joseph, do you think so?
JOSEPH. Babylonia and Britain are only boroughs of you.
Your look dimensions the world. I took once
a northward journey to find fables for the Sultan
and heard a lad on the hill of Faesulae syllabling
a girl of Faesulae who nodded good-morning at him,
and that her form timed the untimed light.
Place must be because grace must be,
and you because of glory. O blessing,
the light in you is more than you in the light.
MARY. The glory is eternal, and not I,
and I am only one diagram of the glory:
will you believe in me or in the glory?
JOSEPH. It is the vision of the Mercy.
MARY. Hold to that.
But for salvation—even of those who believe
that time and place and the one are the whole of love—
Love—O the Mercy! the Protection!—
shall make his flesh as one in time and place.
It shall come in the time of Augustus Caesar,
in the place of Bethlehem of the Holy Ghost,
in the coast of Judaea: not quite Jerusalem,
but not far from Jerusalem, not far but not quite.
O Thou Mercy, is this the secret of Thy might?
When Thou showest Thyself, that Thou art not there
to be found? we find Thee where Thou art not shown.
Thou art flown all ways from Thyself to Thyself,
and Thy ways are our days, and the moment is Thou.
O Thou Mercy, is this the thing to know?
Joseph, come, take me to Bethlehem;
there the apparition and the presence are one,
and Adam's children are one in them;
there is the way of Paradise begun.

[*They move round the stage to the stone. As they go, the* CHORUS *re-enter on all sides*]

THE CHORUS. In Thule, in Britain, in Gaul, in Rome,
among the slim pillars of Bagdad, in round mounds of Caucasia,

we heard the maxim that rules the schools of prophets:
this also is Thou; neither is this Thou.

With double hands and single tongues
the prophets climb the rungs of heaven,
in the might of a maxim gained and given:
this also is Thou; neither is this Thou.

But we who wander outside the rules and schools
compromise and complain,
before the clot in the blood has shot to the heart or brain:
this is not quite Thou and not quite not.

Sister, sister, did you dream?

What did you see on the banks of the body's stream,
in Thule, in Britain, in Gaul, in Rome,
under Bagdad's dome, by the mounds of Caucasia?
SOLO. One came walking over the sand,
one and a shadow from a desert land;
I saw a knife flash in a black hand.

At daybreak a child is born to the woman;
he grows through the noon to his full stature;
she devours him under the moon; then at morn—
THE CHORUS. Save us, Father Adam, or we perish!—
SOLO. or in a mirage of morn the child is reborn.
And to-morrow everything begins again.
THE CHORUS. From bone, from brain, from breasts, from hands,
from the mind's pillars and the body's mounds,
the skies rise and roll in black shadows
inward over the imperial soul:
over our sighs in the moon of dusty sorrow—
O, O, could everything begin before to-morrow;
over the creak of rusty grief—
to-morrow will be soon enough for belief;
over the kitchens of a pot neither cold nor hot,
and the thin broth, and the forming of the clot—
not quite Thou and not quite not.

Father Adam, save us or we perish.

[MARY *sits on the stone,* JOSEPH *stands behind her. From opposite sides two* ROMAN SOLDIERS *run in, turn to the front, and come to the salute*]

FIRST SOLDIER. Octavianus Caesar Augustus,

SECOND SOLDIER. filius Julii divi Augustus,

BOTH SOLDIERS. orders the world in the orbit of Rome.

FIRST SOLDIER. Oaths and service to the lord Augustus;

SECOND SOLDIER. incense and glory to the god Augustus:

BOTH SOLDIERS. to the god Augustus and the Fortune of Rome.

[*They wheel inwards, and fall back on either side.* ADAM *re-enters as* AUGUSTUS, *accompanied by* EVE *and the two* KINGS]

ADAM. I was Julius, and I am Octavianus,
Augustus, Adam, the first citizen,
the power in the world, from brow to anus,
in commerce of the bones and bowels of men;
sinews' pull, blood's circulation,
Britain to Bagdad. I in brawn and brain
set knot by knot and station by station.
I drive on the morrow all things to begin again.
Look, children, I bring you peace;
I bring you good luck; I am the State; I am Caesar.
Now your wars cease; what will you say?

THE TSAR. Hail, Caesar; I am your occupation for the days.

THE SULTAN. I am your sleeping-draught for the nights: hail, Caesar.

THE CHORUS. Hail, Caesar; we who are about to die salute you!

ADAM. I will take now a census of the whole world,
the nations and generations of the living and dead,
to find whether anywhere it has been said
what place or person Paradise lies behind,
even among the prophets who made a formula for the mind.
Each man shall answer, on or under earth,
from Cain and Abel, who were first to explore
womb and tomb, and all whom women bore,

to the pack that died at Alexandria yesterday.
Answer, children, and say, if you can. I know
the thing that was threatened comes; there is still time.
Go!

[*The* SOLDIERS *run out; there is a deep and confused noise.*[1] *Presently they return, bearing papers*]

FIRST SOLDIER. All these millions dead

SECOND SOLDIER. and dying; these thousands dying or dead;

FIRST SOLDIER. these hundreds, and sixteen—

[*He drops his spear towards the nearest of the* CHORUS *on his side, who answers as from a sepulchre*]

ONE OF THE CHORUS. and seventeen

ANOTHER. and eighteen

ANOTHER. and nineteen

[*All answer in turn, as the* FIRST SOLDIER, *and then the* SECOND, *pass, pointing their spears. The* SECOND *comes to* JOSEPH]

JOSEPH [*answering according to the number of the* CHORUS]. and thirty-six [*The* SOLDIER *points to* MARY

JOSEPH [*answering for her*]. and thirty-seven.
Shall I add one more for the child that slumbers in your womb?

MARY. O no, Joseph; he is something different from all numbers;

[1] The producer suggested that something should be added here, and used to prepare for the entrance of the Third King shortly afterwards. C. W. had begun to write this additional matter, but the following fragment is all that we have:

TSAR. When the Archangel spoke to you in the true Paradise
and your heart broke—what did he say, there
under the trees? something you could not hear
about not-dying

SULTAN. When you ran and pushed
your way through hedge and river, when you rushed
down the ledge of rock between the abounding foliage
near the water rounding Paradise and the world outside—
a few leaves of the hedge clung to your coats

TSAR. a few drops of water hung on your skins.
That was the beginning.

SULTAN. Twinning what was one

you cannot tell how or whom. The people are reckoned,
but the child that comes through me
holds infinity in him, and hides in a split second.

[*The* SOLDIERS *return to* ADAM

FIRST SOLDIER. Hail, Caesar; those who are dead

SECOND SOLDIER. and those about to die

BOTH SOLDIERS. salute you.
Octavianus Caesar Augustus;
filius Julii divi Augustus;
gubernator, imperator, salvator, Augustus.

A VOICE [*off*]. What is this difference between the dying and the dead?

[*The* THIRD KING *enters, followed by a* NEGRESS, *carrying a scimitar*]

ALL [*except* JOSEPH *and* MARY, *in a general moan*]. Ah!

THIRD KING [*looking round*]. What provincial talk is this? what academic
pedantic dichotomy? O la, brothers!

[*Seeing the* KINGS *left, right*

THE TWO KINGS. Ah, brother, how did you find us?

THIRD KING. Indeed I might not have done;
but my mother here has eyes and a nose,
and with each sun recognized more strongly
gold's glint and censer's smell.
As the wind of infinity blows
earth is always leaving clues for hell,
and hell has only to follow that news of earth.
[*To the* CHORUS]
No wonder you talk so if you have them here
talking of distinctions and differences, smells and savours,
sight of gold, sniff of incense, flavours
of this or that differing degree of corruption.
[*To the* KINGS]
You left me away in a stony land,
brothers; I was lonely without you.
I came to find this mind of Rome,
this concept, this Augustus, this new Adam.
Why, father! The old Adam, after all!

ADAM. It is you, is it?

THIRD KING. I. You saw me
when you breathlessly slid down the smooth threshold
of Paradise gate? and saw the things that were hid
as God warned you you would? did you know
I was the core of the fruit you ate?
Did you remember, ungrateful that you are,
how you threw me away, with such a swing
I flew over Eden wall, dropped,
and stuck between two stones?
You did not see; you did not look after me!
Smell and taste for you; let the core go to hell.
But God looks after the sparrows.
Presently the sun split the core,
and out grew I, the King of the core.
I have travelled to get back to you ever since.

EVE. And who is she?

THIRD KING. Ah, she!
At the heart of the core, in the core of me,
lived a small worm you could not see.
The sun is a generous sun; he set us both free.
She lives by me, and I by her.
I call her my little mother Myrrh,
because of her immortal embalming. We two
have come, my other mother, to live with you—
if you can call it living.

ADAM. What else?

THIRD KING. O well! She has her own idea of food.
[*He indicates the scimitar*
The nearer the relation, the better the dish.
But you will not *die*; no, I do not think you will *die*.
I did not, and I have been eaten often,
you may imagine; it was a long way from here,
and a long time ago, that we made our start,
and angels on the way delayed us,
with exhortations of earnest heavenly evangels:
but what can angels do against decaying matter?
Matter can only be corrected by matter,

flesh by flesh; we came through and came on,
and I everlastingly perishing. The worm
of that fruit, father, has a great need to feed
on living form. But I do not think you will die.

ADAM [*to the* SOLDIERS]. Seize her.

[*They rush forward. She laughs at them, and they fall back on their knees*]

THIRD KING. Whom are you seeking?
Are you come out with swords and staves to take us?
We were often with you in your temples: now—
Father Adam, you were always a fool,
and it seems at the top of your Roman school
no better; will you arrest the itch
with your great hands? will your bands pitch
their javelins against the diabetes of the damned?
The belly is empty in hell though the mouth is crammed:
a monotonous place!

THE CHORUS. Father Adam, lord Augustus!

THIRD KING. Among the stones and locusts she lived on me;
it is your turn—this is my refrigerium.

[*He draws back. The* TWO KINGS *drop their gold and lute.* EVE *covers her face. The* NEGRESS *walks slowly round, the* CHORUS *falling on their knees as she passes. At last she comes to* MARY. *Meanwhile the* CHORUS]

THE CHORUS. Call the kings!
saints! poets!
prophets! priests!
Call the gospels and the households!
those of Aquino and Assisi!
Stratford! Chalfont St. Giles!
caskets of Caucasia!
censers of Bagdad!

ALL. Help us and save us!

THE TWO KINGS. Balthazar our brother is stronger than we.

THE CHORUS. Call on the households!
harp-stringer of David!

hewer of wood for Joseph!
ink-maker for Virgil!
galley-captain of Caesar!
armour-bearer of Taliessin!

ALL. Come to your defences! all heavenly lords,
stand about us with swords.

THIRD KING. Election is made, capital rather than coast:
she thrives most on the dear titbits of perfection.
Sister, you are lovelier than all the rest,
and like the busy blest. She shall eat you alive
for her great hunger; take pity on her appetite.

[JOSEPH, *drawing his own scimitar, thrusts himself between them*]

JOSEPH [*crying out*]. Ha, ha! to me, my household!
There is no God but God: in the name of God!

[*The scimitars clash; the* THIRD KING *touches* JOSEPH *in the thigh; he stumbles and is beaten down*]

THIRD KING [*dragging him away*]. Little man, martyrs and confessors
are no good here, nor are poets any good.
They are all a part of the same venomous blood.
Come away, come away, and wait your turn quietly.

[MARY *takes a step or two forward*

MARY. Dearest, you will find me very indigestible.
The stomach of the everlasting worm
is not omnivorous; it is a poor weak thing:
nor does the fire of Gehenna do more than redden
the pure asbestos of the holy children; if mine,
is for the fire and your dangerous appetite to find.

[*The* NEGRESS *attacks* MARY *with her scimitar.* MARY *goes back before her, at first slowly, moving round the stage*]

MARY. Sister, how slowly you carve your meat!

THIRD KING. Be easy, sister; you will not get away from us.

MARY. Nor she from me, brother, which is more important.

[*The movement of the two women quickens and becomes a dance; the scimitar flashing round them in a white fire. The* CHORUS *sway to the movement,* ADAM *only remaining motionless*]

MARY [*suddenly breaking into song*]. Parturition is upon me: blessed be He!
Sing, brothers; sing, sisters; sing, Father Adam.
My soul magnifies the Lord.

THE CHORUS [*hesitatingly*]. My spirit hath rejoiced in God my saviour.

MARY [*dancing and singing*]. For he hath regarded the low estate of his handmaid:

THE CHORUS [*gathering strength*]. behold, from henceforth all generations shall call thee blessed.

[MARY *at the door of the stable, where the* ARCHANGEL *is seen, catches the uplifted wrist of the* NEGRESS *in her right hand. They stand rigid, foot to foot*]

MARY [*singing joyously through a profound suspense*]. For he that is mighty hath done to me great things;

THE NEGRESS [*in a shriek of pain and joy*]. and holy is his Name.

[*She faints at* MARY's *feet*

MARY [*leaning towards* JOSEPH]. Joseph!
My son calls to his foster-father: come!
prince of maidens, hasten to the master of maidenhoods, and the pillar of maternity.

JOSEPH [*half-rising*]. O mother of the world's brightness,
I sought uprightness, and yet it failed in the end!

MARY. Most dear friend, my lord, it delayed the scimitar
but till my son took flesh under its flash:
the heavens constrain me to glory: Joseph!

[*He springs up and to her, and takes her into the stable*

ADAM [*in a strong voice*]. His mercy is on them that fear him from generation to generation.

[*The* CHORUS, *singing, gather about the* TWO KINGS, *as at first*]

FIRST CHORUS. He hath showed strength with his arm;

SECOND CHORUS. he hath scattered the proud in the imagination of their hearts.

FIRST CHORUS. He hath put down the mighty from their seats;

SECOND CHORUS. and exalted them of low degree.

FIRST CHORUS. He hath filled the hungry with good things;

SECOND CHORUS. and the rich he hath sent empty away.

THIRD KING [*stretching out his hand towards the* CHORUS]. Are you now so gay?

[*As his hand sinks down, they fall on their knees*

And you, lord Adam,
do not speak too soon; you desired the boon of salvation—
have it! You desired twice—me and not me,
the turn and the Return; the Return is here,
take care that you do not now prefer me.

JOSEPH [*coming from the stable*]. Sir, send a midwife to your daughter.

All things are rigid; only Mary and I
move, and the glory lies even between us.
The Return is at point to issue; befriend salvation.

[*All the figures are rigid, except* JOSEPH *and the* THIRD KING. ADAM *speaks with difficulty and without moving*]

ADAM. Whom shall I send? whom?

THIRD KING. We, call we you father, are not yours;
we are the things thought of before you, brought
into Eden while men were not, when
in the Days hunger was created, and lives
with a need always to feed on each other. This
was felt in the first kiss of man and woman.
Mother, there is a good cake for you now
to take everlastingly; go, kiss her, love
hungers: deliver her and she shall deliver you.

[*The* NEGRESS *leaps up and turns on him*

The eaten are on your left hand, the uneaten on your right;
go—there is no thing living so dextrous as you.

[*The* NEGRESS *and* JOSEPH *go into the stable*

THE ARCHANGEL. Adonai hu ha-elohim!

THIRD KING. What do you see, man? but I see.
Flesh is become that firmament of terrible crystal
your prophet saw: within it wreathed amber
and fire sheathed in the amber; now

the fire and the amber and the crystal are mingled into form;
what do you hear, man? [*He pauses*] but I hear
the terrible sound of the crystal singing as it spins
round the amber where the fire is hidden, and now the amber
is hidden in the crystal, and the crystal spinning into flesh,
twining into flesh: it slows, it stops, it sinks—
what do you know, man? but I know—
it drops into the stretched hands of my mother;
my mother has fetched a child from the womb of its mother;
my mother has taken the taste of the new bread.
Adonai Elohim!

[JOSEPH *comes from the stable*

JOSEPH. Father Adam, come in; here is your child,
here is the Son of Man, here is Paradise.
To-day everything begins again.

[ADAM *goes down to the door of the stable*

MARY [*meeting him and genuflecting*]. Bless me, father: see how
to-morrow is also now.

ADAM [*making the sign of the Cross*]. Under the Protection!
peace to you, and to all; goodwill to men.

[*They go into the stable*

JOSEPH. Our father Adam is gone in to adore.

THE TSAR. Blessed be he who is the earth's core

THE SULTAN. and splits it all ways with intelligible light.

THE CHORUS. Christ bring us all to the sight
of the pattern of glory which is only he.

THE ARCHANGEL. Yeshua!

THE TSAR. Blessed be he whose intelligence came to save
man from the gripping of the grave: blessed be he.

THE SULTAN. Blessed be he who, because he does all things well,
harries hell by his mercy: blessed be he.

THIRD KING. Blessed be he who is the only Necessity
and his necessity in himself alone.

EVE. Blessed be he who is sown in our flesh, grown
among us for our salvation: blessed be he.
THE CHORUS. Christ bring us, by his clean pact,
into the act which is only he.
THE ARCHANGEL. Yeshua!
THIRD KING. He consumes and is consumed.
THE SULTAN. He is the womb's prophecy and the tomb's.
THE TSAR. He creates, redeems, glorifies: blessed be he.
EVE. He is all our heart finds or lacks.
JOSEPH. He frees our souls from hell's cracks.
THE CHORUS. Christ bring us, by his true birth,
into a new heaven and earth.
JOSEPH. Blessed be he whose love is the knowledge of good
and its motion the willing of good: blessed be he.
THE CHORUS. Adore, adore: blessed for evermore
be the Lord God Sabaoth: blessed be He.

RELIGION

THE CROSS

From a symposium, What the Cross Means to Me, *1943*

ANY personal statement on such a subject as the present is bound to be inaccurate. It is almost impossible to state what one in fact believes, because it is almost impossible to hold a belief and to define it at the same time, especially when that belief refers not to objective fact but to subjective interpretation. A rhetorical adjective will create a false stress; a misplaced adverb confuse an emotion. All that can be hoped is that a not too incorrect approximation may eventually appear. And anything that does appear is, of course, to be read subject to the judgement of the Christian Church, by whom all individual statements must be corrected.

Joseph Conrad, in his *Letters to Madame Paradowska*, says: 'Charity is divine and universal Love, the divine virtue, the sole manifestation of the Almighty which may in some manner justify the act of creation.' The last phrase is not perhaps one which would be used by the normal Christian. But the need for some such credible justification of the act of creation is one of which even the normal Christian may, humanly speaking, be very conscious. Many sermons and pious books are devoted to no other end. Much discussion of 'faith' means nothing else. Nor (still speaking in terms of human feeling) is such a justification unnecessary. The original act of creation can be believed to be good and charitable; it is credible that Almighty God should deign to create beings to share His Joy. It is credible that He should deign to increase their Joy by creating them with the power of free will so that their joy should be voluntary. It is certain that if they have the power of choosing joy in Him they must have the power of choosing the opposite of joy in Him. But it is not credible that a finite choice ought to result in an infinite distress; or rather let it be said that, though credible, it is not tolerable (to us) that the Creator should deliberately maintain and sustain His created universe in a state of infinite distress as a result of the choice. No doubt it is possible to Him.

This would be true, even if it were we ourselves who had made that choice. I am far from saying that we did not. It may be that we were 'in' Adam very much more particularly than is often supposed; it may be indeed that we, in that pre-fallen state, *were* Adam, and that it was we who chose. *Fuimus ille unus*, said Augustine, *quando fuimus in illo uno*; we were the one when we were in the one. But popular doctrine in the Church has rather taken the view that we did not consciously choose that original sin, but are at most its successors and inheritors. The vicarious guilt of it is in us; the derived concupiscence is in us. There remains for us the eternal dying which is its result.

This is the law which His will imposed upon His creation. It need not have been. Aquinas said that God wills His own goodness necessarily, but other things not necessarily. Our distress then is no doubt our gratuitous choice, but it is also His. He could have willed us not to be after the Fall. He did not. Now the distress of the creation is so vehement and prolonged, so tortuous and torturing, that even naturally it is revolting to our sense of justice, much more supernaturally. We are instructed that He contemplates, from His infinite felicity, the agonies of His creation, and deliberately maintains them in it. I do not refer merely to the agonies of the present time; they are more spectacular and more destructive, but not more lasting, nor perhaps very much worse, than the agonies of a more peaceful time. But man has not often known a more peaceful time. And if he had, in the times that he has known, the very burden of daily existence too often seems a curse. The whole creation groaneth and travaileth together.

This then is the creation that 'needs' (let the word be permitted) justifying. The Cross justifies it to this extent at least—that just as He submitted us to His inexorable will, so He submitted Himself to our wills (and therefore to His). He made us; He maintained us in our pain. At least, however, on the Christian showing, He consented to be Himself subject to it. If, obscurely, He would not cease to preserve us in the full horror of existence, at least He shared it. He became as helpless as we under the will which is He. This is the first approach to a sense of justice in the whole situation. Whatever He chose, He chose fully, for Himself as for us. This is, I think, unique in the theistic religions of the world. I do not remember any other in which the Creator so accepted His own terms—at least in the limited sense of existence upon this earth. It is true that His life was short. His pains (humanly speaking) comparatively brief. But at least, alone among the gods, He deigned to endure the justice He decreed.

There is another point of the same kind. It is often said that He was put to death by evil men. Caiaphas and Pilate and Herod are denounced. It is, of course, in some sense true that it was evil which persecuted Him. But I have myself felt that the destructiveness was more common to our experience if we hold, as we very well may, that Caiaphas and Pilate were each of them doing his best in the duty presented to them. The high priest was condemning a blasphemer. The Roman governor was attempting to maintain the peace. At the present time, for example, it is clear that one man must suffer for the people—and many more than one man, whether they consent or not. It is, no doubt, inevitable; it may be right. But we can hardly blame those earlier supporters of the same law. Humanly speaking, they were doing the best they could. They chose the least imperfect good that they could see. And their choice crucified the Good.

It is this agonizing fact which is too often present in our own experience. Certainly our sins and faults destroy the good. But our efforts after the good also destroy it. The very pursuit of goodness becomes a hunt; that which was to be our lord becomes a victim. It is necessary to behave well here? We do. What is the result? The destruction of some equal good. There is no more significant or more terrible tale in the New Testament than that which surrounded the young Incarnacy with the dying Innocents: the chastisement of His peace was upon them. At the end He paid back the debt

—to God if not to them; He too perished innocently. With Him also (morally) there was nothing else to be done.

He had put Himself then to His own law, in every sense. Man (perhaps ignorantly, but none the less truly for that) executed justice upon Him. This was the world He maintained in creation? *This* was the world He maintained in creation. This was the best law, the clearest justice, man could find, and He did well to accept it. If they had known it was He, they could have done no less and no better. They crucified Him; let it be said, they did well. But then let it be said also, that the Sublimity itself had done well: adorable He might be by awful definition of His Nature, but at least He had shown Himself honourable in His choice. He accepted Job's challenge of long ago, talked with His enemy in the gate, and outside the gate suffered (as the men He made so often do) from both His friends and His enemies. Which of us has not known and has not been a Judas? He had nowhere to lay His head? And we? 'Behold my mother and my brethren.'

This then has seemed to me now for long perhaps the most flagrant significance of the Cross; it does enable us to use the word 'justice' without shame—which otherwise we could not. God therefore becomes tolerable as well as credible. Our justice condemned the innocent, but the innocent it condemned was one who was fundamentally responsible for the existence of all injustice—its existence in the mere, but necessary, sense of time, which His will created and prolonged.

This is the more objective side; there is the more subjective. Man chooses, in most of his experiences, between the rack and the Cross, between a prolonged lesser and a shorter but greater pain. I do not wish to seem here to become rhetorical; I do not underrate the great and pure beauties which are presented and revealed to us, the virtue and value of fidelity, the appearance of a new kind of goodness where sometimes the old seems to have been exhausted. Yet it is also true that a kind of death attends us all everywhere. Our best knowledge is dimmed with boredom or darkened by destruction. 'A mist goes up from the ground' or an earthquake shakes it. A languor and a reluctance take us as we endure the undestroyed good, or else the demand for its sacrifice preoccupies us. This occurs so often that we feel it to be in the nature of life; this is what life is. Yes then, certainly, this is what Life is. The Cross is the exhibition of Life being precisely that; more—as knowing itself to be precisely that, as experiencing itself as being precisely that. We are relieved—may one say?—from the burden of being naturally optimistic. 'The whole creation groaneth and travaileth together.' If we are to rejoice always then it must be a joy consonant with that; we need not—infinite relief!—force ourselves to deny the mere burden of breathing. Life (experience suggests) is a good thing, and somehow unendurable; at least the Christian faith has denied neither side of the paradox. Life found itself unendurable. Romantically multiplying each side as our feelings may propose, we cannot go beyond that realism. Life itself consents to shrink from its own terrors; it concedes to us its utterance of our own prayer: 'O not *this*! If it be possible, not *this*!' I am not for a moment equating our sorrows with that; the point is that the sorrow is centrally there. Life itself is acquainted with grief.

And not grief alone. Crucifixion was an obscene thing. It was revolting not merely because of the torture and the degradation, but also because of the disgust; or rather it is revolting to us—I do not know that it was revolting to those who saw it. They were as accustomed to it as our fathers were to burning and castration or we to many years' imprisonment or to the gallows. It was, however, definitely more spectacularly obscene than the gallows; we can hardly, in the nature of things, realize it so, and even our best efforts tend to make it a little respectable. But then again life, as we know it, is obscene; or, to be accurate, it has in it a strong element of obscenity. Again and again we become aware of a sense of outrage in our physical natures. Sometimes this is aroused by the events of which we read in the papers, but as often by the events which happen to us. The Family, for example, is a sacred and noble thing, but the things that happen in the Family are the result of blood antagonistic to itself. 'Love', it is said, 'is very near to hate.' Without discussing the general truth of that, it may be allowed that where it is so, the hate is often of a particularly virulent and vehement kind.

I take these two qualities—the sorrow and the obscenity—as examples of that dreadful contradiction in our experience of life which is flatly exhibited in the living of life by Life. I am not unaware that it will be said that That which dies on the Cross was something a great deal more than Life in any sense in which we understand the word. But I am not now talking of Christian dogma, but of a particular sense of the Cross. 'The feeling intellect' of the Faith is a state of a much more advanced nature than anything I can claim to have known.

I say then that the idea of the Cross does, on the one hand, make the idea of justice in God credible; and on the other certifies to us that we are not fools in being conscious of the twisting of all goodness to ignominy. We may (if it may be put so) approach God with that at least cleared up. We are not being unjust to His creation in the distaste we feel for it, nor even in the regret we feel that He allows it to continue. There would be other things to be said were we now discussing the Incarnation as such, but these are the things to be said peculiarly about the Cross. This is what Almighty God, as well as we, found human life to be. We willed it so, perhaps, but then certainly He willed that we should will.

There is, however, more to it than that. There is Easter. It is not possible to separate the idea of Easter from the Cross. Easter is its consequence. But it is a consequence of which many of us have very little apprehension. There are those who find it easy to look forward to immortality and those who do not. I admit that, for myself, I do not. It is true that the gradual stupefaction of the faculties which normally overcomes a man as he grows older seems to make—if not the idea of immortality more attractive—at least the idea of annihilation less so. Possibly curiosity is the last of one's faculties to be stupefied; possibly the natural egotism which has had a free run in one's life accentuates marvellously the idea of self-preservation as one approaches the apparent end of self-preservation. Possibly one is merely more fussy. Whatever is true, the idea of annihilation is more repellent. But I cannot say I find the idea of immortality, even of a joyous immortality, much more attractive. I admit, of course, that this is a failure of intelligence; if joy is joy, an infinite joy cannot be undesirable. The mere fact that our experience on this earth makes it difficult for us to apprehend a good without a catch in it somewhere, is, by definition, irrelevant. It may, however, make the folly more excusable.

Easter, however, is not only a consequence of the Cross; it is also almost an accident of it. It followed the Cross, but also it began in the Cross. I say 'in' rather than 'on', for by the time it began He had become, as it were, the very profoundest Cross to Himself. That certainly He had always been prophetically, but now the exploration of His prophecies was complete. The Cross was He and He the Cross. His will had maintained, or rather His will in His Father's will had maintained, a state of affairs among men of which physical crucifixion was at once a part and a perfect symbol. This state of things He inexorably proposed to Himself to endure; say, rather, that from the beginning He had been Himself at bottom both the endurance and the thing endured. This had been true everywhere in all men; it was now true of Himself apart from all men; it was local and particular. The physical body which was His own means of union with matter, and was in consequence the very cause, centre, and origin of all human creation, was exposed to the complete contradiction of itself. It would be perhaps too ingenious a fancy, which in these things above all is to be avoided, to say that actual crucifixion is a more exact symbol of His suffering than any other means of death. It is, however, with peculiar explicitness in the physical category what His other agony was in the spiritual (so, for a moment, to differentiate them). He was stretched, He was bled, He was nailed, He was thrust into, but not a bone of Him was broken. The dead wood drenched with the blood, and the dead body shedding blood, have an awful likeness; the frame is doubly saved. It was the Cross which sustained Him, but He also sustained the Cross. He had, through the years, exactly preserved the growth of the thorn and of the wood, and had indued with energy the making of the nails and the sharpening of the spear; say, through the centuries He had maintained vegetable and mineral in the earth for this. His providence overwatched it to no other end, as it overwatches so many instruments and intentions of cruelty then and now. The Cross therefore is the express image of His will; it depends in its visible shape and strength wholly on Him.

In the moment, as it were, of the final so-near-to-identity of Himself and His wooden Image, He spoke. He said: 'It is finished.' It is at that moment that Easter began. It is not yet Easter; the Deposition has not yet taken place. He speaks, while yet He can, while He is not yet as speechless as the wood, and He announces the culmination of that experience. Life has known absolutely all its own contradiction. He survives; He perfectly survives. His—I dare not call it victory—is not afterwards, but then. His actual death becomes almost a part of His Resurrection, almost what Patmore called the death of the Divine Mother, a 'ceremony'. Not so, for the ceremony was itself a work and a discovery, but then proper ceremonies are so; they achieve, as this does. The joy of His self-renewed knowledge perfectly exists, and His Resurrection is (in His Father and Origin) at His own decision and by His own will. It is the will of His unalterable joy which, having absorbed, exists.

This moment of consummation is therefore related to man's inevitable demand that all things should be justified in the moment that they happen. We must perhaps, joyously or reluctantly, consent to leave the knowledge of that justification till afterwards, but we must be willing to believe that it is now. Or better, that the result is neither here nor there, neither now nor then, and yet both here and there, both now and then. There has indeed been much admiration, much gratitude, much love, that God should be made like us, but then there is at least equal satisfaction that it is an unlike us who is so made. It is an alien Power which is caught and suspended in our very midst. 'Blessed be God', said John Donne, 'that He is God only and divinely like Himself.' It is that other kind of existence which here penetrates our hearts, and is at all points credibly justified by our justice. The supreme error of earthly justice was the supreme assertion of the possibility of justice. In His mortal life He never pretended, in making all His impossible and yet natural demands, that He judged as we do. The parable of the labourers, the reply to James and John, are alien from our equality; and so is the incredible comment on Judas—'it were good for that man if he had not been born'. And who caused him to be born? Who maintained his life up to and in that awful less than good? It is in the Gospels that the really terrifying attacks on the Gospel lie.

He was not like us, and yet He became us. What happened there the Church itself has never seen, except that in the last reaches of that living death to which we are exposed He substituted himself for us. He submitted in our stead to the full results of the Law which is He. We may believe He was generous if we know that He was just. By that central substitution, which was the thing added by the Cross to the Incarnation, He became everywhere the centre of, and everywhere He energized and reaffirmed, all our substitutions and exchanges. He took what remained, after the Fall, of the torn web of humanity in all times and places, and not so much by a miracle of healing as by a growth within it made it whole. Supernaturally He renewed our proper nature. By so doing, it is true, He redoubled, at least within the Church, our guilt and our distress. When He had made hope a virtue He had prevented it from being a natural habit. In all failures of love there is left to us only a trust in His work; that is what we call 'faith', a kind of quality of action. It is, however, a trust in what is already done. Not only His act, but all our acts, are finished so. 'Thy will be done on earth as it is in heaven' means precisely that at any moment the holy desire is already accomplished—not perhaps in the sense that we desire it, but in the sense that He wills it. It is finished; we too do but play out the necessary ceremony.

As in bombings from the air, cancer, or starvation, for instance? Yes, I suppose so; if at all, then certainly in those examples. The Church (of which He seems to have had a low opinion) is His choice, but nature was His original choice, and He has a supreme fidelity. It is, in fact, that fidelity which causes Him to maintain His creation and to die for His creation and to renew His creation. It may seem that little has been here said about our salvation through His sacrifice. That would not be quite true, for all that has been said concerns our salvation. Our salvation is precisely our reconciliation, to nature and to the Church—not that they are so separate; our reconciliation both to Him and to our present state, both at once and both in one. We are, by that august sacrifice, compelled to concede to Him the propriety of our creation. I do not know that anything greater could be demanded or done. 'It is He that hath made us, and not we ourselves.' We know that very well. But the General Thanksgiving ('general thanksgiving'—incredible words!) goes farther. 'We bless Thee for our creation, preservation . . . for the means of grace and the hope of glory.' It seems that nothing less will do. We are then required to do it because He does; it is at once a duty and a relief. Let Him do it for us, for at least the Life in Him is not separate from our life: we are allowed to repose in His blessing of Himself, and to confirm ours by virtue of His blessing. The duty and the relief do not remain themselves; they are changed as nature is changed, as the elements in the Eucharist are changed. In the Eucharist He withdraws all into His Resurrection, because the Resurrection is in the sacrifice. This is not the place, however, to discuss the Eucharist. It is sufficient to say that there, as everywhere, to be able to bless is to be in a state of salvation, in a state of goodwill towards Him and all His creation, in a state of love. Only beatitude can properly bless, as only Love can love. In so far as we desire to bless, we are at least believers in a state of salvation now.

Our own guilt, natural or supernatural, is only manifested so. We can hardly be in a state of guilt towards something which is not in bearable relations with us. The Crucifixion, restoring those relations, restores very much more. It permits repentance because it enables us to mean something by sin. Without that act, the infliction on us of something terribly like injustice would have made nonsense of any injustice on our side. He restores Himself to us as God with all the qualities of God merely by being content not to be nothing but God. God can pardon, but pardon is only half pardon unless it is desired; the supreme life of it is precisely in the mutual act. There is no lovingness, mortal or divine, which does not, for its mutual quality, depend on that sacrifice of Himself. 'Others He saved; Himself He cannot save.' If He had saved Himself, it seems, He could not have saved others; He did it by His power affirming, in the Crucifixion, its own lack of power. He maintains us, by His will, in the state of sin in which we are; by His act He makes free to us the knowledge of that state, and of that issuing in Him.

'O fools and slow of heart, *ought* not Christ to have suffered these things, and entered into His glory?' Yes; He ought. He said so: 'The Son of Man *must*. . . .' But then also He did. If the glory on which He insists, at such a cost, seems intolerable to us, if the exposition of release from our unhappy state seems as unbearable as the state itself, so that we cannot bear the only alternative to what we already cannot bear, at least that, after all, is the situation; it is He. We may be bold to say that He knows Himself as well as we know Him; after the Cross we can believe that He knows Himself not only as He does, but as we do. In the finishing of that knowledge a little cloud of fresh good arises, the first sense of that cloud into which He was received when He ascended. Whole, He died; whole, He rose; whole, He went up. Not the least gift of the Gospel is that our experiences of good need not be separated from our experiences of evil, need not and must not be. In time they generally are, and even when they are not they are apt to seem unrelated. The authority which the good in our experience seems to have over us, unlike the evil, however much less than the evil it seems to be, is united with that other authority of the God who endured His own. It is the Christian religion that makes the Christian religion possible. Existence itself is Christian; Christianity itself is Christian. The two are one because He is, in every sense, life, and life is He. It is to that, in the Triune Unity, that there is ascribed, beyond all hope, to that only Omnipotence, as is most justly due, all might, majesty, dominion, and power.

NATURAL GOODNESS

From Theology, *October 1941*

IT is a little unfortunate that in ordinary English talk the words 'natural' and 'supernatural' have come to be considered as opposed rather than as complementary. Something like it has happened with those other words 'nature' and 'grace', but less frequently, since the second two are more often used by trained theologians. But certainly the common use of the first two words implies rather a division between their meanings than a union.

This would be more comprehensible if we meant by 'supernatural' only the world of angels and of God. It is true that God is so wholly 'other' that only in the broadest sense can anything we mean by 'supernatural' be applied to Him any more than 'natural'. But of the two terms we must use one rather than the other. And the forces of the world of angels are certainly different from our own 'natural' forces. It is also true that the Christian religion has asserted that those 'natural' forces are but elements, and even infinitesimal elements, in the whole range of creation. But they are so far harmonious with it that they appear contrary only because of that element in man which we call sin, and they are not insignificant or negligible. The 'supernatural' must therefore in some sense include the 'natural'. 'A new earth' was promised as well as 'a new heaven'. Whatever the promise means, that earth is presumably in some relation to this earth.

Matter, certainly, is by definition the opposite of spirit. It is apparently as far the opposite of God (leaving will and morals out of the question) as God chose to create. But it did not therefore become less significant of Him than that less technical opposite which is called spirit. We have, in fact, only lost proper comprehension of matter by an apostasy in spirit. Matter and 'nature' have not, in themselves, sinned;

what has sinned is spirit, if spirit and matter are to be regarded as divided. That they so easily can be is due perhaps to that lack of intellectual clarity produced by the Fall.

There is, I understand, an opinion permissible to the faithful which may be discussed here. I am told that it is related to the great name of Duns Scotus, and no doubt it is, if permissible, familiar to readers of *Theology*. But it is illuminating on this subject and illustrates the problem of natural goodness.

It is, briefly, that the Incarnation is the point of creation, and the divine 'reason' for it. It pleased God in His self-willed activity to be incarnate. But obviously this union of Himself with matter in flesh did not necessarily involve the creation of other flesh. It would have been sufficient to Himself to be Himself united with matter, and that 'united with' means a union very much beyond our powers to conceive; more than a union, a unity. Even now, in spite of the Athanasian Creed, the single existence of the Incarnate Word is too often almost Gnostically contemplated as an inhabitation of the flesh by the Word. But it is not so; what He is, He is wholly and absolutely, and even in His death and in the separation of body and soul He remains wholly and absolutely one. His act could have been to Himself alone. He decreed that it should not be; He determined creation; He determined not only to be incarnate, but to be incarnate by means of a mother. He proposed to Himself to be born into a world.

This decree upon Himself was the decree that brought mankind into being. It was His will to make creatures of such a kind that they should share in that particular joy of His existence in flesh. He bade for Himself a mother and all her companions; perhaps the mystery of the mortal maternity of God was greater even than that, but at least it was that. It was the great and single act of active love, consonant with nothing but His nature, compared to which the Redemption (if indeed He were infinitely to maintain all souls alive) was but a sheer act of justice. Our flesh was to hold, to its degree, the secrets of His own.

Nothing has ever altered, nothing could ever alter, that

decree. I do not, of course, mean even to seem to separate it from His other acts; only one must speak in terms of time. Certainly He acted altogether, He created and redeemed and judged and executed judgement all at once. But it seems that, as far as we are concerned, He also in that act created process and therefore time, time being in this sense the mere measurement of process. Indeed, so determining to be incarnate by a mother, it might perhaps be said that He determined process for Himself also, and even that, for pure increase of joy, He determined that the process should depend on the free will of His mother and of men. He designed exchange of joy; He gave us the final privilege of owing everything to ourselves as well as to Him. This moment was our primal nature, and nothing has ever altered that fact—not though we may wish it had.

There followed, as we know, the chosen catastrophe which we call the Fall. Whether in that state in which mankind was, the Fall was a single act of a single soul, or the simultaneous act of all souls, this is not the place to discuss. It is, I suppose, possible (since it is to be believed that every human creature sins) that in some way every human nature sinned at once; that the whole web was at once and everywhere ruined. That is irrelevant to the fact that, however it happened, it certainly happened. The will of man sinned. But the will of man was a spiritual quality; it was in his soul. It was that power in him which we call the soul that sinned. It was not the power which we call the flesh. It was therefore the 'supernatural' which sinned. The 'natural', as we now call it, did not. They cannot, of course, be separated. But if, in terminology, they can be, then it is the matter of our substance which has remained faithful, and the immaterial which has not.

The definition of the Fall is that man determined to know good as evil. Whether (as may be) it was indeed an affair of the fruit of a tree or whether that is symbolical does not matter. But if the good, which was whole, was to be known as evil, then process must be known as evil; that is, the process must be to a living death. The end would be hell. But all the qualities and all the glories of that human creation were not in one moment changed to a state of hell. So much the decree of process itself forbade. The end might be inevitable, but it had to be gradual.

His nature, as it were, was still implanted in His creatures; it was, indeed, human for divine, their nature. Nor has that foundation ever failed. They devoted it to everlasting death. But the genius of it, so to speak, was of eternal life. He who had desired His creatures to accept His choice now accepted the terms of His creation; He accepted the choice of His creatures. The Incarnation became also the Redemption. He became the new thing. But that did not prevent Him from being the foundation of the old thing. He was, is, and is to be, the light that lighteneth every man.

The Apostolic and Catholic Faith declared the Redemption of fallen nature, but that Redemption was on the principles and to the principles of our first unfallen nature. Man could not longer be innocent; he was corrupt, and his best efforts were, but for the new grace, doomed to death. But his best efforts were, and are, of no other kind than had been decreed. His blood might be tainted, but the source from which it sprang was still the same. His natural life was still, and is now, a disordered pattern of the only pattern, a confused type of the one original; it is full still of glory and of peace, as well as of bloodshed and despair. It contends within itself. The most extreme goodness may be found in it and asserted of it—so long as the absolute invalidity of it apart from the new life is also declared. The most absolute domination of the new life may be asserted, so long as the accidental goodness of the old is never denied.

It is no doubt true that the operations of the Christian Church for two thousand years—sacramental, doctrinal, and moral—have had a greater effect than we generally realize. When all allowances, however, have been made for this, and for the various legal and social systems which, touched by Christianity as well as by civic security, have faintly aimed at goodness, it remains true that the goodness in the 'natural' order often seems to rival and equal the goodness of the 'supernatural'. Something very much like heroic sanctity exists everywhere. This heroic sanctity outside the Christian Church is a thing for which Christians are always 'making allowances'. I use the silly phrase because it is the only one that fits. They do not, perhaps, mean it to sound so; the effect is due to the use of a great vocabulary by inadequate voices. It is also due to the unintentionally insincere claims made by foolish Christians on behalf of their Christian experience. Vigil, heroism, martyrdom, vicarious life, are common to man. In so far as they are possible outside the Church, they are elements of man's original nature operative within him in spite of, but under conditions of, the catastrophe of the Fall. In so far as they are impossible inside the Church, they are the change in man's fallen nature which even grace has not yet renewed. Nature and grace are categories of one Identity.

What, then, are we to hold is the value of the Christian religion? It is applicable far beyond itself, in the sense that what it says is the only final validity of those other great acts of goodness. Union with our sacred Lord is obtained by acts. Belief is, no doubt, an act; proper motive is an act; but also an act is an act. The great doctrines are the only explanation and the only hope. But even the great doctrines are only the statement of something as wide as the universe and as deep as the human heart. They do not deny as Creator that which they adore as Saviour, though the Creator had to become a Saviour lest His creation should be wholly lost. It is to be believed that, except by the Cross and Resurrection, no act is valid; and that by that Cross and Resurrection the proper validity of every act is determined. The Christian Church has been charged with the great secrets which are the only facts of existence. But the visible and vocal Church will have to practise much humility, in itself as well as in its separate members, before it can find itself capable of speaking on equal terms with that nature which it has to regenerate with universal blessing.

The Incarnation of the Son of God led to the Cross because it summed up and prevented the otherwise inevitable end of human process both individual and general. But it is at least a question whether the Incarnation only existed to lead to the Cross or whether it was in fact the original act. The Church is the means of penitence and faith. But the lack of penitence and faith cannot altogether destroy the value of what remains of natural goodness. The transformation of natural goodness into eternal goodness demands all stress on both the Incarnation and the Crucifixion. Our great difficulty is that it is much easier to transform eternal goodness, or what should be eternal goodness, into natural goodness. 'When religion is in the hands of the natural man', wrote William Law, 'he is always the worse for it; it adds a bad heat to his own dark fire and helps to inflame his four elements of selfishness, envy, pride and wrath.' But it was the same William Law who wrote:

> Natural religion, if you understand it rightly, is a most excellent thing, it is a right sentiment of heart, it is so much goodness in the heart, it is its sensibility both of its separation from and its relation to God; and therefore it shows itself in nothing but in a penitential sentiment of the weight of its sins, and in an humble recourse by faith to the mercy of God. Call but this the religion of nature and then the more you esteem it, the better; for you cannot wish well to it without bringing it to the Gospel state of perfection. For the religion of the Gospel is this religion of penitence and faith in the mercy of God, brought forth into its full perfection. For the Gospel calls you to nothing but to know and understand and practise a full and real penitence, and to know by faith such heights and depths of the divine mercy towards you, as the religion of nature had only some little uncertain glimmerings of.

Remove the word 'God' from that description of natural religion, remove the word 'religion', and the principles still hold. Those principles are in our nature because of His, and the Word (and we by the Word) are other than all the vocabularies.

THE INDEX OF THE BODY

From the Dublin Review, *July 1942*

IN the *Prelude* (book viii, ll. 279–81) Wordsworth wrote:

> the human form
> To me became an index of delight,
> Of grace and honour, power and worthiness.

The most important word there is *index*. There are moments in all poetry when the reader has to ask himself whether a word used by the poet is accurate not only for the poet's universe but for the reader's own. It is a secondary decision, since the first must be only of the poetic value, but it is sometimes important. That is so here; the word *index*, pressed to its literal meaning, is a word which demands attention, and afterwards assent or dissent.

It is true that Wordsworth himself did not develop the idea; he is speaking generally, and in other passages his genius suggests that the index is to a volume written in a strange language. This is no weakness in Wordsworth; it was, on one side, his particular business. Thus the image of the Leech-Gatherer in *Resolution and Independence* is drawn at least as inhuman as human; so is the Soldier in Book IV of the *Prelude* who is the cause of such terror, and the other wanderers; the woman with the pitcher, and even Lucy Gray, are of the same kind. They are on the borders of two worlds, which almost pass and repass into each other. Wordsworth, of all the Romantics, came nearest to defining and mapping that border-land.

There are, of course, also his more exclusively human figures—Michael, for instance, in the poem of that name. Here the human form suggests to him the grandeur of the moral virtues; it is the suffering and labouring spirit of man which he sees. That may have been what he had chiefly in mind in the passage I have quoted: man as 'a solitary object and sublime', but man also 'with the most common; husband, father', who

> suffered with the rest
> From vice and folly, wretchedness and fear.

But the passage is capable of another reading, and one which proposes to us a real, if less usual, sequence. It is that reading which I wish now to discuss, and the word *index* is the beginning. The question proposed is whether we shall take that word seriously as a statement of the relation of the human form to 'grace and honour, power and worthiness'. The human form meant, to Wordsworth, the shape of the shepherd seen among the hills. There it was high and distant. It was a whole being significant of a greater whole—which is, in some sense, the definition of objects seen romantically. But the lines might be applied to the same shape, seen near at hand and analytically. They might refer to the body itself; it is that which can be considered as an index.

What then would be meant by the word? Nothing but itself. An index is a list of various subjects, with reference to those places where, in the text of the volume, they are treated at greater length. But, at least, the words naming the subjects are the same; and a really good index will give some idea of the particular kind of treatment offered on the separate pages. Some such idea, Wordsworth's lines suggest, the body and even the members of the body may give of the delight, grace, honour, power, and worthiness of man's structure. The structure of the body is an index to the structure of a greater whole.

I am anxious not to use words which seem too much to separate the physical structure from the whole. The fact of death, and the ensuing separation of 'body' and 'soul', lead us to consider them too much as separate identities conjoined. But I hope it is not unorthodox to say that body and soul are one identity, and that all our inevitable but unfortunate verbal distinctions are therefore something less than true. Death has been regarded by the Christian Church as an outrage—a necessary outrage, perhaps, but still an outrage. It has been held to be an improper and grotesque schism in a single identity—to which submission, but not consent, is to be offered; a thing, like sin, that ought not to be and yet is. The distress of our Lord in His Passion may perhaps not improperly be supposed to be due to His contemplation of this all but inconceivable schism in His own sacred and single identity. If our manhoods were from the first meant indivisibly, how much more His!

It is one of the intellectual results of the Fall that our language has always to speak in terms of the Fall; and that we cannot help our language does not make it any more true. The epigrams of saints, doctors, and poets, are the nearest we can go to the recovery of that ancient validity, our unfallen speech. To treat the body as an index is to assume that, as in an index the verbal element—the *word* given—is the same as in the whole text, so in the physical structure of the greater index the element—the *quality* given—is the same as in the whole structure. Another poet, Patmore, put the thing in a similar light when he wrote that

> from the graced decorum of the hair,
> Ev'n to the tingling sweet
> Soles of the simple earth-confiding feet
> And from the inmost heart
> Outwards unto the thin
> Silk curtains of the skin,
> Every least part
> Astonish'd hears
> And sweet replies to some like region of the spheres.

'The spheres' there are likely to mean, first, the outer heavens. This idea is practically that of the microcosm and the macrocosm: the idea that a man is a small replica of the universe. Man was 'the workshop of all things', 'a little world', *mundus minor exemplum majoris mundi ordine, filius totius mundi*. It is a very ancient idea; it was held before Christianity and has been held during Christianity; it was common to Christians, Jews, and Mohammedans; and, for all I know, the scientific hypothesis of evolution bears a relation to the union of the two. Into that, however, I am not learned enough to go. The idea went through many changes, but its general principle remained constant: that man was the rational epitome of the universe. It led, of course, to many absurdities, and (if you choose—like any other idea) to some evils. Some writers catalogued painstakingly the more obvious fantasies: hair was the grass or the forests; bones were mountains; the sun was the eyes, and so on. Astrology, if not based on it, at least found the idea convenient; however we may reject that ancient study, it had at least this philosophic principle mixed up with it—that each man, being unique, was a unique image of the universe, that the spatially greater affected the spatially lesser, and the calculable influences of the stars were only calculable because each man represented and reproduced the whole. Astrology then was a high and learned science; it was forbidden for good reasons, but it was not fatalistic. It did not say 'this will certainly happen'; it said: 'Given these stellar and individual relations, this result is likely.' But the will of God and the wills of men were allowed much freedom to interfere with the result. *Sapiens dominabitur astris.* The paragraphs in our papers to-day bear as much resemblance to the science as texts lifted up on boards outside churches do to the whole dogmas of the Church. The paragraphs are, I allow, more likely to harm; the texts, on the whole, are innocuous.

Beside, or rather along with, this study went the patterns of other occult schools. The word 'occult' has come into general use, and is convenient, if no moral sense is given it simply as itself. It deals with hidden things, and their investigation. But in this case we are concerned not so much with the pretended operations of those occult schools as with a certain imagination of relation in the universe, and that only to pass beyond it. The signs of the Zodiac were, according to some students, related to the parts of the physical body. The particular attributions varied, and all were in many respects arbitrary. But some of them were extremely suggestive; they may be allowed at least a kind of authentic poetic vision. Thus, in one pattern, the house of the Water-carrier was referred to the eyes; the house of the Twins to the arms and hands; the house of the Scorpion to the privy parts and the sexual organs; and the house of the Balances to the buttocks.

It will be clear that these four attributions at least had a great significance. It will be clear also that in such a poetic (so to call it) imagination, we are dealing with a kind of macrocosmic-microcosmic union of a more serious and more profitable kind than the mere exposition by a debased astrology of chances in a man's personal life. It may be invention, but if so, it is great invention; the houses of the Zodiac, with their special influences ruling in special divisions of the spatial universe, may be but the fables of astronomy; it must be admitted that few certain facts support them. But they are not unworthy fables. They direct attention to the principles at work both in the spatial heavens and in the structure of man's body. Aquarius is for water, clarity, vision; Gemini are for a plural motion, activity, and achievement; Libra is for that true strength of balance on which the structure of man depends.

With this suggestion, we are on the point of deserting the spatial heavens for something else. The like regions of the spheres, of which Patmore spoke, here begin to be transferred to the spiritual heavens. 'As above, so below' ran the old maxim, but even that dichotomy is doubtful. The houses of the Zodiac, in this, do but confuse the issue, except in so far as they, like the whole universe, exhibit the mystery by which spirit becomes flesh, without losing spirit. Perhaps the best verbal example is in the common use of the word 'heart'. Even in our common speech the word is ambiguous. To call Hitler heartless means that he seems to be without the common principle of compassion. It is said that Tertullian (but I have not found the reference) said that 'the supreme principle of intelligence and vitality', 'the sovereign faculty' of man, resided 'where the Egyptians taught—*Namque homini sanguis circumcordialis est sensus*, the sense of man is in the blood around the heart'. At least the pulsating organ presents, for man, his proper physical rhythm in the whole—*mundus minor exemplum majoris mundi ordine*. As our meaning—physical life or compassionate life—so the word *heart*. Compassion is the union of man with his fellows, as is the blood. The permitted devotion to the Sacred Heart is to the source of both. The physical heart is, in this sense, an 'index' to both. Gerard Hopkins wrote, of the Blessed Virgin:

> If I have understood
> She holds high motherhood
> Towards all our ghostly good
> And plays in grace her part
> About man's beating heart,
> Laying, like air's fine flood,
> The deathdance in his blood;
> Yet no part but what will
> Be Christ our Saviour still.

The visionary forms of the occult schools are but dreams of the Divine Body.

All these brief allusions show that there have been some traditions of significance—poetic, occult, religious. Christians, however, may be permitted to press the significance more closely; they may be allowed to ask whether the body is not indeed a living epigram of virtue. There have been doctors who held that Christ would not have become incarnate if man had not sinned; there have been doctors who held that He would. Either way, it is clear that the Sacred Body was itself virtue. The same qualities that made His adorable soul made His adorable flesh. If the devotion to the Sacred Heart does not, in itself, imply something of the sort, I do not know what it does imply. The virtues are both spiritual and physical—or rather they are expressed in those two categories. This is recognized in what are regarded as the more 'noble' members in the body—the heart, the eyes. But it is not so often recognized as a truth underlying all the members—the stomach, the buttocks. That is partly because we have too long equated the body as such with the 'flesh' of St. Paul. But 'flesh' is no more that than (as Mgr. Knox pointed out recently in the *Tablet*) it is 'sex'. The body was holily created, is holily redeemed, and is to be holily raised from the dead. It is, in fact, for all our difficulties with it, less fallen, merely in itself, than the soul in which the quality of the will is held to reside; for it was a sin of the will which degraded us. 'The evidence of things not seen' is in the body seen as this epigram; nay, in some sense, even 'the substance of things hoped for', for what part it has in that substance remains to it unspoiled.

It is in this sense then that the body is indeed an 'index' to delight, power, and the rest. 'Who conceives', wrote Prior,

> 'Who conceives, what bards devise,
> That heaven is placed in Celia's eyes?'

Well, no; not so simply as that. But Celia's eyes are a part of the body which (said Patmore, who was orthodox enough)

> Astonish'd hears
> And sweet replies to some like region of the spheres.

And those spheres are not merely the old spatial macrocosmic heavens, but the deep heaven of our inner being. The discernment of pure goodwill, of (let it be said for a moment) pure love in Celia's eyes, at some high moment of radiant interchange or indeed at any other moment, is no less part of the heavenly vision (so tiny and remote as it may be) because it is a physical as well as a spiritual vision. The word 'sacramental' has perhaps here served us a little less than well; it has, in popular usage, suggested rather the spiritual *using* the physical than a common—say, a single—operation.

Eyes then are compacted power; they are an index of vision; they see and refer us to greater seeing. Nor has the stomach a less noble office. It digests food; that is, in its own particular method, it deals with the nourishment offered by the universe. It is a physical formula of that health which destroys certain elements—the bacteria which harmfully approach us. By it we learn to consume; by it therefore to be, in turn, consumed. So even with those poor despised things, the buttocks. There is no seated figure, no image of any seated figure, which does not rely on them for its strength and balance. They are at the bottom of the sober dignity of judges; the grace of a throned woman; the hierarchical session of the Pope himself reposes on them: into even greater images and phrases we need not now go.

It will be thought I labour the obvious; and I will not go through the physical structure suggesting and propounding identities. The point will have been sufficiently made if the sense of that structure being heavenly not by a mere likeness but in its own proper nature is achieved. It is a point not so much of doctrine as of imagination. That imagination is at once individual and social. The temples of the Holy Ghost are constructed all on one plan: and our duties to our material fellows are duties to structures of beatitude. The relation of the Incarnation to our own mode of generation is blessedly veiled. But its relation to those other identities of power is not at all doubtful. It is not only physical structures we neglect or damage by our social evils; it is living indexes of life. The Virtues exist in all of them materially, but it is the Virtues which so exist. Christ, in some sense, derived His flesh from them, for He derived it from His Mother, and she from her ancestors, and they from all mankind.

The Sacred Body is the plan upon which physical human creation was built, for it is the centre of physical human creation. The great dreams of the human form as including the whole universe are in this less than the truth. As His, so ours; the body, in this sense of an index, is also a pattern. We carry about with us an operative synthesis of the Virtues; and it may be held that when we fall in love (for example), we fall in love precisely with the operative synthesis.

> Grace was in all her steps, heaven in her eye;
> In every gesture dignity and love;

is much more a definite statement of fact than we had supposed; footsteps are astonishing movements of grace. That we cannot properly direct and control our sensations and emotions is not surprising; but the greatness of man is written even in his incapacity, and when he sins he sins because of a vision which, even though clouded, is great and ultimate. As every heresy is a truth pushed disproportionately, so with every sin; at least, with every physical sin. But, however in those states of 'falling in love' the vision of a patterned universe is revealed to us, the revelation vanishes, and we are left to study it slowly, heavily, and painfully. All that the present essay attempts to do is to present a point of view which has behind it, one way and another, a great tradition—a tradition which, for Christians, directs particular attention to the Sacred Body as the Archtype of all bodies. In this sense the Eucharist exposes also its value. The 'index' of our bodies, the incarnate qualities of the moral universe, receive the Archtype of all moralities truly incarnated; and not only the pattern in the soul and will but the pattern in the body is renewed. Or, better, in that unity which we, under the influence of our Greek culture, divide into soul and body. 'Socrates', Dr. William Ellis writes, 'invented the concept which permeates every part of modern thinking, the concept of the twofold nature of man, of man as a union of the active, or spiritual, with the inactive, or corporeal; the concept, in short, of the organism as a dead carcass activated by a living ghost. Even if we repudiate this idea, we are still half-dominated by it, so deeply does it underlie our pattern of culture.'[1] I am far from suggesting that this is the proper Christian view. But there is, I think, no doubt that it is not far from the popular Christian view. The fuss that has been made about Browning's line (not that that was Browning's fault)—'nor soul helps flesh more now than flesh helps soul'—shows that. It was repeated almost as a new revelation, though indeed the Lady Julian had said almost the same thing centuries before. We have to overcome that lazy habit of the imagination—the outrage of death notwithstanding. We experience, physically, in its proper mode, the Kingdom of God: the imperial structure of the body carries its own high doctrines—of vision, of digestion of mysteries, of balance, of movement, of operation. 'That soul', said Dante in the *Convivio*, 'which embraces all these powers [the rational, the sensitive, and the vegetative] is the most perfect of all the rest.' The rational, or self-conscious, power is indeed the noblest, but we must ask from it a complete self-consciousness, and not a self-consciousness in schism.

It was suggested that the stress of this imagination may be

[1] *The Idea of the Soul in Western Philosophy and Science.*

an incentive to our social revolution. For if the body of our neighbour is compact of these heavenly qualities, incarnated influences, then we are indeed neglecting the actual Kingdom of God in neglecting it. It is the living type of the Arch-typal. We have not merely to obey a remote moral law in feeding and succouring and sheltering it. It is the 'index' of power; tear away the index, and we are left without the power; tear away the index, and we are left without the delight. Let the whole to which that index witnesses be as immense as any volume of truth may be, and still the value of that small substance remains. Every student of a learned work uses the index attentively. A good index can indeed be studied in itself. To study the body so is to increase our preparation for the whole great text.

THE WAY OF EXCHANGE

A pamphlet in the New Foundations *series, 1941*

IT has been of old a general complaint against war that it involves many harmless and unwilling persons belonging to different communities in the conflict between those communities. The general discussion whether we are at war with the German people or not is an example of this. Efforts have been made, and abandoned, to show that the German people are not at one with their leader. What is certain is that at present the vast majority of Europeans greatly dislike the conditions in which the vast majority of Europeans live. Nevertheless they assent, passively or actively, to the action of their governments; they are, so far, compelled to be at one with their governments. 'Like ourselves,' wrote Mr. J. L. Garvin in the *Observer* of 16 June 1940, 'many, many millions of the Italian people abhor this tragedy. They neither hate us nor we them. That can make no difference on their side or our side.'

They and we are, in fact, committed by our governments. Those governments, in the nature of modern society, cannot be checked or much controlled, except at serious risk, by their nationals. We may well believe that the present situation of Europe tends to show that our own Government cannot have deceived us. But then we are still affected by the German Government. We are at war because of Hitler, or because of the general tension between all governments; either way, we are not at war directly because of our own wish, but because of others. We depend upon others. The old cry against governments involving their peoples in war may be inapplicable in this war or not. It was sincere, but (as we now see) useless. We are always in the condition that we are because of others.

This is all so elementary as to sound stupid. Yet to accept

this profoundly is difficult. To be in a distressing and painful condition because of others is a thing we all naturally resent. It is often the cause of hatred towards those others, whether in public or private things. Yet until we are willing to accept the mere fact without resentment we can hardly be said to admit that other people exist. We may reject, we may rebuke, we may contend against their action. But the very first condition of admitting that their existence is as real as our own is to allow that they have, as individuals, as much right to act in the way that they decide as we have. They may be wicked and we good or vice versa; that is a question of moral judgement, and therefore another question. The main fact is that we are compelled to admit their decision, and to admit that our lives, and often our deaths, depend on that.

Such a decision, important as it is in war, is, in fact, no less important in peace. We have, first, to learn that others exist by ceasing to resent their existence. Until we have ceased to resent that existence, merely instinctively, we can hardly be said to admit it. But having admitted it, we have then to decide what we are to do about it; what our attitude is to be towards those other existences, what our relation with them. The great philosophies have given various answers; the great religions, on the whole, the same answer. Out of these the good taste of the West (one can hardly call it more) had, until recently, made a general amalgam which it called, roughly, 'tolerance'.

Tolerance meant, at worst, sullenly putting up with what one could not alter; at best, willingly accepting what one could not alter. It was a little limited by the fact that 'to tolerate' was always considered as an active and hardly ever as a passive verb. One always tolerated and rarely was tolerated. The idea that others had, so to speak, to 'put up with' oneself was rarely practised, deeply and consistently. But, such as it is, toleration was, and remains, a noble virtue—yet a virtue which serves best as a guide to something greater than itself.

The great religions had, on the whole, recommended something more active. Much though they differed in their definitions of God, they did, generally, agree on their definitions of our duty towards our neighbour, even if they did not always agree on the exact definition of our neighbour. The Christian idea was expressed in the phrase 'bear ye one another's burdens'. It encouraged, indeed it demanded, a continual attention to the needs of one's neighbour, to his distresses and his delights. And it defined 'neighbour' as meaning anyone with whom one was, by holy Luck, brought into contact. It required, then, an active 'sympathy', and it spoke of something still higher, of an active and non-selfish love. It went even farther. It declared a union of existences. It proclaimed that our own lives depended on the lives of our neighbours. St. Anthony of Egypt laid down the doctrine in so many words: 'Your life and your death are with your neighbour.'

August as that doctrine may have been, it is clear that it very soon became modified. It is regarded as Christian to live 'for' others; it is not so often regarded as Christian doctrine that we live 'from' others—except certainly in rare experiences. There has been, everywhere, a doctrine of unselfishness, but that the self everywhere lives only within others has been less familiar. The 'bear one another's burdens' became, on the whole, an exterior thing. We sympathized; we assisted. We loved—from ourselves. But there had been more than that in the original thought.

Certainly the great Christian doctrine applied first to the 'household of faith'. Our Lord promised to the members of His Church a particular and intense union with each other through Himself. He defined that union as being of the same nature as that which He had with His Father. The later definitions of the inspired Church went farther; they declared not merely that the Father and the Son existed co-equally, but that they existed co-inherently—that is, that the Son existed *in* the Father and that the Father existed *in* the Son. The exact meaning of the preposition there may be obscure. But no other word could satisfy the intellect of the Church. The same preposition was used to define our Lord's relations with His Church: 'we in him and he in us'. It was in that sense that the Church itself in-lived its children: 'we are members one of another'.

It is not, however, entirely necessary to call the Christian Church in evidence that such is the nature of man. It was as clear to the pagans that in society men depended on each other exteriorly as it is to us. The whole natural and social world depended, then as now, on some process of exchange. Human life, in the Roman Empire, had been specialized; not perhaps so much as ours, but it had been specialized. It depended on an exchange of labours. The medium of that exchange, with us, is money. Money has been called, by the economists, 'the means of exchange'. Our social system exists by an unformed agreement that one person shall do one job while another does another. Money is the means by which those jobs are brought into relation. It is, usually, the medium in which particular contracts are formed. And contract, or agreement, is the social fact of 'living by each other'.

This is the widest sense of social exchange. Within smaller groups—families or friends—the same thing is always taking place, sometimes irritably, sometimes happily. The more intense the element of love between two or more persons, the more clear, generally, that exchange of activities is. There certainly, in such states of natural love, doing it 'for' someone else produces precisely that sense of increased well-being, of increased life, which the great doctrine asserts. The difference, of course, is that, in such cases of love, there have arisen naturally the conditions of goodwill towards the 'neighbour'; where, however, those conditions do not naturally exist, love depends upon the will, and the difficulty of believing that we ourselves live by such acts is correspondingly greater, since the will does not, by itself, create emotion.

There is one great natural fact—a fact at the very root of all human facts—which involves a relation very much of the nature of exchange, or of something more than exchange. It is the fact of childbirth. Before any child can be born, the masculine seed has to be received by the feminine vessel. The man is quite helpless to produce a child unless he surrenders the means to someone else; the woman is as helpless unless she receives the means from someone else. It is a mutual act —but not only in the sense that two people agree to do something together. They do do something together, but they do it by an act (as regards the child) of substitution. It is not two people carrying a burden at the same time; the mother carries, literally, the burden. By the substitution of the woman for the man the seed fructifies. New life (literally) exists. It exists by the common operation of the woman and the man, and that operation involves something of the nature of substitution.

That substitution produces the new life. That new life exists literally within its mother; it inheres in its mother. The value of the sexual act itself is a kind of co-inherence; the two participators intend (violence apart) a renewal of mutual vigour from the most extreme intimacy of physical relationships. With conception comes the physical inherence of the child. And this is renewed through all the generations; each generation has inhered in that before it; in that sense without any doubt at all, we carry, if not another's burdens, at least the burden of others.

Such is the natural fact. At the root of the physical nature of man (so long as free choice exists) lie exchange of liking, substitution, inherence. The nature of man which is so expressed in the physical world is expressed after the same manner, only more fully, in the mental and spiritual.

The formal threefold division is a nuisance, but it may momentarily stand. What unites the three worlds is precisely this business of 'living from others'. In the mental world, for example, we derive nourishment, energy, and it is not perhaps going too far to say 'life', from great art. Appreciation of great poetry, for example, gives us this sense that though we read and remember the lines, yet the lines are greater than we are and contain us—'felt in the blood and felt along the heart'. It is not, however, in art, however great, that the secret lies; that cannot be more than a part of it. If this principle of exchange, substitution, and co-inherence (inhering in each other) is at all true, then it is true of the whole nature of man. If it is true, then we depend on it altogether—not as a lessening of individuality or moral duty but as the very fundamental principle of all individuality and of all moral duty.

In the records of the Thebaid, of the strange ascetic monks of the Egyptian desert, followers of St. Anthony, the thing was put plainly enough.

> A certain old man used to say, 'It is right for a man to take up the burden for those who are akin (or near) to him, whatsoever it may be, and, so to speak, to put his own soul in the place of that of his neighbour, and to become, if it were possible, a double man; and he must suffer, and weep, and mourn with him, and finally the matter must be accounted by him as if he himself had put on the actual body of his neighbour, and as if he had acquired his countenance and soul, and he must suffer for him as he would for himself.'[1]

So great a business of exchange and substitution fills the phrase 'bear ye one another's burdens' with a much fuller meaning than is generally ascribed to it. But that fuller meaning is no less practical than the usual meanings of being sympathetic and doing exterior acts 'of kindness and of love'. It is very proper that they should be done. But that is because we ought to be 'members one of another'—*membra*, limbs, not members of the same society. Christians are not members of a club; they are 'members' of the Church, which is not a club. Men and women are not members of a club; they are 'members' of mankind, which is not a club. From childbirth to those (in Dante's phrase) 'adult in love', there is but one Nature. That Nature is not divided from grace; it is indeed (let it be said with submission to the theologians) the nature of grace. The difference, in that sense, is only a difference of power.

How then is this to be practised? By 'bearing one another's burdens' interiorly as well as exteriorly; by the turning of the general sympathy into something of immediate use; by a compact of substitution. It is the word 'compact' that is to be stressed. I am not ignorant that in many cases such a sub-

[1] *The Paradise of the Fathers*, Sir Wallis Budge.

stitution may take place instinctively, by the operation of an instinctive love; a wife for a husband, a lover for a lover, a friend for a friend. Still less am I ignorant of the great operations of this kind—in prayer and sacrifice—carried out by the religious Orders. But we are not dealing here with the most intense states of natural love or with the most advanced sacrificial victims of religion, but with ourselves and with the ordinary man. It is ordinary life which might be, more than it is, shot with this principle; it requires only, I will not say faith, but the first faint motions of faith.

Compacts can be made for the taking over of the suffering of troubles, and worries, and distresses, as simply and as effectually as an assent is given to the carrying of a parcel. A man can cease to worry about *x* because his friend has agreed to be worried by *x*. No doubt this is only a part of casting all our burdens upon the Lord; the point is that it may well be a part of it. No doubt the first man may still have to deal directly with *x*; the point is that his friend may well relieve him of the extra burden. So also one may bind oneself more surely by promises made by another on one's behalf than by one's own promises; one may practise a virtue on behalf of another more easily than for oneself. The mere attention of the mind to such a life of substitution will itself provide instances and opportunities. What is needed is precisely that attention.

And, of course, common sense. There are as many dangers in that life as in any. We have to avoid portentousness; we have not to promise anything we obviously cannot do. But perhaps there is very little that could not be done. It does not follow that the payment must be made in the same kind as the original need. This is probably peculiarly true of physical needs. It is in small things that the practice could be begun—sleeplessness or anxiety or slight pains. It is between friends and lovers that the practice could be best begun; always remembering that in the end he whom holy Luck throws in our way is our neighbour—as much as (but perhaps not more than) he whom we go out of our way to seek. To begin the way in small things conveniently is better than to dream of the remote splendours of the vicarious life; not that they are likely in any case to seem very splendid when they come. To begin by practising faith where it is easiest is better than to try and practise it where it is hardest. There is always somewhere where it can be done.

The doctrine of the Christian Church has declared that the mystery of the Christian religion is a doctrine of co-inherence and substitution. The Divine Word co-inheres in God the Father (as the Father in Him and the Spirit in Both), but also He has substituted His Manhood for ours in the secrets of the Incarnation and Atonement. The principle of the Passion is that He gave His life 'for'—that is, instead of and on behalf of—ours. In that sense He lives in us and we in Him, He and we co-inhere. 'I live; yet not I but Christ liveth in me' said St. Paul, and defined the web of universal power towards substitution. To love God and to love one's neighbour are but two movements of the same principle, and so are nature and grace; and the principle is the Word by whom all things were made and who gave Himself for the redemption of all things. It was precisely the breach in that original nature which the new Nature entered to fulfil. But either way it is our nature that is concerned. Our natural life begins by being borne in another; our mothers have to carry us. This is not (so far as we know) by our own will. The Christian Church demands that we shall carry out that principle everywhere by our will—with our friends and with our neighbours, whether we like our neighbours or not.

Such a labour has, almost immediately, two results. In the first place, it encourages a state of mind which may perhaps be called humility—but not so much as a virtue as a mere fact. Humility, said the author of the *Cloud of Unknowing*, consists in seeing things as they are. If our lives are so carried by others and so depend upon others, it becomes impossible to think very highly of them. In the second place there arises within one a first faint sense of what might be called 'loving from within'. One no longer merely loves an object; one has a sense of loving precisely from the great web in which the object and we are both combined. There is, if only transitorily, a flicker of living within the beloved. Such sensations are, or are not; they are, in themselves, of no importance. But they do for a moment encourage us, and they may assist us to consider still more intensely the great co-inherence of all life.

It is said (among other examples of substitution in the Church) that the blessed St. Seraphim of Sarov laid on a certain nun 'the ascetic discipline of death, that she should die instead of her sick brother Michael, whose work was not yet done'.[1] The deaths of those of the English who are being killed every day are, in their manner, 'instead of' us. Between the two the ladder lies by which our capacities run up and down, like angels; and the Joy of the Word which is the ladder because of the Creation and the Incarnation and the Atonement sustains all. From childbirth to the Divine Trinity Itself the single nature thrives; there is here no difference between that natural and that super-natural.

Our chief temptation is to limit its operation. We can believe it happily of ourselves as regards our lovers and our friends; we can accept the idea, at least, as regards strangers; we cannot so easily as regards those of our 'neighbours' who are, individually or nationally, inimical to us. We feel it as an outrage that we should be intimately interrelated, physically and spiritually, to those who have offended our pride or our principles; our very physical bodies revolt against it. It is why one hears of frustrated lovers committing murder; it is why our Lord warned us that murder was in our hearts. We desire to be free from the necessity of contemplating or practising the awful truth. But the doctrine will not let us escape so. It is not for us to make a division; that power our Lord explicitly reserved to Himself. If we insist on it, we can, in His final judgement, *be* separated. That is hell. But only our selves can put us there, and we cannot put others there. Virtue, in this as in all things, is merely to understand the republican fact.

It is republican because it exists everywhere and at all times. No civil or international war can alter it. No neglect of social duty can change it; if we are guilty of such a neglect

[1] *St. Seraphim of Sarov*, A. F. Dobbie-Bateman.

then it will be we ourselves in whom the co-inherent life will tend to perish, and therefore we who will draw nearer to that 'perishing everlastingly' which will one day be hell. The great Rite of this (as of much else) within the Christian Church is the Eucharist, where the co-inherence is fully in action: 'He in us and we in Him.' The prayer after Communion in the ritual of the Church of England expresses it:

> Almighty and everliving God, we most heartily thank thee, for that thou dost vouchsafe to feed us, who have duly received these holy mysteries, with the spiritual food of the most precious Body and Blood of thy Son our Saviour Jesus Christ; and dost assure us thereby of thy favour and goodness towards us; and that *we are very members incorporate in the mystical body of thy Son, which is the blessed company of all faithful people*; and are also heirs through hope of thy everlasting kingdom, by the merits of the most precious death and passion of thy dear Son. And we most humbly beseech thee, O heavenly Father, so to assist us with thy grace, *that we may continue in that holy fellowship, and do all such good works as thou hast prepared for us to walk in*; through Jesus Christ our Lord, to whom, with thee and the Holy Ghost, be all honour and glory, world without end.

The 'good works which thou hast prepared for us to walk in' are those that belong to 'that holy fellowship'; they are therefore those peculiarly of exchange and of substitution. They are prepared and they are there; we have only to walk in them. A little carrying of the burden, a little allowing our burden to be carried; a work as slow, as quiet, even as dull as by agreement to take up or give up a worry or a pain—a compact of substitution between friends—this is the beginning of the practice. The doctrine will grow in us of itself.

THE WAY OF AFFIRMATION

An article called 'The Church Looks Forward', from the St. Martin's Review, *July 1940*

IN fact, of course, the Church does not, in her full existence, even on earth, look forward. She looks centrally, she looks at that which is not to be defined in terms of place and time. It is either the nature of God at which she looks or the nature of things as known in God. It is *now* that the Kingdom of Heaven is fulfilled, generally and individually.

Even in less absolute terms, the Church must not look forward too much. Her future is in the movement of the Holy Ghost and the resolution of our temporal knowledge into terms of Christ is the doing of the Holy Ghost. But though this is the nature of her life, she knows it in the mode of our more usual life. She does not, and under present conditions she cannot, fully realize that continuity of glory. There is therefore a double sense in which it may be said that the Church does look forward: it may be said to correspond to the two great virtues of faith and hope—faith in the nature of God, hope in the nature of things in God. These virtues are not mere abstractions; they are the names of substantial life in its different preoccupations. They are even the names of the physical body in its proper reaction to actuality; perhaps they have been too confined to the invisible operations of the soul.

The Church is to be distinguished from the world. But the physical bodies of her members relate her very intensely to the world. The union of the Church and the world is material in the flesh. But the world, taken in this sense, is not the only element in the flesh; the flesh, even apart from matters of Redemption, is not wholly fallen. It has indeed been dragged down with the soul. But the soul is illuminated to know the principles of the unfallen flesh, and in the Redemption to recover them after the new method, to discover the substitution of a new kind of experience for an old. Whether we always recognize the experience for what it is is another matter; our business is to pursue it under authority. There are two main directions. The first is concerned particularly with the nature of things in God; the second with the nature of God. Neither, of course, can exist entirely without the other. It is not possible for the Christian to attend only to men and women (say) and not at all to God in Himself. But neither is it possible for him to attend only to God in Himself and not at all to men and women. The most remote hermit generally has to attend occasionally to his own meal, however frugal. The most overworked doctor has to say the Lord's Prayer with its clauses concerning God in Himself.

We may find the intensity of both these great ways of the soul (and of the Church) revivified. It is possible that there may come to exist a fresh impulse of ascetic life in the Church; and by asceticism I do not mean hardships of the body only but of the mind and of the soul: the hardships and martyrdoms necessary to all those who are called to a life of separation (so far as possible) from all 'creatures'. Such outbreaks of austere vocations have occurred often in the history of the Church. This is a matter which can only be recognized by souls capable of and called to that vocation. It is, certainly, the duty of every member of the Church to examine himself or herself whether he or she is called to such an interior work. And it is also a duty to give the correct answer without any regret or dissatisfaction. It is a duty if the answer is 'no' quite as much as if it is 'yes'. There is likely to be as much rejection of ourselves on the one way as on the other.

It was once suggested—and the suggestion was made neither profanely nor scandalously—that among all the Orders of the Christian Church there lacked one to our Sacred Lord as 'a gluttonous man and a wine-bibber'. Considering that the very term Christian rose as a term of abuse and was then adopted, these other terms of abuse may not be without their own value and instruction for us. Food and wine are here the definite symbols of the 'creature', more so as a divine Way than the locusts and wild honey of the Precursor. It is the following of our Lord in this knowledge of the creature which has been a part of the work of Christendom and may well be a greater part in the future. The doctrine of our Lord as God with its corollaries took centuries to work out. It is, certainly, now attacked. It is in dispute between Christendom and all that is not Christendom. But it is not in dispute within Christendom; all that has been finished with. The other doctrine of His Manhood, with its corollaries, has still to be worked out and put into action.

Its corollaries have indeed arisen during the last century, even more clearly than ever before. More and more Christians have felt it their absolute religious duty to ensure, as far as possible, the existence of a just State. Mr. Middleton Murry has pointed out that, under present conditions, we only succeed in establishing anything like a just State under immediate pressure of war. Until that pressure exists we are content to leave a heavy proportion of our citizens in a state of direct or indirect despair; in a state, that is to say, in which, humanly speaking, any gospel, even the Christian, is bound to be incapable of reception. It is forbidden to the Christian to entertain despair: how much more to inflict it!

Despair is infectious; a State in which it is unconsciously permitted to exist is lost. We may, however, leave that particular prospect for others: it is sufficient to say that the duty there incumbent on us arises as much from our Lord's physical relation to men and women as from the order of His Deity.

It is something of the same sense that lies at the beginning of another problem to which the members of the Church will have to address themselves—the problem of marriage. Speaking generally, we have up to the present time insisted on the morals of marriage but we have not based them on any doctrine of love. We have rejected divorce but we have done so without any clear idea of the reason; and it is much to be feared that, in rejecting it, we have called in the help of all kinds of fallacies, inaccuracies, and even definite untruths. Natural life produces a vision of beauties, energies, and glories about which the comments of the officers of the supernatural life seem anxiously inadequate. When the same inadequate voices declare that the corollary of those strange benefits must be a lifelong fidelity, they must expect to be asked why. One answer is that it has been proved socially desirable, which seems doubtful and even unlikely. Another is that it is the Will of God, which (if likely) is inexplicable. A labour of intellects is required. There have already appeared recently several books on the subject of marriage. I cannot discuss them for I have not read them. They may remain few, they may be the precursors of many more.

The last sentence brings us to a point of looking forward on which a great deal depends in all the preoccupations of the Church. Her missionary and her contemplative activities depend, it is agreed, on the Holy Ghost. The activities of the Holy Ghost depend on nothing but Itself. But the success of the activities of the Holy Ghost (within the Church) does depend on a something beside Itself—it depends on the honesty of Christians. The honesty of Christians is a very desirable and also a very difficult thing. There can be few Christians alive who have not been aware, in themselves or in each other, of that great temptation—'to lie on the Lord's behalf'. It has in the past done untold harm to the Church, and it will again unless it can be overcome. It takes many shapes. It is apt to *pretend*—to pretend that intellectual arguments are valid when it should be clear that they are fallacious, that moral iniquity exists where there is no proof of it, and so on. An extremely distinguished dignitary of the Church once printed the statement that the proportion of happiness to unhappiness in a man's life was as nine to one—an absolutely unjustified statement. (I do not say it was false: the whole point is that one ought not to make that sort of generalization at all; it is unprovable.) This kind of thing is still too common. Accuracy, accuracy, and again accuracy! Accuracy of mind and accuracy of emotion. If the Church is to look forward to a wholesome mental life her members must discipline themselves to honesty. The indulgence of any prejudice must be regarded as sinful, and an intellectual sin is as bad as a physical.

Yet the life of the Church is single and not divided into intellectual and physical, and in her (militant here upon earth) the two affect each other as much as in any of her children. If her honesty can be recovered there might be recovered with it the fullness of her charismatic and prophetic ministry. It is not in any sense to deny the order which has developed in the Church to say that the New Testament seems to contemplate the charismatic ministry as being the common possession of all believers. Whatever texts may be regarded as symbolic and whatever as literal, it is hardly possible to regard as other than literal the promise of a new life which shall be unharmed by earthly accidents, though not perhaps by earthly malignity. The disciples may be put out of the synagogues or even killed by the hatred (the righteous hatred) of those who conceive that they are doing God service so. But the casual 'deadly things'—the serpent or the accidental venom—are to be harmless as far as they are concerned. And if those, then perhaps the accidental diseases and dangers of ordinary human life also—unless indeed those were, in certain cases, deliberately welcomed on behalf of others and in the cause and name of charity.

The rediscovery of such a high power as normal to the operative Christian is far enough away at present, and it is difficult to imagine how it might come. Nor indeed is it altogether desirable to imagine it coming; it is probably true that we shall never reach that state unless and until we are willing to welcome those distresses on behalf of others. We have lost, I think, to a very large extent the idea that we can effectively welcome them; it lingers chiefly in the intuitive natural desire of men and women at rare moments and under rare conditions. But conditions which are comparatively rare in the life of 'the flesh' should be comparatively common in the life of 'the spirit'—not meaning, by those words, the visible and invisible parts of our organism. What is necessary is the life of 'faith', the substantial existence in us which we call faith. It is our business to recover *that*. The Holy Ghost will then do what He will, and it seems possible that we may humbly believe that at the right hour He shall teach us 'what we shall speak'—when to make offers and when to receive offers, when to dismiss 'devils' and when to endure them.

The doctrine of the Christian Church depends on the substitution, in the last experiences, of our sacred Lord for us. The activity of the Christian Church may have to recover, more than is commonly supposed, our substitution, one for another. The most important thing is to get our minds accustomed to the idea of that activity: attention without fever, speed without haste. The Atonement of our Lord restored this power to man; the Holy Ghost now, as originally, confirms, nourishes, and directs it. In the old legend Adam and Eve were, originally, one being. It is a profound symbol. Justice, charity, union; these are the three degrees of the Way of the Affirmation of Images, and all of us are to be the images affirmed.

POETRY

INTRODUCTION

What then is the achievement of the Grail?

From Arthurian Torso, *edited by C. S. Lewis*

DANTE, in a later century, was to put the height of human beatitude in the understanding of the Incarnation; in a lesser, but related, method Angela of Foligno was to speak of knowing 'how God comes into the Sacrament'. To know these things is to be native to them; to live in the world where the Incarnation and the Sacrament (single or multiple) happen. It is more: it is, in some sense, to live beyond them, or rather (since that might sound profane) to be conscious of them as one is conscious of oneself, Christ-conscious instead of self-conscious. The achievement of the Grail is the perfect fulfilment of this, the thing happening.

It is to the French poets and romancers that we owe the bringing of this high myth into relation with Arthur, King of Britain or Logres; as it is to Geoffrey of Monmouth that we owe the development of the figure of Arthur the king out of the doubtful records of the Captain-General of Britain; and as we owe to Sir Thomas Malory the most complete version of the whole in the English language. Much was modified and much added by others. It is perhaps worthwhile to reshape the whole tale here once more. But we cannot go back behind the royalty which Geoffrey invented. No one can ever uncrown Arthur. The king may have—and indeed must have—the qualities of the Captain-General, but he must be the king.

At a time then when the Roman and Christian civilization in Britain was seriously endangered by the invasions of the pirate and pagan forces, there arose a patriotic movement of considerable force. It was at first led by Aurelius Ambrosius, of a noble Romano-British family; after his death his brother

Uther, called Pendragon, succeeded to the leadership and by his victories was named for a brief period king of all Britain. He was the father—canonically, but with some strangeness about the birth—of a son, Arthur. At that time the centre of the Roman *imperium* lay in Byzantium. The Empire was Christian, and not only Christian but orthodox and Trinitarian. The Arian heresies had been defeated. Christ was adored as God and not as a created being. The variations of this which were called Nestorianism had also been overcome.[1] It had been determined that the mystery of redemption lay not only in the operation of true God but by that operation in flesh and blood. It was generally accepted, though not yet defined, that the Incarnacy deigned to maintain Himself (in His Passion and Resurrection) in His Eucharists. The Pope was in possession of Rome; about both his figure and that of the remote Emperor in Byzantium there lay something of a supernatural light—at best mystical, at worst magical. There was, for all disputes between East and West, as yet no great schism in Christendom. The prince Arthur grew to youth in that Catholic world; and this is, eastward from Logres, the condition of his life and reign. But as this is the historic relation, so on the other—westward from Logres—there is the mythical. In a sense, of course, history is itself a myth; to the imaginative, engaged in considering these things, all is equally myth. We may issue from it into other judgements—doctrinal, moral, historic. But so doing we enter into another kind of thought and judge by other tests—more important perhaps, but not the same. In the myth we need ask for nothing but interior consistency; thus, if we choose to have it so, there is no reason why Julius Caesar should not hear the souls of the dead putting off in spectral boats from the shores of Gaul. There is no reason why Camus and St. Peter should not both lament Lycidas (for whom, after all, rather than Edward King, Milton supposed himself to be sorrowing. But Edward King *is* Lycidas ? it is certain that Lycidas is something more than Edward King). It is in an ocean

[1] It is possible that Charles Williams intended to mention more than one heresy, but the text, as it stands, can be defended. [C. S. L.]

where such tales are relevant that Britain lies; that is why it is Logres, which is Britain in an enlarging world—Britain and more than Britain. It is more like that mysterious Albion of which Blake wrote in another geography.

There lie then near Logres—and they must lie to the west, for to the east we come into history and doctrine and Europe—other places of the myth. There is the mysterious forest of Broceliande: there are the seas on which the ship of Solomon is to sail; beyond them is Sarras. It is certainly true that Sarras was originally on the borders of Egypt, but that cannot now be helped, for the lords of the Quest must go there in a ship, and it must lie beyond Carbonek. To send the ship back from Carbonek through the Mediterranean to Egypt—I will not say it could not be done, for anything can be done that can be done, but it seems less convenient than to remove Sarras; especially as Sarras can be spiritually reached anywhere, but it is not quite suitable that the High Prince should return to the world. He who does that is Bors.

Carbonek itself must be, if not in, at least on the borders of Broceliande. It is the castle of the Hallows; there are in its chapel the Grail and the Spear. The Spear is that which pierced the heart of Christ; the Grail is the vessel used at the Last Supper, in which also the blood from the wounded heart was caught. The Keeper of the Castle is the King Pelles, and in the processions of the Grail it is carried by his daughter Helayne. She is maiden, and all but vowed to maidenhood; only there lies over her the rejection of that desired life; she is to be the mother of the Grail-lord. It would be perhaps a pity to lose from the tale the other name of Castle Mortal and its king; but if it is to be kept, there is only one figure who can occupy it, and that is the brother of Pelles, the invisible knight, who is called Garlon. That castle too must stand in Broceliande.

It is indeed in that forest, inextricably mingled with the mystical sea spiritual distance,[1] that all these places of marvel must lie. It is, after all, one of the great forests of myth—greater because of its hidden mysteries than Arden or Bir-

[1] 'Sea spiritual' (or 'sea-spiritual') is, I think, an adjective. [C. S. L.]

nam or Westermain. The wood of Comus may be compared with it; and indeed is poetically a part of it, except that it is a holy place and uninhabited by such sorcerers. But some of the outlying parts might be given up to him—until the Judgement. A nobler comparison is with that forest which Dante found at the foot of the Mount of Purgatory and where he came again to himself, or that other on the height of the Mount where Beatrice came again to him. But it is not proper to do more than shyly observe comparisons between such myths. It is a place of making and of all the figures concerned with making.

Of these one of the most mysterious is Nimue, the Lady of the Lake. Swinburne's great description of her is too effective to be lost. Tennyson turned her into a kind of allegory of the Church, and (if baptism were involved) this might be well enough. But of the two Swinburne's is the greater, for the ecclesiastical and religious figures are already patterned, and the High Prince himself has his own Way, not to be confused. So that Nimue is the great mother and lady of Broceliande—Nature, as it were, or all the vast processes of the universe imaged in a single figure.

There is, however, a problem about Merlin. He is so very much a preparation for the Grail that his earlier diabolic birth seems almost improper to so high a vocation, though it might be worked in well enough. On the other hand there is something attractive in a small invention which would be inconsistent with this diabolic conception. The central fact of the conception of Galahad depends partly on the strange drink given to Lancelot by Brisen, the nurse of Helayne. She in fact prepares within Carbonek what Merlin prophesies and prepares (by his calling of Arthur) in Logres. It might be permissible to make them twins, children of some high parthenogenetical birth of Nimue in Broceliande. They would come then almost like Time and Place to their mission, to prepare in Carbonek and Camelot for the moment of the work.

The calling of Arthur, and the freeing of Logres (or Britain) from the pagans and tyrants is the first movement of the mystery. The Matter of Britain begins with this, leading to the coronation of the king; when, in the old phrase, 'he put on his crown'. What, however, obviously ought not to happen, and what in Malory and Tennyson is already an almost minor episode, is his war against the Emperor. This was very well in the chivalric battles of Geoffrey, though Nationalism (too often attributed only to the Renascence) is already there getting slightly out of hand. But a kind of supreme worldly glory is Arthur's climax. Even then—by accident or design—he was never allowed to meet the Emperor in battle, and all that Tennyson says is that 'Arthur strove with Rome'. It had better be dropped. No national myth was ever the better for being set against a more universal authority—in our own day we have learnt that—though it might be desirable to heighten the *imperium* in order conveniently to include this royalty within it. But in a myth Byzantium may be many things. It may also be urged, for what the point is worth, that it was in fact this Roman and universal authority for which, in however shadowy a way, the historic Arthur was fighting against the barbarians; it is not for him himself to fight against it. Nor, now, to win conquests over other nations as such. He is a champion, not a conquistador.

It is in fact here that the centre of the myth must be determined. The problem is simple—is the king to be there for the sake of the Grail or not? It was so the Middle Ages left it; but since then it has been taken the other way. The Grail has been an episode. This may still be so, but it can no longer be accidentally so. Tennyson, in that sense, was right; he meant to make the Grail an episode, and he did. He said it was only for certain people, and he modified the legend accordingly. If it is to be more, it must take the central place. Logres then must be meant for the Grail. (There is a difficulty here about the Dolorous Blow which may be mentioned in a moment.) This indeed must be the pure glory of Arthur and Logres. Vessels of plenty have nothing to do with it; were it true (as it is not) that the Grail had developed from them, it would still have developed out of all common measurement.

It is the central matter of the Matter of Britain. We may, if we choose, reasonably and properly refuse it, but we can hardly doubt that if we do we shall have no doubt a consistent, but a much smaller myth.

For the Grail, so understood, must itself be—I will not say enlarged, for that is impossible, but it must be understood in all its meanings and relationships. It is the tale of Galahad; it is the tale of the mystical way; but also it is the tale of the universal way. It is not, as in Tennyson, only for the elect; it is for all. It is in this sense that the three lords of the Quest are of importance. Bors is in the chapel at Sarras as well as Galahad and Percivale. This is what relates the Achievement to every man. The tale must end, and that part of it when the holy thing returns again to earth—when Galahad is effectually in Bors as Bors is implicitly in Galahad—cannot be told until the clause of the Lord's prayer is fulfilled and the kingdom of heaven is come upon earth, perhaps not until there is a new heaven and a new earth. It must therefore vanish: and Bors must return—in spite of the fact that there are hints, even in Malory, that the mere passage of the Grail destroyed the kingdom. Since the *Grand St. Graal* nothing has ever been quite the same. That romance worked on the literature the effect which the Grail worked on Logres. The only question is whether that work is a necessary part of the Achievement.

If then the Grail is to be fully accepted, in every sense, it must be accepted from the beginning. I have sometimes thought that the best way would be to imagine that Logres was designed to be a place for the coming of the Grail. The immediate expectation of the Second Coming had faded, but the vision of it remained as it has always remained in the Church. It might be taken that the King Pelles, the Keeper of the Hallows, was at the proper time, when Merlin had brought Arthur into his royalty and Logres had been cleared and established, to emerge from Carbonek into Logres, directing the processions of the Grail and the prelude of the Second Coming. Logres was to be blessed thus, and he who said Mass in Sarras would say it in Caerleon and Camelot as he did in Jerusalem. This, however, is but one means to making the tale coherent, and need not be pressed. The more urgent problems are the place of the unasked question and of the Dolorous Blow. They are, of course, strictly speaking, alternatives. It is certain that we must keep the Dolorous Blow; a loss of that would mean a loss of the Wounded King, which cannot be imagined. The only question is whether we can have the unasked question also.

It would not be impossible, if the whole thing were regarded as a tale of the Fall—individual or universal. The union would be in the fact that the lack of the question would mean the lack of an answer, and hence an ignorance of the true nature of the Invisible Knight. This was one of the secrets Gawaine should have learned and reported; not learning and not reporting, he left the Court ignorant and Balin the Savage free to avenge his host's son. The refusal to ask the question is precisely that refusal to inquire which accompanies so many a temptation and encourages so many a sin. 'What serves the Grail?' The answer is 'You and all Logres'. It is not so much the encouragement of a sin that is so often sinful as a refusal to encourage the counter-movement, the opposite of a sin. After that, the ignorant savage is free.

The Dolorous Blow consisted in the wounding of the royal Keeper of the Hallows with the Sacred Spear. The Spear was that which had wounded the side of Christ, and it bled continually at the point. It was then aimed at the central heart. But when Balin le Sauvage used it, he used it for his own self-preservation. It is this turning of the most sacred mysteries to the immediate security of the self that is the catastrophic thing. It is indeed, morally, precisely the wounding of the Keeper of the Hallows which then takes place. Man wounds himself. It is an image of the Fall; it is also an image of every individual and deliberate act of malice, though the deliberation is here but passionate and not coldly angry.

It has, of course, every excuse. The mystery of the Invisible Knight—say, the Invisible Slayer—is abroad in the world. He might have been explained, had the question been asked. As it is, he rides destructively, but in the hall of Carbonek he is at last seen and known; it may be that even there he was a dark knight, and perhaps the King or Duke of Castle Mortal, since one must not over-multiply the title of king. There is here a certain similitude to the figure of the Holy Ghost, as It exercises Its operations in the world. For Balin actually to kill an inhabitant of Broceliande can hardly be allowed: the forest and its people are not of a kind that could be overcome in that manner. But the ever-bleeding wound of the Keeper is exactly symbolical, and so is the ruin that falls on Logres. A new darkness and sterility begin to creep through the land from which the pagans have been expelled. The outer conquests are not the inner. Victory is being still celebrated in Camelot when defeat issues from Carbonek.

This, even in the direct incidents of the tale, is not an exaggeration. One incident is directly the consequence of the Dolorous Blow; and there is another like it which should be. The first is that Balin the Savage in ignorance kills his own brother Balan, and Balan him. The natural pieties begin to be lost, and there is incivility in the blood. It is in fact the further externalization of the Wounded King. But the disorder spreads farther. In the first tales Mordred was the king's nephew; in later versions he became the king's son by incest, but unknown incest. The queen Morgause of Orkney, the wife of King Lot, was Arthur's sister. But he does not know this when she comes to his court, and he tempts her to lie with him. The birth of that incestuous union is Mordred, and the fate of the Round Table comes into the world almost before the Table has been established; say, at the very feast of the crowning of Arthur and the founding of the Table. The seed of its destroyer lies in the womb of Morgause while she watches the ceremonies. This is not irony; it is something beyond irony. No doubt the wise young master Merlin knows, but it is not for him to speak, or only in riddles. He knows that the egress of the Grail from Carbonek has now been prevented, but also he prepares the Perilous Seat. He sets that empty chair among all the chairs; he promises an achievement, and a restoration from a destruction which is known then to him alone.

This now is the double way of Logres, of the Table, and of the king. The glory of Arthur continues. He marries Guinevere—the most beautiful woman. He has for friend and chief lord Lancelot, the bravest and noblest man. Lancelot is chief in the heart of both the king and the queen. It was a wise instinct that kept the old writers from making Arthur himself a lord in love between a man and a woman. It is the high brotherhood of arms and friendship in which he is noble; that is his own personal share in the glory of his kingdom. But it is an actual kingdom and an actual glory: that is, Lancelot has his proper duties to the State. The political side of the kingdom is not to be denied or despised, and the Table itself is a part of the settlement. All the champions are still to be champions of the good; in that Tennyson was right, though he perhaps a little slurred the inevitable dullness of their duty. The Table is a gathering of the realm as well as of knighthood, and if Lancelot is not a Chancellor or Prime Minister he is not unlike. It is observable that in the great parting with Guinevere in Malory he tells her that he would have achieved the Grail 'had not your lord been'. This may refer to the love-conflict, but then one would have expected 'had not you been'. It may again be an error,[1] but if it is not, then it is important. For then we have a definite relation of Lancelot to a more complete way of the Affirmation of Images than has been allowed to him. It is not only to do with a woman, but with men and women; not only with the queen but with the Republic.

The speech of Sir Ector over the dead Lancelot confirms this. Lancelot, for all the errands upon which he rides, is never merely a knight-errant. He affirms friendship, courtesy, justice, and nobility—in all the references allowed them. He is almost the active centre of that kingdom of which Arthur is, in a sense, the passive. Arthur, of course, is no such poor thing, but it is true he does not *seem* to act.

[1] It almost certainly is. Malory XXI. ix reads *lord*, but Winchester MS. (ed. F. Vinaver, Oxford, 1947, vol. iii, p. 1253) reads *love*. The Winchester text was, of course, inaccessible when Charles Williams wrote. [C. S. L.]

Lancelot then is the chief figure of the Way of Affirmations. The great Arthuriad is no longer a division between this and its opposite and complementary companion—the Way of Rejections. The tales of Arthur and of the Grail, of Camelot and Carbonek, may have been as antagonistic in their first invention as scholars maintain. They are now no longer so. There is, no doubt, a separation, but the separation is the union; and this is not so alien from our experience that we need reject in myth what we have to accept in mere living. The moral of the whole is as firm as ever Tennyson would have made it, but it is deeper in its metaphysic.

Between Guinevere and Lancelot there has risen this fatal love—fatal but not fated. No magical potion has been its source, such as Tristram and Iseult drank between sea and sky. The spring, and young blood, and generous hearts, are its beginning. Guinevere has always been a slight difficulty, for in the situation of the tale, she has nothing to do but to be in love with Lancelot. He can ride out, and have adventures, and return, but she can only sit and work at embroideries and love. It is therefore only in relation to that that she has hitherto existed. I suppose something more might be done with her; her royalty might be stressed in actions. But it has not yet happened. Her phrases are love's phrases—embittered or noble. 'And so I report me unto all the Table Round', &c. She retains to the end that capacity for stabbing at Lancelot; it is to be forgiven because of her very great dolour, and because it is not for us to revenge what Lancelot accepted.

I am not sure that, for all Chrétien de Troyes and the others did with it, the great love-tale comes properly now under the heading of Romantic Love, either in the historic or the metaphysical sense. It began certainly with Romance. But Malory, as was said, has made it different. It is the affirmation of one kind of image and not of another. It is certainly not any nonsense of the 'death-wish' as M. de Rougemont suggests. Malory knows nothing of lovers who desire to perish. Subconsciously? Nor that; through all their beings these great lovers desire life, honour, and reciprocal joy. Some such element might—though I do not much believe it—be felt in the Tristram drink, though in Malory Tristram shows little enough awareness of it. But Lancelot and the queen are simply not of that kind at all. Any more than we are—in spite of our occasional dark indulgence of ourselves in our sorrows.

It is indeed their situation—in life and desire for life—which in Malory offers such profound hints. The soul, affirming the validity of those images which appear to it, finds itself, physically or mentally, caught in its own desire to appropriate them. The temptation of the king—were it stressed, but it is not—would be to be too much himself the State; to appropriate Logres to himself. The temptation of Lancelot is to appropriate the queen. It is no less a temptation of the soul that it appears as a temptation of the body. It is a temptation of power. Power is not something that one has; it is something one is. The desire for power is always being thwarted by this misunderstanding. One is not powerful. But if one had *x* one would be powerful. Power (as Wordsworth showed us) is in one's capacities. The capacities of Lancelot and the queen are distracted.

It is, however, by indirect means that these two great Powers are fulfilled. One must learn to think properly of the personages of the myth, and not less mightily than the names deserve. The Arthuriad recedes into dim forests and seas, and the ship of Solomon driving into the last Mysteries, and in the foreground is a Saracen knight hunting a strange beast which is known by the sound of barking dogs. It is called the Blatant Beast, and when Spenser took it over he turned it into the mob, but it is not that in Malory; it is only a figure of fable, except that its Paynim pursuer will not be christened till he has overcome it. But he has another quality too, which is his hopeless love for the queen Iseult, but it was Tristram whom she loved and she took no care for Palomides. (And a distinction between ways of thought is between Malory and Austin Dobson's short poem.) These two might well, in some way, be one; and it is perhaps significant that Palomides is at last christened after his reconciliation with Tristram (but not with Mark—but of Mark we need say nothing), and that nothing in the end is heard of any seizing of the Blatant Beast.

There is, however, another point where Palomides comes violently into the myth. It is at the famous—and oddly named—Tournament of Lonazep. It is there that Palomides does his greatest deeds—'it is his day', said Sir Dinadan—but also his worst; for he overthrows Lancelot by falsehood.[1]

Malory and the Grail Legend

From the Dublin Review, *April 1944*

THE Twelfth Book of Malory's *Morte D'Arthur* ends with the following words: 'And here followeth the noble tale of the Sangreal, that called is the holy vessel: and the signification of the blessed blood of our Lord Jesus Christ, blessed mote it be, the which was brought into this land by Joseph of Aramathie.' The Seventeenth Book ends: 'Thus endeth the story of the Sangreal, that was briefly drawn out of French into English, the which is a story chronicled for one of the truest and the holiest that is in this world.' The five books between are occupied with Galahad and the achievement of the Quest.

It is not my purpose here to discuss the origins of the Grail story—Celtic, Classical, or Christian. Much attention has been given them. The Grail itself has been traced back to 'heirlooms belonging to the house of Atreus' and to 'the wars of the ancient Irish gods'. The first view was put forward by Mr. Charles B. Lewis,[2] the latest discussion of the second is in the recently published *Origin of the Grail Legend* by Professor Arthur Brown. It is, no doubt, true that Chrétien de Troyes, who seems to have begun the Tale, may have been vaguely influenced from both sources. Writers are apt to take over agreeable ideas from any source. Thus Professor Brown

[1] This was the point in his book *The Figure of Arthur* which Williams had reached at the time of his death. [A. R.]

[2] *Classical Mythology and Arthurian Romance*, published for St. Andrews University; Oxford University Press, 1932.

discusses the four-sided fairy cup of plenty in Irish mythology, and points out the insistence on the number four in Chrétien's *Percival.* This is exactly the kind of detail which might easily have appealed to and been taken over by a Christian writer; the Evangelists, the four-sided City, &c. On the other hand, when Professor Brown speaks of a castle surrounded by a river which is crossed by a bridge and writes: 'H. R. Patch has argued that the river and the bridge that often accompanies it are oriental material worked over by the Irish', he gives Mr. Patch too much importance. Houses on islands, even if supposed to be in the Other World, must have been too natural to Chrétien for him to need suggestions from the marvels of the Oriental and the Celt. He could do that sort of marvel by merely looking out of his medieval window.

There is perhaps still room for some consideration of the Tale as it has existed in the English imagination. There are a number of texts, even without involving those of the Middle Ages. They occur mostly in the Victorian poets—Hawker, Morris, Tennyson, Swinburne—and they are mostly unsatisfactory. There is, however, no need to explain this by dragging in religion; it is much more easily and truly explained by saying that none of these poets had the full capacity of the mythical imagination. If we can read the *Idylls of the King* without remembering what critics have said about them, we shall find a great deal of good stuff. But it is true that Tennyson was really writing (and very properly) a modern moral story, as he said he was. He could not—he did not try to—get the Myth. Thus Balin, in the Grail Castle, instead of wounding the King with the Sacred Lance, uses it as a jumping-pole. This is a serious lapse. Morris arranged a highly decorative and highly delicate pageant of Galahad. The poet who, in an occasional touch, gets nearest to the tone of the Myth is Swinburne. This will seem odd unless we realize that the poetic capacity for Myth is quite different from the human capacity for religion; a fact not without relevance to our general belief in religion as well as to our criticism of verse.

But it is, of course, in prose rather than in verse that the thing has remained for us in English; it is in Malory, and in Sebastian Evans's translation of a part of Chrétien's *Percival* under the title of the *High History of the Holy Graal*. The latter book is a very noble piece of work. But it is, as it were, a detail; the whole grand Myth—or at least much of it—is in Malory. There is, however, even in Malory, a certain suggestiveness which Malory does not seem altogether to have understood. The present article does not intend to discuss how far these significances are in Malory's originals; its writer would be incapable, and the discussion would be irrelevant. The point is not where they came from but what they have become.

One main fact, however, must be mentioned. There are, in the history of the European imagination, a few moments when a superb invention of the very first importance takes place. I doubt whether there has ever been one of more real power than that of the invention of Galahad; not even excluding that of Dante's discovery of Beatrice as the theme of the *Commedia*. That, one really feels, must, sooner or later, have happened; there were so many poets in love. But the invention of Galahad as the son of Lancelot might easily not have happened. Someone—M. Vinaver[1] says a Cistercian—at some time in some place thought of it; it was a moment as near to divine inspiration as any not technically so called can be. It is, of course, necessary to speak cautiously here. M. Vinaver himself opposes the idea, put forward by other writers, that there is any 'mystic affiliation' between Lancelot and Galahad. He properly distinguishes between the Court of Arthur and the Court of Heaven. 'The author of the *Queste* [the Galahad romance]', he says, 'was conscious of an acute conflict between the two kinds of chivalry, and never derived the one from the other. Galahad's mysticism can by no means be fathered upon Lancelot.' This is certainly true. But it is equally true that Galahad himself has certainly been fathered upon Lancelot, and that therefore their relation—even in division—is a very particular relation. Their distinc-

[1] *Malory*, Clarendon Press, 1929.

tion exists in a kind of imaginative union; the greater (however much greater) derives, in that Myth, for ever from the lesser, and something in each of their differing hues illumines the other.

Malory took the tale over. He either took over with it, or else he invented, certain details. It may be objected that my choice of these details is arbitrary, and I entirely agree that there are many insignificant details in Malory. He fills his pages with all sorts of things which may be fascinating but are not (in our sense) mythical. But there are some which are mythical in the sense that they seem to have a profound spiritual relevance. The whole question of Courtly Love may be ruled out at once. Malory was not concerned with that technique, any more than (at least, directly) with the greater passion and truer vision of the Dantean Romantic Love. Lancelot and Guinevere do not develop that. But they are still passionately and permanently in love. It is almost impossible for either of them to alter the exterior situation. A very little extra touch here and there in the *Morte* would have made it quite impossible—a little heightening of the realistic side of the kingdom of Arthur. The chief man in the kingdom after the King cannot throw up his job at once, and the Queen can certainly not throw up hers. The struggle after virtue, the happiness-unhappiness, the mere infinite tiresomeness, and the beauty, are all in the situation.

But there are (and here we begin the Myth as Malory has it) other people about. One of these is the Saracen knight Palomides. Palomides is in love with the Queen Iseult, but she is married to Mark and in love with Tristram. That, however, is not relevant to the Myth, except that the misery of Palomides accentuates his bitterness. He will not be christened, 'howbeit in my heart I believe in Jesu Christ and his mild mother Mary', till he has done certain great deeds, and overcome the questing beast (which is not without a likeness to the inner agony he suffers). At the seven-days' tournament at Lonazep, in that discourtesy to which he is prone, he commits an outrage against the laws of chivalry, and insults and injures Lancelot. Lancelot forgives him—

'Sithen my quarrel is not here, ye shall have this day the worship as for me . . . it were no worship for me to put you from it.' But Lancelot carries his courtesy farther, for soon after the tournament is closed he finds Palomides in the hands of those who are about to put him to death, and rescues him from twelve knights; 'and Palomides kneeled down upon his knees and thanked Sir Lancelot'.

Lancelot in fact had a great many activities besides being in love with Guinevere: 'thou were', said Sir Ector of him, 'the courteousest knight that ever bare shield. And thou were the truest friend to thy lover that ever bestrod horse. And thou were the kindest man that ever struck with sword.' It is immediately after his exhibition of courtesy towards someone who has injured him—this is the significant, if accidental, detail—that we find Lancelot riding towards the mysterious castle of King Pelles, who is the Keeper of the Grail; it is shown between the hands

of a damozel passing fair and young. O Jesu, said Sir Lancelot, what may this mean? This is, said the king, the richest thing that any man hath living. And when this thing goeth about, the Round Table shall be broken; and wit ye well, said the king, this is the holy Sangreal that ye have seen. . . . The king knew well that Sir Lancelot should get a child upon his daughter, the which should be named Sir Galahad, the good knight, by whom all foreign country should be brought out of danger, and by him the Holy Greal should be achieved.

There is about this a known predestination: 'the king knew well that Lancelot should'. Lancelot is here the predetermined father of the great Achievement; he is the noblest lord in the world, the kindest, the bravest, the truest. But he will not have to do with any woman but the Queen: 'when was Lancelot wanderingly lewd?' And Galahad must certainly be the child of the Grail-princess and certainly not of Guinevere. How is it to be done? It is brought about by holy enchantment and an act of substitution. Lancelot is deluded (as it were, by a courtesy of terrible condescension) into riding 'against night' to another castle, where he is received 'worshipfully with such people to his seeming as were about

Queen Guinevere secret'. He is given a cup of enchanted wine and taken to the room where the supposed Queen is: 'and all the windows and holes of that chamber were stopped that no manner of day might be seen'.

I am not unaware that the substitution of one woman for another is common enough in the romances; it is the kind of substitution that makes this so thrilling. The vision is of 'the best knight', labouring in that threefold consciousness of God, the King, and Guinevere, received into the outlying castle of the Mysteries, and then by the deliberate action of spiritual powers drawn on into a deeper operation. He dismounts: around him are those who seem to be the Queen's servants, but it is not so; the assumed forms, the awful masks, of this sacred mystery attend him; he is taken to a chamber as dark as the dark night of the soul; and there the child who is to achieve the Grail is begotten.[1]

And the next morning? Here, it must be admitted, Malory fell away from what the Myth demanded. He sends Lancelot back to the Court, sends the Princess after him, describes the anger of Guinevere, enchants Lancelot all over again, causes him to meet the Queen, and then drives him mad because of his disloyalty to her. There is some very good writing, but it will not do. What must obviously happen is that immediately on waking in the Castle of the Substitution, Lancelot realizes the deception; which he does—'anon as he had unshut the window the enchantment was gone; then he knew himself that he had done amiss. Alas, he said, that I have lived so long; now I am shamed.' It is then that his mind should be overthrown; it is very proper that he should leap from that window of awful realization 'into a garden, and there with thorns he was all to scratched in his visage and his body; and so he ran forth he wist not whither, and was wild wood as ever was man; and so he ran two years, and never man might have grace to know him'.

So far as I can see, there is no particular reason for two

[1] It is necessary to guard, through the whole Myth, against any identification of Galahad with Christ. Galahad is only that in the human soul which finds Christ.

years; nine months would have been a better time. Presently he comes again to the house of the Grail, and there 'by force Sir Lancelot was laid by that holy vessel; and there came a holy man, and unhylled that vessel, and so by miracle and by virtue of that holy vessel Sir Lancelot was healed and recovered'. He remains for some time in disguise and seclusion, calling himself only 'Le Chevalier Mal Fet, that is to say, the knight that hath trespassed'. The trespass is, no doubt, chiefly his unintentional falsity to Guinevere, but then in Malory truth is part of his passion; Lancelot does not believe that he will become true to the King by being untrue to the Queen. He may fail to manage to be true to both, but this is his intention. He is merely overthrown by that element in him which, because of his love and courtesy, is predetermined 'where Will and Power are one' to make him the father of Galahad. There is no compromise with the sin, but there is every charity towards the virtue.

At last Lancelot meets with Percivale and returns with him to the Court. The name of Percivale brings us to the second part of the Myth. Time has gone by, but time is not in Malory very strictly attended to. Galahad is taken to a Convent of White Nuns, where he is brought up. But the tale passes on from Lancelot's return almost directly to the coming to the Court of the High Prince: not indeed that in Malory 'the High Prince' is Galahad's title at all; it belongs to Galahault, who is quite a different person, and not of much importance. He had once been; it was he who had brought Lancelot and Guinevere to their first kiss in one of the love-romances where the greater interpretations were not imagined. As a result he had gained a literary immortality, for he had been given a famous line in the *Inferno*: 'Galeotto fu il libro e chi lo scrisse.' It is proper that the title should pass from him; in a myth there ought to be more than charm, sweetness, and physical delight to justify such a phrase.

It is Pentecost; the King holds his court. One rite has already been solemnized. Palomides has been reconciled with Tristram and has been baptized by 'the suffragan of Carlisle'. 'And so the king and all the court were glad that Sir

Palomides was christened. And at the same feast in came Galahad and sat in the siege perilous.' The second sentence is premature, but the tale passes on to give a full account. A fair gentlewoman who says she has come on King Pelles' behalf (Pelles is the Grail King) asks for Lancelot and carries him off to a nunnery in a forest. It is a brief episode, but very moving, for there Lancelot unknowingly knights his son—'seemly and demure as a dove, with all manner of good features'. 'On the morn, at the hour of prime, at Galahad's desire, he made him knight and said: God make him a good man, for of beauty faileth you not as any that liveth.' Lancelot's consent goes with Galahad's desire; he does not know what he does, but he does what courtesy and largesse demand; and both he and his son are the more advanced in the Way.

In the tale of Galahad himself at Camelot it might be held that there has been since Malory a certain alteration in values. We are not so much affected by the pulling of swords out of stones floating on rivers (besides, there have been too many of them) as by such other things of possible significance as the coming to every knight at the feast of what food he desired, and of the laying to rest of the High Prince in the King's bed. The first and dominating fact is, of course, the sitting of Galahad in the Siege Perilous. But the meaning of this would require a whole thesis of the meaning of the Siege and of its making by Merlin. The magical foreknowledge of Merlin is certainly not ordinary magic; it is not contrary to grace, though Merlin himself is somehow apart from the whole question of sin and grace. He is rather as if time itself became conscious of the future and prepared for it. The sitting of Galahad in the Siege is the condition precedent to all achievement; and Tennyson's phrase may serve for the moment—that he cried: 'If I lose myself I find myself.' At the supper there is a blast of thunder and a beam of seven-times-clear sunlight; all the lords see their companions fairer than before, and all have the meats and drinks that they love best. I have wondered if this second result would not be more convenient if it were taken to mean that what each had actually before him was precisely to his most satisfaction. It would fit the first better; it is what is there that is fairest. The world is in the Grail, which then appears, but it appears covered and carried invisibly. It must, of course, be so, or there would be no further achievement, and the tale would have to stop. But in every great Myth the technique and the meaning are one; only it does us no harm to realize that the tale, as well as the meaning, has to be kept going. This is the world in the Grail, but it is (also and therefore) at first the world clothing the Grail, so that it cannot be seen in itself. Vows are taken by the lords to seek it out, much to the King's sorrow, for he knows that this will break up the great fellowship. The Queen has a brief interview with Galahad in which she declares him to be Lancelot's son, but 'as to that, he said neither yea or nay'. 'And in the honour of the highness of Galahad he was led into King Arthur's chamber, and there rested in his own bed.'

This is a very great sentence, for it is at once the fulfilment and the frustration of the three lordliest personages, whether they like it or not. There lies in the King's bed that which is the consummation and the destruction of the Table. To Lancelot it is the visible defeat of his treasured fidelity, and the success and defeat of his own life. And to the Queen it is her lover's falsity and her lover's glory. The Queen has some glorious phrases: 'I may well suppose that Sir Lancelot begat him on King Pelles' daughter, by the which he was made to lie by enchantment, and his name is Galahad. I would fain see him, said the queen, for he must needs be a noble man, for so is his father that him begat, I report me unto all the Table Round.'

It is then this living, tragic, and joyous Resolution of all their loves that now enters on its own adventure. They had all talked of love; let them now love this. Its quest begins, and must be passed over here. Towards the conclusion the High Prince reaches Sarras with two companions; they are Percivale and Bors. There seems a significant reason, though Malory does not develop it, why it should be so. Galahad, of course, has no relation with human loves (except Lancelot);

his whole function is the Quest. But Percivale finds a lady who declares herself to be his sister. Obviously in the tale this is meant literally, but in the Myth it has not so much the significance of kinship in blood as of kinship in spirit. It is a human relationship, but it is one known only in the companionship of the quest; it is conjoined love, but love conjoined in the Grail. The lady is of a holy temper; on the journey she dies by giving her blood for another lady who is sick. 'She said to the lady, Madam, I am come to the death for to make you whole; for God's love pray for me.' This again is an act of substitution, but clear and without deceit. Her body is found again when the three lords reach Sarras, though indeed it might well have been taken with them in the ship that carries them across the last ocean, and have made a fourth to the living three.

But the third, Bors? Bors, one might say, is the ordinary fellow. Malory (and here he allows the Grail fellowship rather more than he need have done) does not say he was married. But he does say he had a son by another Elayne, 'and save for her, Sir Bors was a clean maiden'. The Princess of the Grail was called Elayne, and though it is an unimportant point it is admirably right that a wife, for there is no need to deny her the marriage which the tale implies in principle, should have the same name. But if we allow Sir Bors his marriage and his work in the world and his honest affections, see how perfect the companionship of the three lords becomes! There is the High Prince, wholly devoted to his end in the Grail; and there is Percivale with his devout and selfless spiritual sister; and there is Bors with his wife and child. These are functions each of the others. The High Prince is at the deep centre, and the others move towards him; but also he operates in them towards the world. These are three degrees of love. Their conclusion is proper to them. Galahad is assumed into the Grail. Percivale after that assumption remains a hermit by the City of Sarras, where that other sacrificed flesh of his sister is buried. Bors returns to Camelot, joins Lancelot, is made a king, goes on a crusade, and in the last sentence of the book dies, with Sir Ector, Sir Blamore, and Sir Bleoberis, fighting against the Turks, 'upon a Good Friday, for God's sake'.

The conclusion of the Quest itself is found in Sarras, which is beyond and across the sea from the house of the Grail. There is a suggestion that though the Grail in Logres is the consummation of the life of Camelot, yet the Grail beyond seas is only the beginning of the life of Sarras. Galahad is the living suggestion of that other life. When he and Percivale and Bors reach Sarras, they are put into prison by 'the king of the city', who is a 'tyrant', but after a year he dies, and Galahad is made king. This might indeed be thought to have a great meaning in religious experience: after the endurance of tyranny comes the time of sovereignty. Another year of this brings them to their end. Joseph of Arimathie says Mass—only he ? only he in Malory, but there is a phrase which suggests more: 'a man kneeling on his knees in likeness of a bishop, that had about him a great fellowship of angels *as it had been Jesu Christ himself; and then he arose and began a mass of Our Lady*'. The italics are mine; they will suffice to suggest that at that moment something like the Creation and the Redemption exist at once. Galahad is called; after Communion he parts from his companions; and it is then that one of the greatest phrases in Malory is used. Galahad says to Bors: 'Fair lord, salute me to my lord Sir Lancelot my father, and as soon as ye see him bid him remember of this unstable world.'

If the state of these great mysteries, where one like Christ begins a mass of Our Lady, is recognized, that final salutation has its full value. It is then that the High Prince remembers, recognizes, and salutes his father. The times have been changed since the love of Guinevere and the enchanted darkness of the chamber of Elayne, but Galahad derives from all. 'The unstable world'—yes; but it was thence that he himself came. The rejection of importunate love—yes; Guinevere herself is to say so;[1] but it is through the mystical

[1] 'Therefore, Sir Lancelot, I require thee and beseech thee heartily, for all the love that was betwixt us, that thou never see me more in the visage. Well, madam, said he, God defend but I should forsake the world as ye have done.'

substitution which lies even there that the High Prince was begotten. Lancelot was a master of courtesy, and it is so that Galahad is fathered on him. He himself never achieves the Grail, but at the point of a greater achievement than any he could have known, his son's greeting (full and ungrudging) reaches him, through another (still and always through another), 'Fair lord, salute me to my lord Sir Lancelot my father.'

POEMS

FROM *TALIESSIN THROUGH LOGRES*[1]

Prelude

I

RECALCITRANT tribes heard;
orthodox wisdom sprang in Caucasia and Thule;
the glory of the Emperor stretched to the ends of the world.

In the season of midmost Sophia
the word of the Emperor established a kingdom in Britain;
they sang in Sophia the immaculate conception of wisdom.

Carbonek, Camelot, Caucasia,
were gates and containers, intermediations of light;
geography breathing geometry, the double-fledged Logos.

II

The blind rulers of Logres
nourished the land on a fallacy of rational virtue;
the seals of the saints were broken; the chairs of the Table
reeled.

Galahad quickened in the Mercy;
but history began; the Moslem stormed Byzantium;
lost was the glory, lost the power and kingdom.

Call on the hills to hide us
lest, men said in the City, the lord of charity
ride in the starlight, sole flash of the Emperor's glory.

[1] The brief notes which Williams placed at the end of *Taliessin through Logres* are here added to the relevant pages.

III

Evil and good were twins
once in the alleys of Ispahan; the Moslem
crying *Alla il Alla* destroyed the dualism of Persia.

Caucasia fell to the Moslem;
the mamelukes seized the ancient cornland of Empire.
Union is breached; the imams stand in Sophia.

Good is God, the muezzin
calls, but lost is the light on the hills of Caucasia,
glory of the Emperor, glory of substantial being.

Taliessin's Return to Logres

THE seas were left behind;
in a harbour of Logres
lightly I came to land
under a roaring wind.
Strained were the golden sails,
the masts of the galley creaked
as it rode for the Golden Horn
and I for the hills of Wales.

In a train of golden cars
the Emperor went above,
for over me in my riding
shot seven golden stars,
as if while the great oaks stood,
straining, creaking, around,
seven times the golden sickle
flashed in the Druid wood.

Covered on my back,
untouched, my harp had hung;
its notes sprang to sound
as I took the blindfold track,

The images in the third and fourth stanzas are those used of a particular state of being in *Comus*, the *Nightingale Ode*, the *Prelude*, and the *Divine Comedy*.

the road that runs from tales,
through the darkness where Circe's son
sings to the truants of towns
in a forest of nightingales.

The beast ran in the wood
that had lost the man's mind;
on a path harder than death
spectral shapes stood
propped against trees;
they gazed as I rode by;
fast after me poured
the light of flooding seas.

But I was Druid-sprung;
I cast my heart in the way;
all the Mercy I called
to give courage to my tongue.
As I came by Broceliande
a diagram played in the night,
where either the golden sickle
flashed, or a signalling hand.

Away on the southern seas
was the creaking of the mast;
beyond the Roman road
was the creaking of the trees.
Beyond the farms and the fallows
the sickle of a golden arm
that gathered fate in the forest
in a stretched palm caught the hallows.

At the falling of the first
chaos behind me checked;
at the falling of the second
the wood showed the worst;
at the falling of the third
I had come to the king's camp;
the harp on my back
syllabled the signal word.

I saw a Druid light
burn through the Druid hills,
as the hooves of King Arthur's horse
rounded me in the night.
I heard the running of flame
faster than fast through Logres
into the camp by the hazels
I Taliessin came.

The Vision of the Empire

α

THE organic body sang together;
dialects of the world sprang in Byzantium;
back they rang to sing in Byzantium;
the streets repeat the sound of the Throne.

The Acts issue from the Throne.
Under it, translating the Greek minuscula
to minds of the tribes, the identities of creation
phenomenally abating to kinds and kindreds,
the household inscribes the Acts of the Emperor;
the logothetes run down the porphyry stair
bearing the missives through the area of empire.

Taliessin walked through the hither angels,
from the exposition of grace to the place of images.
The morn brightened on the Golden Horn;
he heard behind him the chariots' clatter
that bore a new matter to all the dialects;
he saw the nuntii loosened on the currents
over the sea, in the mechanism of motion,
rowers' arms jointed to the imperial oars.
Chariots and galleys sprang from the shores;
the messengers were borne over sea and land.
The king's poet gazed in the mirror of the Horn.

β

The morn rose on the Golden Horn.
I saw the identities imaged in a sapphire sea:
beyond Sinai Ararat, beyond Ararat Elburz—
light-sprinkling, flaked-snow-sparkling,
chastities of ranged peaks of Caucasus,
snow's glow on the world's brows
changed with deep vales of verdure.
The missives of identity came from the scribes
where the tribes gather and keep holiday
on the name-day and birthday of their father the Emperor.
The Empire's sun shone on each round mound,
double fortalices defending dales of fertility.
The bright blades shone in the craft of the dancing war;
the stripped maids laughed for joy of the province,
bearing in themselves the shape of the province
founded in the base of space,
in the rounded bottom of the Emperor's glory.
Spines were strengthened, loves settled;
tossed through aerial gulfs of empire
the lost name, the fool's shame,
fame and frame of lovers in lowlands of Caucasia,
rang round snowy Elburz.
The organic body sang together.

γ

Elburz rose in the Golden Horn.
South from the sea-bone, Thule, the skull-stone,
herbage of lone rock,
the scheme of Logres, the theme of the design of the Empire,
rose in balance and weight, freight of government with glory.
Merlin, time's metre, climbs through prisms and lines;
over near Camelot and far Carbonek,
over the Perilous Sell, the See of union,
the phosphor of Percivale's philosophical star shines.
Lancelot's lion, bewildered by the smell of adoration,

roars round Guinevere's lordly body.
Merlin defines, in blazons of the brain,
shield upon shield, station upon station;
and the roads resound with the galloping lords.
The swords flash; the pirates fly;
the Table stands rigid in the king's hall,
and over their seats the plotted arms of the soul,
which are their feats and the whole history of Logres.
Down the imperial highroad the white nuntius rides
to heighten the hearts of Lateran, Gaul, and Logres.

δ

The milk rises in the breasts of Gaul,
trigonometrical milk of doctrine.
Man sucks it; his joints harden,
sucking logic, learning, law,
drawing on the breasts of *intelligo* and *credo*.
I, Taliessin, born of the Druids by the sea,
drank also in the schools of Gaul;
I have drunk at the tables of all the doctors;
I have modulated song to the waters of Logres,
the running of Thames, the tidal basins.
I heard the iron chariots on the roads of Gaul,
but the fleets took me, distances of the sea;
the dialect of Logres was an aspect of Byzantium;
the grand art was taught in the heart of the harbours of
Arthur.

ε

The mist rolled down the edge of an old sun;
mammoth and bear prowled on the broad ledge of the
shoulders.
Strength articulated itself in morals
of arms, joints, wrists, hands;
the planes of palms, the mid-points of hid cones,
opened in Lombardy, the cone's point in Rome,

seminal of knowledge, pontifex of the Arval college
of spiralling instincts, all roads (active and passive) from
Rome,
to be bridge-builders in Gaul, clerks of audience in Byzantium.
Finger-nails, weaklings of seedtime, scratched the soil
till by iron nails the toil was finished in the time of our need,
the sublime circle of the cone's bottom, the seed-springing
surrender:
hands of incantation changed to hands of adoration,
the quintuple psalm, the pointing of Lateran:
active and passive in a single mystery,
a single sudden flash of identity,
the heart-breaking manual acts of the Pope.

ζ

Why moves the Pope in the marches of the Empire?
why do the golden palaces pale to the Papal
vesture, flesh and bone of reparation?
what was the crossing of the will of the Emperor?

η

The Adam in the hollow of Jerusalem respired:
softly their thought twined to its end,
crying: *O parent, O forkèd friend,*
am I not too long meanly retired
in the poor space of joy's single dimension?
Does not God vision the principles at war?
Let us grow to the height of God and the Emperor:
Let us gaze, son of man, on the Acts in contention.

The Adam climbed the tree; the boughs
rustled, withered, behind them; they saw
the secluded vision of battle in the law;
they found the terror in the Emperor's house.

The tree about them died undying,
the good lusted against the good,
the Acts in conflict envenomed the blood,
on the twisted tree hung their body wrying.

Joints cramped; a double entity
spewed and struggled, good against good;
they saw the mind of the Emperor as they could,
his imagination of the wars of identity.

He walked slowly through his habitation
in the night of himself without him; Byzantium slept;
a white pulsing shape behind him crept,
the ejection to the creature of the creature's rejection of
salvation.

Conception without control had the Adam of the error;
stifled over their head, the tree's bright beam
lost in the sides of the pit its aerial stream;
they had their will; they saw; they were torn in the terror.

θ

Elburz sinks through the Golden Horn:
the feet of creation walk backward through the waters.

The single galley hardly moves,
the stiffening mechanic of arms and oars fails;
patched with undyed canvas the purple sails
drag at the flagging hands of man;
the sea's unaccumulated distance drags at the sailor's hearts.

The sea-borne Asian mine,
stuff of Caucasia fashioned in Byzantium,
earth's gold sprinkled over the sea
and plated round the poop of the visionary spirit,
shines no longer nor lustily gleams.

On the brazen deck blasts of hot ashes
fall from unseen volcanoes; harsh birds,
stabbing at sea-broods, grating their mating calls,
cover it; down their flight gusts drove once the galley.

Phosphorescent on the stagnant level
a headless figure walks in a crimson cope,
volcanic dust blown under the moon.
A brainless form, as of the Emperor,
walks, indecent hands hidden under the cope,
dishallowing in that crimson the flush on the mounds of
Caucasia.

His guard heaves round him; heaven-sweeping tentacles
stretch, dragging octopus bodies over the level;
his cope by two is lifted from his body,
where it walks on the sinking floor of antipodean Byzantium.
Let us gaze, son of man, on the Acts in contention.

Phosphorescent gleams the point of the penis:
rudiments or relics, disappearing, appearing,
live in the forlorn focus of the intellect,
eyes and ears, the turmoil of the mind of sensation.

Inarticulate always on an inarticulate sea
beyond P'o-l'u the headless Emperor moves,
the octopuses round him; lost are the Roman hands;
lost are the substantial instruments of being.

ι

The organic body sang together;
the Acts of identity adored their Lord;
the song sprang and rang in Byzantium.

O you shoulders, elbows, wrists,
bless him, praise him, magnify him for ever;
you fittings of thumbs and fingers,
bless ye the Lord;
sockets and balls in knees and ankles,
bless ye the Lord;
hips, thighs, spine in its multiples,
bless him, praise him, magnify him for ever;
bless him in Caucasia, bless him in Lateran,

bless him in the blazons of London-in-Logres,
if there be worlds of language beyond Logres,
bless him, praise him, magnify him for ever;
if there be wit in the rolling mass of waters,
if any regimen in marshes beyond P'o-l'u,
if any measurement among the headless places,
bless him, praise him, magnify him for ever.

The Calling of Arthur

ARTHUR was young; Merlin met him on the road.
  Wolfish, the wizard stared, coming from the wild,
  black with hair, bleak with hunger, defiled
from a bed in the dung of cattle, inhuman his eyes.

Bold stood Arthur; the snow beat; Merlin spoke:
  Now am I Camelot; now am I to be builded.
  King Cradlemas sits by Thames; a mask o'ergilded
covers his wrinkled face, all but one eye.

Cold and small he settles his rump in the cushions.
  Through the emerald of Nero one short-sighted eye
  peers at the pedlars of wealth that stand plausibly by.
The bleak mask is gilded with a maiden's motionless smile.

The high aged voice squeals with callous comfort.
  He sits on the bank of Thames, a sea-snail's shell
  fragile, fragilely carved, cast out by the swell
on to the mud; his spirit withers and dies.

He withers; he peers at the tide; he squeals.
  He warms himself by the fire and eats his food
  through a maiden's motionless mouth; in his mood
he polishes his emerald, misty with tears for the poor.

The waste of snow covers the waste of thorn;
  on the waste of hovels snow falls from a dreary sky;
  mallet and scythe are silent; the children die.
King Cradlemas fears that the winter is hard for the poor.

Draw now the tide, spring moon, swing now the depth;
  under the snow that falls over brick and prickle,
  the people ebb; draw up the hammer and sickle.
The banner of Bors is abroad; where is the king?

Bors is up; his wife Elayne behind him
  mends the farms, gets food from Gaul; the south
  is up with hammer and sickle, and holds Thames mouth.
Lancelot hastens, coming with wagons and ships.

The sea-snail lies by Thames; O wave of Pendragon,
  roll it, swallow it; pull the mask o'ergilded
  from the one-eyed face that blinks at the comfort builded
in London's ruins; I am Camelot; Arthur, raise me.

Arthur ran; the people marched; in the snow
  King Cradlemas died in his litter; a screaming few
  fled; Merlin came; Camelot grew.
In Logres the king's friend landed, Lancelot of Gaul.

Mount Badon

THE king's poet was his captain of horse in the wars.
He rode over the ridge; his force
sat hidden behind, as the king's mind had bidden.
The plain below held the Dragon in the centre,
Lancelot on the left, on the right Gawaine,
Bors in the rear commanding the small reserve:
the sea's indiscriminate host roared at the City's wall.
As with his household few Taliessin rode over the ridge,
the trumpets blew, the lines engaged.

Staring, motionless, he sat;
who of the pirates saw? none stopped;
they cropped and lopped Logres; they struck deep,
and their luck held; only support lacked:

Bors was the nephew of Lancelot, and the companion of Galahad and Percivale. He had two children by Elayne, the daughter of King Brangoris, 'and sauf for her syre Bors was a clene mayden'.

neither for charge nor for ruse could the allied crews
abide the civilized single command;
each captain led his own band and each captain unbacked;
but numbers crashed; Taliessin saw Gawaine
fail, recover, and fail again;
he saw the Dragon sway; far away
the household of Lancelot was wholly lost in the fray;
he saw Bors fling
company after company to the aid of the king,
till the last waited the word alone.

Staring, motionless, he sat.
Dimly behind him he heard how his staff stirred.
One said: 'He dreams or makes verse'; one: 'Fool,
all lies in a passion of patience—my lord's rule.'
In a passion of patience he waited the expected second.
Suddenly the noise abated, the fight vanished, the last
few belated shouts died in a new quiet.
In the silence of a distance, clear to the king's poet's sight,
Virgil was standing on a trellised path by the sea.
Taliessin saw him negligently leaning; he felt
the deep breath dragging the depth of all dimension,
as the Roman sought for the word, sought for his thought,
sought for the invention of the City by the phrase.
He saw Virgil's unseeing eyes; his own,
in that passion of all activity but one suspended,
leaned on those screened ports of blind courage.
Barbaric centuries away, the ghostly battle contended.

Civilized centuries away, the Roman moved.
Taliessin saw the flash of his style
dash at the wax; he saw the hexameter spring
and the king's sword swing; he saw, in the long field,
the point where the pirate chaos might suddenly yield,
the place for the law of grace to strike.
He stood in his stirrups; he stretched his hand;
he fetched the pen of his spear from its bearer;
his staff behind signed to their men.

The Æneid's beaked lines swooped on Actium;
the stooped horse charged; backward blown,
the flame of song streaked the spread spears
and the strung faces of words on a strong tongue.
The household of Taliessin swung on the battle;
hierarchs of freedom, golden candles of the solstice
that flared round the golden-girdled Logos, snowy-haired,
brazen-footed, starry-handed, the thigh banded with the
Name.

The trumpets of the City blared through the feet of brass;
the candles flared among the pirates; their mass broke;
Bors flung his company forward; the horse and the reserve
caught the sea's host in a double curve;
the paps of the day were golden-girdled;
hair, bleached white by the mere stress of the glory,
drew the battle through the air up threads of light.
The tor of Badon heard the analytical word;
the grand art mastered the thudding hammer of Thor,
and the heart of our lord Taliessin determined the war.

The lord Taliessin kneeled to the king;
the candles of new Camelot shone through the fought field.

The Crowning of Arthur

THE king stood crowned; around in the gate,
midnight striking, torches and fires
massing the colour, casting the metal,
furnace of jubilee, through time and town,
Logres heraldically flaunted the king's state.

The lords sheathed their swords; they camped
by Camelot's wall; thick-tossed torches,
tall candles flared, opened, deployed;
between them rose the beasts of the banners;
flaring over all the king's dragon ramped.

Wars were at end; the king's friend stood
at the king's side; Lancelot's lion
had roared in the pattern the king's mind cherished,
in charges completing the strategy of Arthur;
the king's brain working in Lancelot's blood.

Presaging intelligence of time climbed,
Merlin climbed, through the dome of Stephen,
over chimneys and churches; from the point of Camelot
he looked through the depth to the dome of Sophia;
the kingdom and the power and the glory chimed.

He turned where the fires, amid burning mail,
poured, tributaried by torches and candles,
to a point in a massive of colour, one
aureole flame; the first shield's deep azure,
sidereally pointed, the lord Percivale.

Driving back that azure a sea rose black;
on a fess of argent rode a red moon.
The Queen Morgause leaned from a casement;
her forehead's moon swallowed the fires,
it was crimson on the bright-banded sable of Lamorack.

The tincture changed; ranged the craft
of the king's new champion in a crimson field;
mockery in mockery, a dolphin naiant;
a silver fish under bloody waters,
conquered or conquering, Dinadan laughed.

A pelican in golden piety struck well
the triple bloody drops from its wound;
in strong nurture of instinct, it smote
for its young its breast; the shield of Bors
bore its rich fervours, to itself most fell.

Lamorack was the brother of Percivale and Blanchefleur. He was the lover of the queen Morgause of Orkney, Arthur's sister. The two were killed by her sons, Gawaine and Agravaine, for the honour of the house of Orkney.

Shouldering shapes through the skies rise and run,
through town and time; Merlin beheld
the beasts of Broceliande, the fish of Nimue,
hierarchic, republican, the glory of Logres,
patterns of the Logos in the depth of the sun.

Taliessin in the crowd beheld the compelled brutes,
wildness formalized, images of mathematics,
star and moon, dolphin and pelican,
lion and leopard, changing their measure.
Over the mob's noise rose gushing the sound of the flutes.

Gawaine's thistle, Bedivere's rose, drew near:
flutes infiltrating the light of candles.
Through the magical sound of the fire-strewn air,
spirit, burning to sweetness of body,
exposed in the midst of its bloom the young queen Guinevere.

Lancelot moved to descend; the king's friend kneeled,
the king's organic motion, the king's mind's blood,
the lion in the blood roaring through the mouth of creation
as the lions roar that stand in the Byzantine glory.
Guinevere's chalice flew red on an argent field.

So, in Lancelot's hand, she came through the glow,
into the king's mind, who stood to look on his city:
the king made for the kingdom, or the kingdom made for the
king?
Thwart drove his current against the current of Merlin:
in beleaguered Sophia they sang of the dolorous blow.

Doom in shocks sprinkled the burning gloom,
molten metals and kindling colours pouring
into the pyre; at the zenith lion and dragon
rose, clawed, twisted, screamed;
Taliessin beheld a god lie in his tomb.

At the door of the gloom sparks die and revive;
the spark of Logres fades, glows, fades.
It is the first watch; the Pope says Matins in Lateran;
the hollow call is beaten on the board in Sophia;
the ledge of souls shudders, whether they die or live.

Bors to Elayne: on the King's Coins

I CAME in; I saw you stand,
in your hand the bread of love, in your head lightness of
law.
The uprightness of the multitude stood in your figure;
my fieldsmen ate and your women served,
while you watched them from the high seat.
When you saw me a southern burst of love
tossed a new smile from your eyes to your mouth,
shaping for that wind's while the corn of your face.
It was said once that your hair was the colour of corn;
he who said so was capable only to adorn
the margin of parchments drawn in schools of Gaul;
their doctrine is your hands' main. I am come again
to live from the founts and fields of your hands;
colour is art, but my heart counts the doctrine.

On the forms of ancient saints, my heroes, your thumbs,
as on a winch the power of man is wound
to the last inch; there ground is prepared
for the eared and seeded harvest of propinquant goodwill,
drained the reeded marches, cleared the branched jungles
where the unthumbed shapes of apes swung and hung.
Now when the thumbs are muscled with the power of goodwill
corn comes to the mill and the flour to the house,
bread of love for your women and my men;
at the turn of the day, and none only to earn;
in the day of the turn, and none only to pay;
for the hall is raised to the power of exchange of all
by the small spread organisms of your hands; O Fair,
there are the altars of Christ the City extended.
I have ridden all night from organization in London,
ration and rule, and the fault in ration and rule,
law and the flaw in law, to reach to you,
the sole figure of the organic salvation of our good.

The king has set up his mint by Thames.
He has struck coins; his dragon's loins
germinate a crowded creaturely brood
to scuttle and scurry between towns and towns,
to furnish dishes and flagons with change of food;
small crowns, small dragons, hurry to the markets
under the king's smile, or flat in houses squat.
The long file of their snouts crosses the empire,
and the other themes acknowledge our king's head.
They carry on their backs little packs of value,
caravans; but I dreamed the head of a dead king
was carried on all, that they teemed on house-roofs
where men stared and studied them as I your thumbs' epigrams,
hearing the City say *Feed my lambs*
to you and the king; the king can tame dragons to carriers,
but I came through the night, and saw the dragonlets' eyes
leer and peer, and the house-roofs under their weight
creak and break; shadows of great forms
halloed them on, and followed over falling towns.
I saw that this was the true end of our making;
mother of children, redeem the new law.

They laid the coins before the council.
Kay, the king's steward, wise in economics, said:
'Good; these cover the years and the miles
and talk one style's dialects to London and Omsk.
Traffic can hold now and treasure be held,
streams are bridged and mountains of ridged space
tunnelled; gold dances deftly across frontiers.
The poor have choice of purchase, the rich of rents,
and events move now in a smoother control
than the swords of lords or the orisons of nuns.
Money is the medium of exchange.'

Taliessin's look darkened; his hand shook
while he touched the dragons; he said 'We had a good
thought.
Sir, if you made verse you would doubt symbols.

I am afraid of the little loosed dragons.
When the means are autonomous, they are deadly; when
words
escape from verse they hurry to rape souls;
when sensation slips from intellect, expect the tyrant;
the brood of carriers levels the good they carry.
We have taught our images to be free; are we glad?
are we glad to have brought convenient heresy to Logres?'

The Archbishop answered the lords;
his words went up through a slope of calm air:
'Might may take symbols and folly make treasure,
and greed bid God, who hides himself for man's pleasure
by occasion, hide himself essentially: this abides—
that the everlasting house the soul discovers
is always another's; we must lose our own ends;
we must always live in the habitation of our lovers,
my friend's shelter for me, mine for him.
This is the way of this world in the day of that other's;
make yourselves friends by means of the riches of iniquity,
for the wealth of the self is the health of the self exchanged.
What saith Heracleitus?—and what is the City's breath?—
dying each other's life, living each other's death.
Money is a medium of exchange.'

I have come now to kiss each magnanimous thumb,
muscles of the brain, functions of the City.
I was afraid the Council had turned you into gold,
as was told of Midas who had ass's ears.
What can be saved without order? and how order?
Compact is becoming contract; man only earns, and pays,
the house outside the City burns but the house within is
enslaved.
What without coinage or with coinage can be saved?
O lady, your hand held the bread
and Christ the City spread in the extensor muscles of your
thumbs.

The quotation from Heracleitus was taken from Mr. Yeats's book, *A Vision.*

Say—can the law live?
can the dead king's head live?
Pray, mother of children, pray for the coins,
pray for Camelot, pray for the king, pray.

Taliessin in the School of the Poets

THROUGH Camelot, which is London-in-Logres,
  by Paul's and Arthur's door,
Taliessin came to the school of the poets;
through an exposition of song,
over a glamour of golden-work,
  his shadow fell on the floor.

Phœbus there in mid-mosaic
  on a mud-born Python trod;
his beams about him enmeshed the world,
London, Rome, and the underseas;
the moving shadow over all
  lapped the edge of the god.

Dusk deepened in the work's width;
  from rituals and prophecies,
from skins of runes and vellums of verse,
the children of song to the brass of a man,
searching the dark of Phœbus' style,
  turned attentive eyes.

Their hearts ached, their thoughts toiled,
  with sorrows and young loves;
within verse they were teased by verse;
Taliessin stood by the chair of the poets;
in the court beyond the lattice
  cooed the king's doves.

Butterfly fancies hovered
  round the edged Phœbean shape.
'Fortune befall,' the king's poet said,

'the weighed gold of butterflies' wings,
the measure of the swaying hazel's shade,
  or of light in the neck's nape.

'Skeined be the creamed-with-crimson sphere
  on a guessed and given line,
skeined and swirled on the head-to-heel,
or the radial arms' point-to-point;
reckoned the rondures of the base
  by the straight absolute spine.

'Swung be the measuring hazel wand
  over thighs and shoulders bare,
and grace-pricked to gules the field
by the intinctured heart's steel;
but best they fathom the blossom
  who fly the porphyry stair.

'At the huge and heavy stair's head
  all measures, to infinite strength,
from sapphire-laced distances drawn,
fill the jewel-joint-justiced throne;
adored be God and the Emperor
  for the gathering of the *n*th.

'From the indulged Byzantine floor
  between right and left newel
floats the magnanimous path of the stair
to a tangle of compensations,
every joint a centre,
  and every centre a jewel.

'Each moment there is the midmost
  of the whole massive load;
impulse a grace and wonder a will,
love desert, and sight direction,
whence the Acts of Identity issue
  in the Pandects and the Code;

'while in the opposite shires of Logres
  the willows of the brook sway
by the tribal tracks and the Roman roads
in the haze of the levels and the lengthening lines,
and the nuts of the uncut hazel fall
  down the cut hazel's way.'

Taliessin's voice sharpened
  on Virgil's exact word;
he uttered Italy seen from a wave;
he defined the organisms of hell.
Blindfold on their perches
  the king's falcons stirred.

The darkened glamour of the golden-work
  took colour from each line;
dimly the gazing postulants saw
patterns of multilinear red
sprinkled and spreading everywhere,
  and spaced to one design.

The king's poet stood by the sovereign chair;
  in a harsh voice he cried
of the stemming and staling of great verse,
of poetry plunged into the void
where Virgil clutched at clumps of song
  when that master of poets died.

Tendebantque manus—there
  in the broad Phœbean ground
they saw the macrocosm drawn;
they heard the universal sigh
in the balance of changing levels
  and complemented sound.

Infinite patterns opened
  in the sovereign chair's mass;
but the crowned form of anatomized man,

bones, nerves, sinews,
the diagram of the style of the Logos,
  rose in the crimson brass.

Breathless explorers of the image,
  innocent, lucent-eyed,
the young poets studied precision;
Taliessin remembered the soul:
Sis salvator, Domine,
  the king's poet sighed.

The Son of Lancelot

THE Lupercalia danced on the Palatine
among women thrusting under the thong; vicars
of Rhea Silvia, vestal, Æneid, Mars-seeded,
mother of Rome; they exulted in the wolf-month.
The Pope's eyes were glazed with terror of the Mass;
his voice shook on Lateran, saying the Confiteor.
Over Europe and beyond Camelot the wolves ranged.

Rods of divination between Lupercal and Lateran:
at the height of the thin night air of Quinquagesima,
in Camelot, in the chamber of union, Merlin dissolved
the window of horny sight on a magical ingress;
with the hazel of ceremony, fetched to his hand—cut,
smoothed, balsamed with spells, blessed with incision—
he struck from the body of air the anatomical
body of light; he illustrated the high grades.
In the first circle he saw Logres and Europe
sprinkled by the red glow of brute famine
in the packed eyes of forest-emerging wolves,
heaped fires in villages, torches in towns,
lit for safety; flat, frozen, trapped
under desecrated parallels, clawed perceptions
denounced to a net of burning plunging eyes,
earth lay, at the knots the protective fires;

and he there, in his own point of Camelot,
of squat snow houses and huddled guards.

Along the print of the straight and sacred hazel
he sent his seeing into the second sphere:
to the images of accumulated distance, tidal figures
shaped at the variable climax of temperatures; the king
dreaming of a red Grail in an ivory Logres
set for wonder, and himself Byzantium's rival
for men's thuribled and throated worship—magic
throws no truck with dreams; the rod thrust by:
Taliessin beneath the candles reading from Bors
letters how the Moslem hunt in the Narrow Seas
altogether harried God and the soul out of flesh,
and plotting against the stresses of sea and air
the building of a fleet, and the burning blazon-royal
flying on a white field in the night—the hazel
drove, slowly humming, through spirals of speculation,
and Merlin saw, on the circle's yonder edge,
Blanchefleur, Percivale's sister, professed at Almesbury
to the nuns of infinite adoration, veiled
passions, sororal intellects, earth's lambs,
wolves of the heavens, heat's pallor's secret
within and beyond cold's pallor, fires
lit at Almesbury, at Verulam, at Canterbury, at Lateran,
and she the porter, she the contact of exchange.

Merlin grew rigid; down the implacable hazel
(a scar on a slave, a verse in Virgil, the reach
of an arm to a sickle, love's means to love)
he sent his hearing into the third sphere—
once by a northern poet beyond Snowdon
seen at the rising of the moon, the *mens sensitiva*,
the feeling intellect, the prime and vital principle,
the pattern in heaven of Nimue, time's mother on earth,
Broceliande. Convection's tides cease
there, temperature is steady to all tenderness

'the feeling intellect' is from the *Prelude*, Book 14.

in the last reach of the hazel; fixed is the full.
He knew distinction in three abstractions of sound,
the women's cry under the thong of Lupercal,
the Pope's voice singing the Glory on Lateran,
the howl of a wolf in the coast of Broceliande.
The notes of Lupercal and Lateran ceased; fast
Merlin followed his hearing down the wolf's howl
back into sight's tritosphere—thence was Carbonek
prodigiously besieged by a feral famine; a single
wolf, grey and gaunt, that had been Lancelot,
imbruted, watching the dark unwardened arch,
crouched on the frozen snow beyond Broceliande.

Pelles the Wounded King lay in Carbonek,
bound by the grating pain of the dolorous blow;
his flesh from dawn-star to noontide day by day
ran as a woman's under the moon; in midsun
he called on the reckless heart of God and the Emperor;
he commended to them and commanded himself and his
land.
Now in the wolf-month nine moons had waned
since Lancelot, ridden on a merciful errand, came
that night to the house; there, drugged and blurred
by the medicated drink of Brisen, Merlin's sister,
he lay with the princess Helayne, supposed Guinevere.
In the morning he saw; he sprang from the tall window;
he ran into a delirium of lycanthropy; he grew
backward all summer, laired in the heavy wood.
In autumn King Pelles' servants brought him news
of a shape glimpsed on the edge of Broceliande,
a fear in the forest, a foe by the women's well.

Patient, the king constrained patience, and bade
wait till the destined mother's pregnancy was done.
All the winter the wolf haunted the environs of Carbonek;
now what was left of the man's contrarious mind
was twinned and twined with the beast's bent to feed;
now it crept to swallow the seed

of love's ambiguity, love's taunt and truth.
Man, he hated; beast, he hungered; both
stretched his sabres and strained his throat; rumble
of memories of love in the gaunt belly told
his instinct only that something edible might come.
Slavering he crouched by the dark arch of Carbonek,
head-high howling, lusting for food, living
for flesh, a child's flesh, his son's flesh.

And infinite beyond him the whole Empire contracted
from (within it) wolves, and (without it) Moslems.
The themes fell back round separate defensive fires;
there only warmth dilated; there they circled.
Caucasia was lost, Gaul was ravaged, Jerusalem
threatened; the crescent cut the Narrow Seas,
while from Cordovan pulpits the iconoclastic
heretical licentiates of Manes denounced union,
and only Lupercal and Lateran preserved Byzantium.

Helayne, Lancelot's bed-fellow, felt her labour.
Brisen knelt; Merlin watched her hands;
the children of Nimue timed and spaced the birth.
Contraction and dilation seized the substance of joy,
the body of the princess, but in her stayed from terror,
from surplus of pain, from outrage, from the wolf in flesh,
such as racked in a cave the Mother of Lupercal
and now everywhere the dilating and contracting Empire.
The child slid into space, into Brisen's hands.
Polished brown as hazel-nuts his eyes
opened on his foster-mother; he smiled at space.
Merlin from the hazel's divination saw
the child lie in his sister's hands; he saw
over the Empire the lucid flash of all flesh,
shining white on the sullen white of the snow.
He ran down the hazel; he closed the window; he came
past the royal doors of dream, where Arthur, pleased
with the Grail cooped for gustation and God for his glory,
the æsthetic climax of Logres, softly slept;

but the queen's tormented unæsthetic womanhood
alternately wept and woke, her sobs crushed
deep as the winter howls were high, her limbs
swathed by tentacles, her breasts sea-weighed.
Across the flat sea she saw Lancelot
walking, a grotesque back, the opposite of a face
looking backward like a face; she burst the swollen sea
shrieking his name; nor he turned nor looked,
but small on the level dwindled to a distant manikin,
the tinier the more terrible, the sole change
in her everlastingness, except, as Merlin passed,
once as time passed, the hoary waters
laughed backward in her mouth and drowned her tongue.

Through London-in-Logres Merlin came to the wall,
the soldiers saw him; their spears clapped.
For a blade's flash he smiled and blessed their guard,
and went through the gate, beyond the stars' spikes—
as beyond palisades to everywhere the plunging fires,
as from the *mens sensitiva*, the immortal tenderness,
magically exhibited in the ceremonial arts,
to the raging eyes, the rearing bodies, the red
carnivorous violation of intellectual love,
and the frozen earth whereon they ran and starved.
Far as Lancelot's dwindling back from the dumb
queen in a nightmare of the flat fleering ocean,
the soldiers saw him stand, and heard as if near—
far to sight, near to sound—the small
whistling breath in the thin air of Quinquagesima
of the incantation, the manner of the second working.
Then the tall form on the frozen snow
dilated to monstrosity, swelling as if power
entered it visibly, from all points of the wide
sky of the wolf-month: the shape lurched and fell,
dropping on all fours, lurched and leapt and ran,
a loping terror, hurtling over the snow,
a giant white wolf, diminishing with distance,
till only to their aching eyes a white atom

spiralled wildly on the white earth, and at last
was lost; there the dark horizontal edge
of a forest closed their bleak world.

Between the copses on the coast of Broceliande
galloped the great beast, the fierce figure
of universal consumption, Lupercal and Lateran,
taunt of truth, love's means to love
in the wolf-hour, as to each man in each man's hour
the gratuitous grace of greed, grief, or gain,
the measure pressed and overrunning; now the cries
were silent on Lupercal, the Pope secret on Lateran.
Brisen in Helayne's chamber heard the howl
of Lancelot, and beyond it the longer howl of the air
that gave itself up in Merlin; she felt him come.
She rose, holding the child; the wolf and the other,
the wind of the magical wintry beast, broke
together on her ears; the child's mouth opened;
his wail was a song and a sound in the third heaven.
Down the stair of Carbonek she came to the arch
and paused beneath; the wolf's hair rose on his hackles.
He dragged his body nearer; he was hungry for his son.

The Emperor in Byzantium nodded to the exarchs;
it was night still when the army began to move,
embarking, disembarking, before dawn Asia
awoke to hear the songs, the shouts, the wheels
of the furnished lorries rolling on the roads to the east,
and the foremost outposts of mountaineers scanning
the mouths of the caves in snowy Elburz, where hid
the hungry Christian refugees, their land
wholly abandoned to beast and Manichæan:
the city on the march to renew the allegiance of Caucasia.

A white wolf drove down the wood's path,
flying on the tender knowledge of the third heaven
out into moonlight and Brisen's grey eyes.
She called: 'Be blessed, brother'; the child sang:

'blessed brother,' and nestled to its first sleep.
Merlin broke from the wood and crouched to the leap;
the father of Galahad smelt his coming; he turned,
swerving from his hunger to the new danger, and sprang.
The driving shoulder of Merlin struck him in mid-air
and full the force of the worlds flung; helpless
he was twisted and tossed in vacancy; nine yards off
the falling head of Lancelot struck the ground.
Senseless he lay; lined in the lupine shape,
dimly, half-man, half-beast, was Lancelot's form.
Brisen ran; with wrappings of crimson wool
she bound the child to her crouching brother's back;
kissed them both, and dismissed; small and asleep,
and warm on a wolf's back, the High Prince rode into Logres.

Blanchefleur sat at Almesbury gate; the sleeping
sisters preserved a dreamless adoration.
Blanchefleur prayed for Percivale and Taliessin,
lords in her heart, brothers in the grand art,
exchanging tokens; for the king and queen; for Lancelot
nine months lost to Logres; for the house-slaves
along whose sinewy sides the wolf-cubs leapt,
played in their hands, laired in their eyes, romped
in the wrestle of arms and thighs, cubs of convection,
haggard but held in the leash, foster-children
of the City, foster-fellows of the Merciful Child.
Suddenly, as far off as Blanchefleur deep
in exchange with the world, love's means to love,
she saw on the clear horizon an atom, moving,
waxing, white in white, speed in snow,
a silver shape in the moonlight changing to crimson,
a line of launched glory.

The child of Nimue
came, carrying the child of grace in flesh,
truth and taunt inward and outward; fast
Merlin ran through Logres in the wolf-month
before spring and the leaf-buds in the hazel-twigs.

Percivale's sister rose to her feet; her key
turned, and Almesbury gate opened; she called:
'Sister,' but the white wolf lay before her; alone
she loosened the crimson wrappings from the sleeping
Galahad;
high to her breast she held the child; the wolf
fled, moving white upon motionless white,
the marks of his paws dark on the loosening snow,
and straight as the cross-stamped hazel in the king's house.
The bright intellects of passion gathered at the gate
to see the veiled blood in the child's tender cheeks;
glowing as the speed in the face of the young Magian
when at dawn, laughing, he came to London-in-Logres;
or the fire built in Carbonek's guest-chamber
where Lancelot lay tended, housed and a man,
to be by Easter healed and horsed for Logres;
where at Easter the king's whole household
in the slanting Latin of the launched legions sang

Gaudium multum annunciamus;
nunc in saecula servi amamus;
civitas dulcis aedificatur;
quia qui amat Amor amatur.

Palomides Before his Christening

WHEN I came out of the cave the sky had turned.
I have climbed since down a dead mountain,
over fossils of space in the petrifaction of time,
by the track at the slant-eyes' edge to the city of astrologers.

Astrologers and astronomers alike would starve here;
the rocks are too hard to give any roots room.
No earth-shock alters the infinite smooth formation,
nor anywhere in the monstrous markings are lifting latches.

I determined, after I saw Iseult's arm,
to be someone, to trap the questing beast
that slid into Logres out of Broceliande
through the blank between the queen's meaning and the queen.

Having that honour I would consent to be christened,
I would come then to the Table on my own terms,
bringing a capture by which Christendom might profit,
which Pelles the wounded master could not recover.

But things went wrong; Tristram knocked me sprawling
under the tender smile of Iseult; my manhood,
chivalry, and scimitar-play learned from the Prophet,
could not gain me the accurate flash of her eyes.

Once I overthrew Lancelot by cheating at a tourney,
whence, enraged, fleeing, I was taken by pirates;
Lancelot freed me—he rode on to Carbonek;
Did I smile when I heard that he my saviour was mad?

For bees buzzed down Iseult's arm in my brain;
black gnats, whirring mosquitoes; the cream
everywhere dissolved into a spinning cloud;
and I thought if I caught the beast they would cease certainly.

They would vanish; the crowd's mass of open mouths,
the City opening its mouth, would certainly swallow them.
There would be nothing but to admire the man
who had done what neither Tristram nor Lancelot did.

In the blank between the queen's meaning and the queen
first I followed my self away from the city
up a steep trail. Dinadan rode past me,
calling: 'Friend, the missing is often the catching.'

But I climbed; I bruised my ankles on gaunt shapes,
knees, wrists, thighs; I climbed up a back;
my feet jarred on the repetition of shoulders;
crevasses showed their polished slippery sides.

At other times I clambered over house-roofs,
without doors; on their blank sides
the king's knights were flat cracks, chinks,
rubbed patches, their heads grey blobs.

At last, above them all, I came to a cave,
and a heap of twigs some traveller had left;
I rubbed a fire and sat within; the beast
lay at the cave's mouth; I was glad of its company.

The fire burned awhile; now I know
time was petrifying without. I sat and scratched.
Smoke in a greasy thickness rolled round the cave,
from flames of fierce fancy, flesh-fire-coloured.

Fire of the flesh subsided to ache of the bone;
the smoke rolled out, faded, died;
the beast, as the smoke thinned, had disappeared;
starveling, I lay in bone on the cave's floor.

Bone lay loving bone it imagined near it,
bone of its hardness of longing, bone of its bone,
skeleton dreaming of skeleton where there was none.
From the cave the greasy smoke drifted slowly outward.

Skeleton dreamed of skeleton it loved to neighbour,
thigh yearning for thigh, humerus for humerus;
by infinitesimal jerks on the cave's floor
it thrust sideways to the shining cates it imagined.

Bones grew brittle; sinews yielded; spirit
hated the air, the moving current that entered,
movements in the cubical plot of the cave, when smoke
emptied, and bones broke; it was dull day.

Spirit spread in the cave, hating the air.
Bat-like, it hung to the roughness of rock; it lay
sucking the hollow cavities, less than a bat,
in bones where once it had found a nourishing marrow.

At last the bats frightened me; I left
my pretties; airy currents blew my light
flimsy ash to the cave's mouth. There
was the track; it went over the mountain to Caerleon.

The sky had turned round; I could not think
why I should not be christened in the city of astrologers.
It was true I should look a fool before everyone;
why not look a fool before everyone?

The Chi-Ro is only a scratching like other scratchings;
but in the turn of the sky the only scratching—
in a world of rock and one thing other than rock,
the small, slender, pointed, crimson beast;

the scratching, biting, sliding, slithering thing,
whisking about in unreachable crevasses and cracks,
in cliffs and boulders; the smooth-backed head-cocked
snout, and fat rump, and claws on the rock;

the blatant agile beast. The lord Dinadan
laughed for joy when once I triumphed in the tourney;
he called to the lords: 'This is his day'; to me:
'Catch as catch can; but absence is a catch of the presence.

'Sir, if ever in a blank between this and that,
the sky turns on you, and the path slides
to the edge not the front of the eyes, come and be christened.
I will stand your godfather at the pool in Caerleon.'

Dull, undimensioned, I ride at last to Dinadan;
he is the only lord without a lady;
he fights and is not enclosed in fight; he laughs
but he has not the honour and the irony of the court of culture.

The Coming of Galahad

IN the hall all had what food they chose;
they rose then, the king, Lancelot, the queen;
they led the young man Galahad to Arthur's bed.
The bishops and peers, going with the royalties, made
ceremony; they created a Rite. When he was laid,
and the order done, the lords went to their rooms.
The queen all night lay thinking of Lancelot's son.

At their rising the king's poet alone had gone
another way; he took the canals of the palace,
the lower corridors, between maids and squires,
past the offices and fires of the king's kitchens,
till he came by a door cleft in a smooth wall
into the outer yards, the skied hall of the guards,
grooms, and scullions. He looked above; he saw
through the unshuttered openings of stairs and rooms
the red flares of processional torches and candles
winding to the king's bed; where instead
of Arthur Galahad that night should lie,
Helayne's son instead of the king's, Lancelot's
instead of Guinevere's, all taken at their word,
their professions, their oaths; the third heaven heard
their declarations of love, and measured them the medium of
exchange.

He stood looking up among the jakes and latrines;
he touched his harp, low-chanting a nursery rhyme:
'Down the porphyry stair the queen's child ran;
there he played with his father's crown . . .'
A youth came up in the dark, the king's scavenger,
large-boned, fresh-coloured, flame-haired,

Galahad came to Caerleon after Palomides had been christened on the Feast of Pentecost. 'In the honour of the hyghness of Galahad he was ledde in to kinge Arthurs chamber and there rested in his own bedde' (*Morte D'Arthur*, Book XIII). The image of the stone and shell is from the *Prelude*, Book 5.

Gareth, a prince and a menial, the son of Morgause,
sent from Orkney and the skull-stone in the sea,
to be for cause of obedience set to the worst work.
None at Caerleon knew him but his brother Gawaine
and the king's poet who saw the profile of his mother,
in a grace of fate and a face too soon to be dead.
Hearing him now, Taliessin half-turned his head,
saying: 'Sir ?' Gareth said, looking at the light:
'Lord, tell me of the new knight.'

Taliessin answered, sounding the strings still:
'Is it not known he is strange, being nurtured till,
men say, but yesterday, among the White Nuns,
by the sister of Percivale, the'—his harp sang—'princess
Blanchefleur ?'

Gareth said: 'Lord, bless me with more.
Among the slaves I saw from the hall's door
over the meal a mystery sitting in the air—
a cup with a covered fitting under a saffron veil,
as of the Grail itself: what man
is this for whom the Emperor lifts the Great Ban ?'
'My lords and fathers the Druids between the hazels
Taliessin stayed the music; he said:

touched poems in chords; they made tell
of everywhere a double dance of a stone and a shell,
and the glittering sterile smile of the sea that pursues.'

Gareth answered: 'I heard it read from a book
by a Northern poet, and once I seemed to look
on Logres pouring like ocean after a girl
who ran in the van, and her hands before her stretched
shone—bright shell, transparent stone,
and the sea touched her, and suddenly by a wind was blown
back, and she mounted a wind and rode away,
and measurement went with her and all sound,
and I found myself weeping there like a fool.'

'To-day
the stone was fitted to the shell,' the king's poet said;
'when my lord Sir Lancelot's son sat in the perilous sell,
if he be Sir Lancelot's; in Logres the thing is done,
the thing I saw wherever I have gone—
in five houses, and each house double: the boughs
of the Druid oak, the cover of gay strokes in the play
of Caucasia, the parchments of Gaul, the altar-stone
in Lateran or Canterbury, the tall Byzantine hall—
O the double newels at the ground of the porphyry stair!
O there the double categories of shell and stone,
and the Acts of Identity uttered out of the Throne.'

'And I among dung and urine—am I one
with shell or stone,' Gareth asked, 'in the jakes?'
But Taliessin: 'And what makes the City? to-morrow
you shall be a prince of Orkney again; to-night
abandon the degrees of Gawaine your brother; consent
to be nothing but the shape in the gate of excrement,
while Galahad in peace and the king's protection sleeps:
question and digestion, rejection and election,
winged shapes of the Grail's officers, double
grand equality of the State, common of all lives,
common of all experience, sense and more;
adore and repent, reject and elect. Sir,
without this alley-way how can man prefer?
and without preference can the Grail's grace be stored?'

A girl said suddenly beside them: 'Lord,
tell me the food you preferred——'; and he: 'More
choice is within the working than goes before.
The good that was there—and did I well then? yes?'
She said: 'Yes; yet has all food one taste?
felicity does not alter?' He answered in haste:
'Felicity alters from its centre; but I—free
to taste each alteration, and that within reach
then and there; why change till the range twirls?' The girl's
eyes turned to the black palace and back.

She said: 'This morning when the Saracen prince was christened
dimly the lord Percivale's pentagram glistened
in the rain-dark stones of his eyes: what food there?'

Taliessin answered: 'Five cells the world
gave me, five shells of multiple sound;
but when I searched for the paths that joined the signs,
lines of the pentagram's frame, the houses fled
instead to undimensioned points; their content slid
through the gate of the winged prince of the jakes; pale
they fluttered in an empty fate; the Child lay dead
in his own gate of growth—and what then,
lady, for you or me or the Saracen,
when the cut hazel has nothing to measure?' 'I have known,'
she said, with the scintillation of a grave smile,
'the hazel's stripes on my shoulders; the blessed luck
of Logres has a sharp style, since I was caught free
from the pirate chaos savaging land and sea;
is the shell thus also hidden in the stone?'
'Also thus,' he said, 'if the heart fare
on what lies ever now on the board, stored
meats of love, laughter, intelligence, and prayer.
Is it thus?' and she: 'Who knows?—and who does not care?—
yet my heart's cheer may hope, if Messias please.
Is this the colour of my lord Galahad's eyes?'

He said: 'The eyes of my lord are the measure of intensity
and his arms of action; the hazel, Blanchefleur, he.
The clerks of the Emperor's house study the redaction
of categories into identity: so we.
Give me your hand.' Lightly she obeyed, and he
as lightly kissed: 'O office of all lights
from the king's scavenger to the king's substitute, mean
of the merciful Child, common of all rites,
winged wonder of shell and stone, here
a shoot of your own third heaven takes root in Logres.'

Gareth said: 'Lord, before the meal,
when he washed his hands, the water became phosphorescent;
did you not see?' and he: 'Sanctity
common and crescent! I have seen it flushed anew
in each motion and mode of the princess Blanchefleur;
who walked dropping light, as all our beloved do.
It is the shell of adoration and the grand art.
But I looked rather to-night at the queen's hand
lying on her heart, and the way her eyes scanned
the unknown lord who sat in the perilous sell.
The bone of the fingers showed through the flesh; they were
claws
wherewith the queen's grace gripped: this was the stone
fitting itself to its echo.'
He turned to the gate
into the outer air; she let cry:
'Lord, make us die as you would have us die.'

But he: 'Proofs were; roofs were: I
what more? creeds were; songs were. Four
zones divide the empire from the Throne's firmament,
slanted to each cleft in each wall, with planets planted:
Mercury, thinning and thickening, thirsting to theft;
Venus preference—though of the greatest, preference;
O Earth between, O seen and strewn by the four!
Jupiter with a moon of irony and of defeated irony,
and Saturn circled, girdled by turned space.
The moon of irony shone on Lancelot at Carbonek,
the moon of defeated irony on Blanchefleur at Almesbury;
her hands and head were the shell bursting from the stone
after it has bred in the stone; she was bright with the moon's
light
when truth sped from the taunt; well she nurtured Galahad.
Logres is come into Jupiter; all the zones
circle Saturn, spinning against the glory,
all the Throne's points, themes of the Empire.'

Emeralds of fire, blank to both, his eyes
were points of the Throne's foot that sank through Logres.

The Departure of Merlin

THE Pope stands at Lateran's stone; man's
heart throbs from his vicarious hands.
The themes are pointed with a new device of brightness,
Trebizond with sun, Archangel with ice.

The blessing of Byzantium befriends the world's ends;
the great heretical doctors, Moslem and Manichæan,
fly; in time-spanned Camelot the Table changes;
the method of phenomena is indrawn to Broceliande.

Merlin bore Lancelot's child to a moon of white nuns,
a knot of nurture in a convent of spirits and suns;
thence in the perilous throne is the Child's moon risen,
pillars of palace and prison changed to the web of a wood.

The joyous moon waxes in the chair;
the blessed young sorcerer, a boy and less than a boy,
rose and ran, turning on the roads; he span
into the heart's simultaneity of repose.

Joseph of Nazareth, Joseph of Arimathea,
came dancing through the coeval-rooted world's idea.
They saw Merlin descending: they met him in the wood,
foster-fathers of beatitude to the foster-father of Galahad;

twin suns of womb and tomb; there no strife
is except growth from the roots, nor reaction but repose;
vigours of joy drive up; rich-ringed moments
thick in their trunks thrive, young-leaved their voices.

Moons and suns that rose in rites and runes
are come away from sequence, from rules of magic;
here all is cause and all effect; the laws
of Merlin's boyhood are unknown in Nimue's wood.

The variation of the Merlin tale is due to Swinburne (but this Merlin is young): *Tristram of Lyonesse*, Books 1 and 6.

I saw from the deck of a galley becalmed in the seas
Merlin among the trees; the headless form faded;
throngs of trunks covered the volcanic waters;
only the flat djongs float into alien P'o-l'u.

The sailors stared at the thick wood; one,
ghastly and gaping, despaired of joy; he yelled
for horror and leapt from the deck to the phosphorescence,
to the wreck of wisdom, the drowned last of love.

The purple sail moved in the wind of Broceliande;
the sailors sprang to the oars; the sea-call sang
bidding tack—near and far infinite and equal—
on the visionary ocean track to the port of Byzantium.

More than the fable of Dryads is troth to the Table
in the growth of hazel and elm, oak and bamboo;
voice of all moments covers who hears as he goes
rich-ringed, young-leaved, monstrous trunks rejoice.

Time's president and precedent, grace ungrieved,
floating through gold-leaved lime or banked behind beech
to opaque green, through each membraned and tissued
experience
smites in simultaneity to times variously veined.

She who is Nimue, lady of lakes and seas,
articulation of limbs, accumulation of distance,
brings all natural becoming to her shape of immortal being,
as to a flash of seeing the women in the world's base.

Well has Merlin spoken the last spell,
worked the last image, gone to his own:
the moon waxes and wanes in the perilous chair,
where time's foster-child sits, Lancelot's son.

The Death of Palomides

AIR strives with wings, wings with air.
In the space of the glory the stresses of power contend;
through the kingdom my heart's revolutions ascribe to the
    power
quicken the backward wings of passages and paths.

Once, when the Prophet's shout had taken Cordova,
north I rode through a moon of Spanish winter,
and lay for a night in a lodging of ancient Israel,
twins of Levi, under the height of Monsalvat.

Sea-grey was one and sea-wrinkled,
one burned sun-black, with clawed hands;
guttural, across the charcoal fire, their chant
dropped into pauses, poured into channelled names.

The first mathematics of Ispahan trembled
before the intoned formulæ; their smiles cast
totals from a myriad intricate calculations,
while the screams of eagles in conflict shook the Sierras.

I sat and heard, aloof in my young seed-mail,
scornful of my secret attention; the hut shook,
the air span, with titles of cherubim and seraphim;
the voices rose into clearness; they pronounced *Netzach.*

Sharply I shouted into the sound: *Netzach?*
What is Netzach? Together and deeply they answered:
Netzach is the name of the Victory in the Blessing:
For the Lord created all things by means of his Blessing.

One now, sea-grey and wave-wrinkled,
calls through all my body to the sun-blackened:
The Lord created all things by means of his Blessing,
and they float upwards; the paths open between.

Netzach is a station on the Sephirotic Tree; its quality is Victory.

Once the paths were interminable; paths were stations.
Unangelical speed loitered upon them,
supposing the everlasting habitations had received it;
only the dolphin Dinadan swam and smiled.

Then Iseult was living; then was the tournament;
then I longed, feared, fought, was angry.
Now if still I fight, fear, am angry,
I know those terminable paths are only paths.

Loneliest of lords, Dinadan smiled; I feared.
Now no sound is near but aerial screams,
no soft voices, nothing except the harsh
scream of the eagle approaching the plateau of Netzach:

its scream and its passage approaching its primal station
backwards; about me a scintillation of points,
points of the eagle's plumes, plumes that are paths;
paths and plumes swoop to the unbelieved symbol.

I left the Prophet; I lost Iseult; I failed
to catch the beast out of Broceliande;
Lancelot forgave me; if I was christened in that pardon
it was half because I was a greater fool so.

I have gone back, down the road of Logres, the arm
of Iseult, the pass of Monsalvat, into the hut;
I sit with the old men, as they were; we sing:
The Lord created all things by means of his Blessing.

I utter the formula; the formula is all that lives:
sharply the Prophet, Iseult, Lancelot, Dinadan,
call to me this at my dying, and I to them:
The Lord created all things by means of his Blessing.

If this is the kingdom, the power, the glory, my heart
formally offers the kingdom, endures the power,
joins to itself the aerial scream of the eagle . . .
That Thou only canst be Thou only art.

Percivale at Carbonek

IN the rent saffron sun hovered the Grail.
Galahad stood in the arch of Carbonek;
the people of Pelles ran to meet him.
    His eyes were sad; he sighed for Lancelot's pardon.

Joy remembered joylessness; joy kneeled
under the arch where Lancelot ran in frenzy.
The astonished angels of the spirit heard him moan:
    Pardon, lord; pardon and bless me, father.

Doubtfully stood the celestial myrmidons, scions
of unremitted beauty; bright feet paused.
Aching with the fibrous infelicity of time,
    pierced his implacability, Galahad kneeled.

The passage through Carbonek was short to the house of the
        Grail;
the wounded king waited for health; motionless
the subdued glory implored the kingdom
    to pardon its power and the double misery of Logres.

Under the arch the Merciful Child
wept for the grief of his father in reconciliation;
who was betrayed there by Merlin and Brisen
    to truth; he saw not; he was false to Guinevere.

Between the Infant and Bors and myself on each hand
under the arch I heard the padding of paws,
woven between us, and the faint howl of the wolf.
    The High Prince shivered in the cold of bleak conjunction.

His hand shook; pale were his cheeks;
his head the head of a skull, flesh
cleaving to bone; his dry voice rattled;
    'Pardon, Lord Lancelot; pardon and blessing, father.'

He knelt silent among the circles of the wolf.
Until the lover of Guinevere acknowledged his son
a bitter frost crept in the bones of Galahad.
  The Host in the Lateran lay in a hid sepulchre.

Stiffly the Child's head turned; the drawn engine
slewed to his left, to Bors the kin of Lancelot.
He said 'Cousin, can you bear pardon
  to the house of Carbonek from the fallen house of Camelot?'

Bors answered: 'What should we forgive?'
'Forgive Us,' the High Prince said, 'for Our existence;
forgive the means of grace and the hope of glory.
  In the name of Our father forgive Our mother for Our birth.'

'Sir,' Bors said, 'only God forgives.
My lord Sir Lancelot my cousin is a lover and kind.
I assent to all, as I pray that my children assent
  and through God join with me in bidding their birth.'

The Infant said: 'Go, cousin.' Bors
stepped from the arch; the angelic household met him.
The High Prince stepped in his footprints; into the sun
  Galahad followed Bors; Carbonek was entered.

The Last Voyage

THE hollow of Jerusalem was a ship.

In the hall of Empire, on the right wall from the stair,
Solomon was painted, a small city and temple
rose beyond, reaching the level of his knee;
all on a deck floated in a sea of dolphins.
His right hand, blessing, whelmed the djinn
who sank impotently around and drowned in the waters.
Rigid his left arm stretched to the queen Balkis;

where her mouth on his hand tasted effectual magic,
intellectual art arm-fasted to the sensuous.
Solomon was the grand master of all creaturely being
in sublime necromancy, the rule and road of seeing
for those who have no necessity of existence in themselves;
On the opposite wall, in a laureate ceremony,
Virgil to Taliessin stretched a shoot
of hazel—the hexameter, the decasyllabic line—
fetched from Homer beyond him; by the king's poet
were the poets of Logres, Britain, and the ninefold isles:
the isles floated beyond them in a sea of dolphins.
But the actual ship, the hollow of Jerusalem,
beyond the shapes of empire, the capes of Carbonek,
over the topless waves of trenched Broceliande,
drenched by the everlasting spray of existence,
with no mind's sail reefed or set, no slaves at the motived oars,
drove into and clove the wind from unseen shores.
Swept from all altars, swallowed in a path of power
by the wrath that wrecks the pirates in the Narrow Seas,
now in the confidence of the charge, the thrust of the trust,
seizing the sea-curve, the shortest way between points,
to the point of accumulated distance, the safe tension
in each allotted joint of the knotted web of empire,
multiple without dimension, indivisible without uniformity,
the ship of Solomon (blessed be he) drove on.

Fierce in the prow the alchemical Infant burned,
red by celerity now conceiving the white;
behind him the folded silver column of Percivale,
hands on the royal shoulders, closed wings of flight,
inhaled the fine air of philosophical amazement;
Bors, mailed in black, completing the trine,
their action in Logres, kneeling on the deck to their right,
the flesh of fatherhood, unique as they in the Will,
prayed still for the need and the bliss of his household.
By three ways of exchange the City sped to the City;
against the off-shore wind that blew from Sarras
the ship and the song flew.

An infinite flight of doves from the storming sky
of Logres—strangely sea-travellers when the land melts—
forming to overfeather and overwhelm the helm,
numerous as men in the empire, the empire riding
the skies of the ocean, guiding by modulated stresses
on each spoke of the helm the vessel from the realm of Arthur,
lifted oak and elm to a new-ghosted power.
The hosted wings trapped the Infant's song;
blown back, tossed down, thrown
along the keel, the song hastening the keel
along the curve of the sea-way, the helm fastening
the whole ship to the right balance of the stresses;
as the fine fair arm of pine-changed Cymodocea,
striking from the grey-green waters of tossed Tiber,
thrust the worshipful duke to the rescue of Rome;
as the arm of the queen, finger-latched to Solomon's,
matched power to purpose and passion to peace.
The wonder that snapped once in the hollow of Jerusalem
was retrieved now along the level of the bulwark
to where the hands of Galahad were reeved on the prow:
the hollow of Jerusalem was within the hollow of his
shoulders,
the ban and blessing of the empire ran in his arms,
from his feet the deck spread that was fleet on the sea.
The ship of Solomon (blessed be he) drove on.

Before the helm the ascending-descending sun
lay in quadrilateral covers of a saffron pall
over the bier and the pale body of Blanchefleur,
mother of the nature of lovers, creature of exchange;
drained there of blood by the thighed wound,
she died another's death, another lived her life.
Where it was still to-night, in the last candles of Logres,
a lady danced, to please the sight of her friends;
her cheeks were stained from the arteries of Percivale's sister.

Blanchefleur died from a letting of blood to heal a sick lady; her body was taken by the three lords of the quest, and buried 'in the spyrytual place'.

Between them they trod the measure of heaven and earth,
and the dead woman waited the turn and throe of the dance
where, rafting and undershafting the quadruplicate sacrum,
below the saffron pall, the joyous woe of Blanchefleur,
the ship of Solomon (blessed be he) drove on.

Dinadan was lord of something more than irony,
he died in the deep schismatic war, when Gawaine
hewed the Table in twain, by a feud with his fellows
making peace with his doctrine: he pursued Lancelot
for the Throne's honour, by a side-path with his own.
His brother Agravaine caught the king's dolphin
on the sea-shore, in a track of the bewildered wood,
when by an ambush Lamorack was shot in the back
by the sons of the queen Morgause who slew their mother,
to clean their honour's claws in the earth of her body.
They drew Dinadan to broil on a bed of coals;
their souls were glad to destroy the pertinence of curiosity;
the merciful heaven drove the thick smoke to choke him.
But the Infant's song was thick with a litany of names
from the king and the king's friend to the least of the slaves.
He was borne through the waves to his end on a cry of substitution.
When he uttered Agravaine's name a light low
covered with flame the spread saffron veil;
the heart of the dead Dinadan burned on the sun,
and gathered and fled through the air to the head of Percivale,
flew and flamed and flushed the argentine column.
The ship of Solomon (blessed be he) drove on.

Through the sea of omnipotent fact rushed the act of Galahad.
He glowed white; he leaned against the wind
down the curved road among the topless waters.
He sang *Judica te, Deus*; the wind,
driven by doves' wings along the arm-taut keel,
sang against itself *Judica te, Deus.*
Prayer and irony had said their say and ceased;

the sole speech was speed.
In the hollow of Jerusalem the quadrilateral of the sun
was done on the deck beyond Broceliande.
In the monstrum of triangular speed,
in a path of lineal necessity,
the necessity of being was communicated to the son of
Lancelot.
The ship and the song drove on.

In Logres the King's friend landed, Lancelot of Gaul.
Taliessin at Canterbury met him with the news
of Arthur's death and the overthrow of Mordred.
At the hour of the healing of Pelles
the two kings were one, by exchange of death and healing.
Logres was withdrawn to Carbonek; it became Britain.

Taliessin at Lancelot's Mass

I CAME to his altar when dew was bright on the grass;
he—he was not sworn of the priesthood—began the Mass.
The altar was an ancient stone laid upon stones;
Carbonek's arch, Camelot's wall, frame of Bors' bones.

In armour before the earthen footpace he stood;
on his surcoat the lions of his house, dappled with blood,
rampant, regardant; but he wore no helm or sword,
and his hands were bare as Lateran's to the work of our Lord.

In the ritual before the altar Lancelot began to pass;
all the dead lords of the Table were drawn from their graves
to the Mass;
they stood, inward turned, as shields on a white rushing deck,
between Nimue of Broceliande and Helayne of Carbonek.

In Blanchefleur's cell at Almesbury the queen Guinevere
felt the past exposed; and the detail, sharp and dear,
draw at the pang in the breast till, rich and reconciled,
the mystical milk rose in the mother of Logres' child.

Out of the queen's substitution the wounded and dead king
entered into salvation to serve the holy Thing;
singly seen in the Mass, owning the double Crown,
going to the altar Pelles, and Arthur moving down.

Lancelot and Arthur wove the web; the sky
opened on moon and sun; between them, light-traced on high,
the unseen knight of terror stood as a friend;
invisible things and visible waited the end.

Lancelot came to the Canon; my household stood
around me, bearers of the banners, bounteous in blood;
each at the earthen footpace ordained to be blessed and to
bless,
each than I and than all lordlier and less.

Then at the altar We sang in Our office the cycle of names
of their great attributed virtues; the festival of flames
fell from new sky to new earth; the light in bands
of bitter glory renewed the imperial lands.

Then the Byzantine ritual, the Epiclesis, began;
then their voices in Ours invoked the making of man;
petal on petal floated out of the blossom of the Host,
and all ways the Theotokos conceived by the Holy Ghost.

We exposed, We exalted the Unity; prismed shone
web, paths, points; as it was done
the antipodean zones were retrieved round a white rushing
deck,
and the Acts of the Emperor took zenith from Caucasia to
Carbonek.

Over the altar, flame of anatomized fire,
the High Prince stood, gyre in burning gyre;
day level before him, night massed behind;
the Table ascended; the glories intertwined.

'the unseen knight' was Garlon, the brother of King Pelles. It was through the quarrel with him that Balin the Savage came to strike the dolorous blow at Pelles 'with the same spere that Longeus smote oure lord to the hearte', so that 'he myght never be hole tyl Galahad the haute prince heled him in the quest of the Sangraille'.

The Table ascended; each in turn lordliest and least—
slave and squire, woman and wizard, poet and priest;
interchanged adoration, interdispersed prayer,
the ruddy pillar of the Infant was the passage of the porphyry
stair.

That which had been Taliessin rose in the rood;
in the house of Galahad over the altar he stood,
manacled by the web, in the web made free;
there was no capable song for the joy in me:

joy to new joy piercing from paths foregone;
that which had been Taliessin made joy to a Joy unknown;
manifest Joy speeding in a Joy unmanifest.
Lancelot's voice below sang: *Ite; missa est.*

Fast to the Byzantine harbour gather the salvaged sails;
that which was once Taliessin rides to the barrows of Wales
up the vales of the Wye; if skill be of work or of will
in the dispersed homes of the household, let the Company
pray for it still.

FROM *THE REGION OF THE SUMMER STARS*

PREFACE

THESE poems are part of a series of poems which began with *Taliessin through Logres*,[1] but these, generally, are incidental to the main theme.

That theme is what was anciently called the Matter of Britain; that is, the reign of King Arthur in Logres and the Achievement of the Grail. Logres is Britain regarded as a province of the Empire with its centre at Byzantium. The time historically is after the conversion of the Empire to Christianity but during the expectation of the Return of Our Lord (the Parousia). The Emperor of the poem, however, is to be regarded rather as operative Providence. On the south-western side of Logres lies the region of Broceliande, in which is Carbonek where the Grail and other Hallows are in the keeping of King Pelles and his daughter Helayne. Beyond the seas of Broceliande is the holy state of Sarras. In the antipodean seas is the opposite and infernal state of P'o-l'u.

Nothing more is, I think, necessary to these poems. But in general the argument of the series is the expectation of the return of Our Lord by means of the Grail and of the establishment of the kingdom of Logres (or Britain) to this end by the powers of the Empire and Broceliande. Logres, however, was distracted by its own sins, and the wounding of King Pelles (the Keeper of the Hallows) by the Lord Balin the Savage was the Dolorous Blow which prevented the union of Carbonek and Logres and therefore the coming of the Grail. There followed, by a heavenly substitution, the begetting of Galahad by Lancelot on the Princess Helayne in an enchantment. Galahad is brought up in a Convent of White Nuns under the care of Dindrane, Percivale's sister.

[1] Oxford University Press, 1938.

Afterwards he goes to the court of Arthur and then departs, together with Percivale and Bors, for Carbonek and Sarras where he finally achieves the Grail. Meanwhile wars break out between Arthur and Lancelot through which, and through the treachery of Mordred the King's bastard son, Logres is overthrown and afterwards becomes the historical Britain, in which the myth of its origin remains.

1944 C. W.

Prelude

IRONY was the Fortune of Athens; Rome came
to pluck the Fortune of Athens, and stand embattled
as in arms, so in mind against evil luck.
A few wise masters devised for the heart
a road from the universe into dematerialized spirit,
but most prattled cunning preventive doctrine;
till on a day from a hill in the middle of Athens
where men adored Irony the unknown lord,
Paul sent over Athens and Rome his call:
'Whom ye ignorantly worship, him I declare.'

The crooked smiles of the Greeks
fled from their faces while thorned-in-the-flesh the Apostle
against their defensive inflections of verb and voice,
their accents of presaged frustration, their sterile protections,
named in its twyfold Nature the golden Ambiguity.
Then for the creature he invented the vocabulary of faith;
he defined in speech the physiological glory
and began to teach the terms of the work of glory.
The young Church breakfasted on glory; handfasted,
her elect functioned in the light. But the ancient intellect
heard, delaying and playing with its archives, and demurred
that pain was easy, and completeness of belief costly,
and flesh too queasy to bear the main of spirit.

The converted doctors turned to their former confessions,
the limitary heresiarchs feared the indiscretions of matter,
and the careful Nestorius, coming to befriend peace,
preached in Byzantium. Before the sermon was at end
the metaphysicians, sitting to note him, heard
from the City the roar of burning and bundled torches
rise through the fixed stars: *Theotokos*, *Anthropotokos*;
his disciples shrank from the blood-stream where the full
torches

ruddily poured round the eikon of Mary-in-blessing.
Professing only a moral union, they fled
from the new-spread bounty; they found a quarrel with the
Empire
and the sustenance of Empire, with the ground of faith and
earth,
the golden and rose-creamed flesh of the grand Ambiguity.

Fast as they, the orthodox imagination
seized on the Roman polity; there, for a day,
beyond history, holding history at bay,
it established through the themes of the Empire the condition
of Christendom
and saw everywhere manumission of grace into glory.
Beyond the ancient line of imperial shapes
it saw the Throne of primal order, the zone
of visionary powers, and almost (in a cloud) the face
of the only sublime Emperor; as John once
in Patmos, so then all the Empire in Byzantium:
the Acts of the Throne were borne by the speeding logothetes,
and the earth flourished, hazel, corn, and vine.

The Empire, in the peace of the Emperor,
expected perfection; it awaited the Second Coming
of the Union, of the twy-natured single Person,
centuries-belated, now to be; but how
only a few saints knew, in Apennine
or Egypt or Cappadocia, monk or nun,
slave or princess or poet, or, white in Lateran,
like the ghost of man awaiting his body, the Pope.
Hope, as by night the first of the summer stars
in the universal sky high hung,
in them looked on the sea, and across the sea
saw coming, from the world of the Three-in-One,
in a rich container, the Blood of the Deivirilis,
communicated everywhere, but there singly borne,
and the morn of the Trinity rising through the sea to the sun.

The Empire lay in the imposed order; around
the Throne the visionary zone of clear light
hummed with celestial action; there the forms
of chamberlains, logothetes, nuncios, went and came,
diagrams of light moving in the light; they lacked
the flesh and blood, the golden cream and the rose
tinctures; these dwelled in Byzantium; they were held
in men and women, or even (as named qualities)
in the golden day and the rose-gardens of Caucasia.
But also in the mind of the Empire another kind
of tale lay than that of the Grail; those
who worked in the ports heard shipmen say
that in the antipodean ocean was a sight
known only to the Emperor's lordliest admirals
who, closeliest obeying command, passed
near to the harbour and vile marshes of P'o-l'u;
there on the waves a headless Emperor walked
coped in a foul indecent crimson; octopods
round him stretched giant tentacles and crawled
heavily on the slimy surface of the tangled sea,
goggling with lidless eyes at the coast of the Empire.

This, fable or truth, none knew
except the high sea-lords; enough
that in the stuff of the Empire the quality of irony
flickered and faded before the capacity of faith;
all the peoples awaited the Parousia, all
the themes vibrated with duty and expectation
of the coming of the vessel where, ere the Deposition,
the blood of the golden single-personed Ambiguity
fulfilled its commission and was caught; then for a season
was hidden in its own place, till at last (bidden
by ultimate Reason) it deigned at last emerge
out of the extreme verge of the west and the east;
priest and victim. Only the women of earth,
by primal dispensation, little by themselves understood,
shared with that Sacrifice the victimization of blood.

The Calling of Taliessin

BY some it was said that Taliessin
was a child of Henwg the saint, bred in Caerleon,
and thence come, miracle-commissioned; by some
that he sprang from the bards, the ancient guards of the
cauldron
called of Ceridwen; she goddess or priestess,
Tydeg Voel's wife, whose life was legend,
and he if her son then so by magic: none
knew; no clue he showed when he rode down the Wye
coracle-cradled, and at the weir was seen
by Elphin the son of Gwyddno and drawn to shore.
The men with Elphin then could only stare
at the bright forehead of the lonely river-fugitive,
the child coming from the wild Druid wood.
Could they believe in the light that lived from his brow?
decision, there as here, was the mind's election,
the arbitration of faith, the erection of the City.
But Elphin was a man of the tribes, his vocation the blood's,
nor could feel, in more than a chorus after a meal,
verse; vainly Taliessin's first song
through river-mated rhythms while he smiled at the sky
pulsated; only in the song a recurrent code
showed the child already initiated
in the changes of the cauldron of Ceridwen, from the fish to
the frog,
from the frog to the crow, from the crow to the leaping
roe,
from the roe to the kindled fire, from fire to wheat,
from the wheat to the cooked loaf, from shapes that eat
to shapes that are eaten, and then to the fish split
to be at once on the dish and again in the sea—
the fated cycle communicated in heathen secrets;
for the Lord God had not yet set him at liberty,
nor shown him the doctrine of largesse in the land of the
Trinity.

In Elphin's house he grew and practised verse;
striving in his young body with the double living
of the breath in the lung and the sung breath in the brain,
the growing and the knowing and the union of both in the
 showing,
the triune union in each line of verse,
but lacking the formulæ and the grand backing of the Empire.
Yet then his heart, ears, and eyes were wise
from Druid secrets in the twilight and the sun-dawn;
his hearing caught each smallest singular cry
of bird and beast; almost he talked their talk;
his sight followed each farthest flight, each small
insect-dance-pattern in the air; he knew
correspondence and the law of similitudes; he had seen the
 cauldron
of poetry and plenty; he heard now dimly
of the food that freed from the cycle, of the butteries of the
 monks
and the baps and beans of hermits in Thule and the Thebaid.
When Elphin asked him his lineage, he sang riddling:
'My heritage is all men's; only my age is my own.
I am a wonder whose origin is not known.
I carried in battle a banner before Lleon of Lochlin,
and held in the sleeping-chamber a mirror for his queen.
I am more than the visions of all men and my own vision,
and my true region is the summer stars.
I suffered in dreams derision for the son of a virgin,
yet I stood in the Galaxy at the throne of the Distributor
and flew over the waves when the world was in flood.
I rose to the third heaven with her of the penitence
and was tangled through every sense by the hazel bush;
I was mangled for a night and a day by black swine,
yet my true region is the summer stars.
I was thrall to Ceridwen and free in the manger of an ass.
Before speech came to pass, I was full of the danger of
 loquacity.
It is a doubt if my body is flesh or fish,
therefore no woman will ever wish to bed me

and no man make true love without me.
All the doctors come to stand about me,
yet I shall never have any near me to need me.
Every king shall call me Taliessin,
and till the doom I am handfast with all the dead.'

Before Wye from his father Henwg, or else
from a wandering priest among the vales of Wye
Taliessin heard a word of the Empire; he heard
tales of the tree of Adam, and the rare superfluity
of moral creation, till the will of the superfluity
turned the tree to a rood for itself and Another
and envenomed its blood with mood; then the will of its
    Origin
shared the blood and fared forth well from the tree.
Dim and far came the myth to Taliessin
over the dark rim of the southern sea.
Poor, goetic or theurgic, the former spells
seemed beside the promise of greater formulæ;
poor—control or compact—the personal mastery,
the act of magic, or the strain of ancient verse
beside the thickening dreams of the impersonal Empire
and the moulded themes of the Empire; and they all
from Gaul to Jerusalem enfolded in the infinite hall
of the Sacred Emperor at operative Byzantium.
His heart turned to know more than could be learned
by Wye of that white healing metaphysic;
he sought the sea and the City; he was caught by a rumour.

On his shoulder a covered harp, and he cloaked
over his tunic; laced boots of hide
on his feet, and a sword of Rome slung by his side,
he turned to the towns of the coast; shipping had failed,
yet sometimes a vessel sailed to the ports of Gaul
from the southern edge of the Isle of the Sea; there
he looked to find passage and then to forage
in holy luck—by singing verses, by writing
letters or carrying, by script-copying or fighting,—

nay, if need were, by currying horses
for the dukes of the Empire whose courses took them to
Byzantium.
As he came on the third day down the way to the coast
he saw on his left a wilderness; Logres lay
without the form of a Republic, without letters or law,
a storm of violent kings at war—smoke
poured from a burning village in the mid-east;
transport had ceased, and all exchange stilled.
On the other hand was the wood of Broceliande.

Dangerous to men is the wood of Broceliande.
Hardly the Druid, hardly a Christian priest,
pierced it ever; it was held, then as now,
by those few who in Britain study the matter of the marches
that there the divine science and the grand art,
if at all below the third heaven, know
their correspondence, and live in a new style—
many a mile of distance goes to the making:
but those fewer, now as then, who enter
come rarely again with brain unravished
by the power of the place—some by grace dumb
and living, like a blest child, in a mild and holy
sympathy of joy; but the rest loquacious with a graph
or a gospel, gustily audacious over three heavens.

Between the anarchy of yet unmade Logres
and the darkness of secret-swayed Broceliande
Taliessin took his way; his way curved
on that stormy day so near the wood that he saw
a dark rose of sunset between tree and tree
lie on the sea, the antipodean ocean
beheld there in thrusting inlets; his heart
beat lest dread or desolation wrecked his mind
so that he fell from his kind, and the grand art failed—
control lost and all sense crossed;
or else he quit no more for a thrilling rhyme,
fulfilling a time of attention, but O pledged

beyond himself to an edged anguish dividing
word from thing and uniting thing to word—
each guiding and each fighting the other.
'It is a doubt if my body is flesh or fish,'
he sang in his grief; 'hapless the woman who loves me,
hapless I—flung alive where only
the cold-lipped mermen thrive among staring creatures
of undersea, or lost where the beast-natures
in a wood of suicides lap at the loss of intellect.'
Obscurely his future—the king's poet's future—
shook in his blood; his look was held by the flood
angrily rose-darkened down the inlets of the wood.

He forced his eyes again to the road; far
before him, on to the road from the wood's mass,
he saw a form pass; it hovered and turned
towards him along the road, as if to challenge,
check, or wreck his journey. The sun had sunk,
the rose vanished from the under-sea—and he
banished there between Logres and Broceliande
to feel before him the road threaten ravage
and the power of universal spirit rise
against him to be wild and savage on his lonely spirit;
all things combined, and defined themselves in that moment
hostile to him and the burning homes of Logres.
He saw draw towards him a faint light
clearer and sharper than sun or moon; nearer
as it drew it grew double; his hand found
his sword, his heart sang an invocation
of the woman whose name he had heard in a tale of the myth,
of Mary Magdalene who had charity for Christ—she
to him in his grief as he to her in her sin.
Bright-keen at first, the light grew soft;
the double aureole was entwining a double shape,
gently-shining—as in the days to be
the king's poet himself at the court of Camelot
might seem (could his heart have guessed) to his true lovers.
The double shape divided to a man and a woman,

pricking his eyes with the quiet shining of their skin,
tall, slender, black-haired; they spared a width
between themselves and him, coming to a pause,
and he also, prepared for any chance.

Time and space, duration and extension, to a child
are in the father's voice, the mother's face,
and to us in things passing or pausing in passing,
amassing themselves in that pause to a new energy
for or against the soul's motion; Taliessin
felt before him an accumulation of power
tower in the two shapes, so deep in calm
that it seemed the word of the heart and the word of the
voice
must find, in each and in both, correspondence there
more than even the grand art could know or show
for all similitudes; he heard speech flow
out of the masculine mouth of the twinned form
as the south wind, stirring the tiny waves, shows
and shakes the stillness of the wide accumulated air.
'Whither, Taliessin—whither, son of the bards—
moves the song that blows you along our marches?'
Taliessin said: 'Who asks?' and the other: 'Merlin
am I; she Brisen my sister; we are free
of the forest, parthenogenetical in Broceliande
from the Nature, from Nimue our mother; sent are we
to build, as is willed, Logres, and in Logres a throne
like that other of Carbonek, of King Pelles in Broceliande,
the holder of the Hallows; my sister shall stand in his house
to tend his daughter in the day of her destiny, but I
make haste to Logres, to call and install King Arthur;
at whose board you and I, lord, again may meet.'
Taliessin said: 'Are you mortal? Are you a friend?
I do not know Arthur; I go from Wye
to find beyond sea a fact or a fable.'
Merlin answered: 'A friend, mortal or immortal,
if you choose; we bear no arms; and for harms spiritual
we two can placably receive the Names spoken

in Byzantium, which shall be by Thames; it is ordered that
soon
the Empire and Broceliande shall meet in Logres,
and the Hallows be borne from Carbonek into the sun.
Therefore Nimue our mother directs in Carbonek
the maidenhood of Pelles' daughter Helayne, and I
go to prepare Logres for the sea-coming
from Sarras.' Taliessin said: 'Where is Sarras?'
But Merlin: 'Hush; formulæ and rhymes are yours
but seek no more; fortunate the poet who endures
to measure in his mind the distance even to Carbonek;
few dare more—enough. The Peace be with you.'
Taliessin gazed at the twins and his heart was stilled;
he said: 'And with you be the Peace.' Then Brisen: 'Sleep
we three here to-night and wait for the day.'

Done was the day; the antipodean sun
cast earth's coned shadow into space;
it exposed the summer stars; as they rose
the light of Taliessin's native land
shone in a visible glory over him sleeping.
Rarely through the wood rang a celestial cry,
sometimes with a like reply, sometimes with none.
The trees shook, in no breeze, to a passage of power.
Under the ground was the sound of great waves
breaking round huge caves, ancient sepulchres,
where Ocean, a young child of making, held
talk with the first mother of making, Nimue:—
or so might seem to the dream of the young poet;
or else the noise gave voice to the image in his brain,
an image springing from a tangle of ringing names—
Thames, Camelot, Carbonek, Pelles and Arthur,
Logres, Wye, Helayne, Broceliande,
Byzantium, the Empire . . . the Empire . . . 'this', the voice
sang, 'is the Empire; what serves the Empire?' The youth
was caught by a pulse of truth in the image; he saw
Merlin and Brisen rise from their sleep and kiss.
He saw in the light of the stars above him Merlin

draw near and stoop; he felt the black-haired wizard
breathe on his eyes, saying: 'Do not wake, king's poet.
Fate is for you to find but for us to make.
Dream—or see in dream. The rite opens.
Lie you still to-night, as in vales of Wye.'

The cone's shadow of earth fell into space,
and into (other than space) the third heaven.
In the third heaven are the living unriven truths,
climax tranquil in Venus. Merlin and Brisen
heard, as in faint bee-like humming
round the cone's point, the feeling intellect hasten
to fasten on the earth's image; in the third heaven
the stones of the waste glimmered like summer stars.
Between wood and waste the yoked children of Nimue
opened the rite; they invoked the third heaven,
heard in the far humming of the spiritual intellect,
to the building of Logres and the coming of the land of the
Trinity
which is called Sarras in maps of the soul. Merlin
made preparation; on the ground he drew the pentagram,
at four corners he dropped the sacred herbs,
sharp odours; under his hands they became
flame of potential intellect becoming actual,
allaying the mortal air with purification.
At the fifth angle, naked in the hypnotic trance,
hands caught behind her at the base of sense
as at the centre of space, Brisen stood,
the impassioned diagram of space; her shadow fell
east into Logres, cast by the fourfold fire.
The abstract gaze of Merlin overlooked
his sister, as time space; the elementals became
the magical continuum, where Merlin saw the place
to prepare, and himself to fare to the preparation.
He lifted the five times cross-incised rod
and began incantation; in the tongue of Broceliande
adjuring all the primal atoms of earth
to shape the borders of Logres, to the dispensation

of Carbonek to Caerleon, of Caerleon to Camelot, to the union
of King Pelles and King Arthur, to the sea-coming of Sarras
which beneath the Throne is shown in mosaics to Byzantium.

The weight of poetry could not then sink
into the full depth of the weight of glory.
For all the codes his young tongue bore
Taliessin could not think in Merlin's style,
nor his verse grow mature with pure fact.
Many a mile of distance in the Empire was to go
to the learning, many a turn of exchange in the need
of himself or others or the Empire, much speed
in chariots and ships by the Golden Horn, and the high
cliffs and gardens of Caucasus, and the sky of Rome
where the hands of the Pope are precise in the white sacrifice.
The operation of Merlin passed through his sleep
by accidents, not by events; nor could his heart
elect and effect the full purpose of formulæ.
But the accidents hinted the events. He saw the pillared
back of Brisen ruddy in the fires' glow,
and the fires' glow reddening the snow of mountains
where his track ran—no more a back, but himself
climbing from meadow-grasses to the rough passes
of frosty heights, crossing Apennine, or tossing
under forked lightning on Caspian below Caucasus.
Everywhere his road ran ranging the themes,
and near a clear city on a sea-site
in a light that shone from behind the sun; the sun
was not so fierce as to pierce where that light could
through every waste and wood; the city and the light
lay beyond the sun and beyond his dream,
nor could the weight of poetry sink so far
as the weight of glory; on the brink of the last depth
the glory clouded to its own covering and became
again the recapitulatory body of Brisen,
the engine of the First Mover, fit to his wit
that works in earth the birth of superfluous good:

fair let the creature follow that Nature. Taliessin
began then to share in the doctrine of largesse
that should mark in Camelot the lovers of the king's poet;
he saw again the wide waste of Logres
under the dark and mighty shadow of Brisen,
cast by the clear assuaging fires; in the shadow
the stones of the waste glimmered like summer stars;
he heard again the presaging spell of Merlin
foretell and furnish the lofty errand of Logres.

The stars vanished; they gone, the illumined dusk
under the spell darkened to the colour of porphyry,
the colour of the stair of Empire and the womb of woman,
and the rich largesse of the Emperor; within was a point,
deep beyond or deep within Logres,
as if it had swallowed all the summer stars
and hollowed the porphyry night for its having and holding—
tiny, dark-rose, self-glowing,
as a firefly's egg or (beyond body and spirit,
could the art of the king's poet in the court of Camelot,
after his journeys, find words for body or spirit)
the entire point of the thrice co-inherent Trinity
when every crown and every choir is vanished,
and all sight and hearing is nothing else.
It burned for a moment as short as itself tiny,
and inturned to its disappearing, as the voice of Merlin
sang: 'Go, son of the bards; king's poet,
go; propolitan are the porphyry chambers; see
and know the Empire; fulfil then an errand;
rescue the king at Mount Badon; stand by the king,
Arthur, the king we make, until the land
of the Trinity by a sea-coming fetch to his stair.
Sarras is free to Carbonek, Carbonek to Camelot;
in all categories holds the largesse of exchange,
and the sea of Broceliande enfolds the Empire.'

The shadow of Brisen lay on the whole of Logres,
but the shadow was a flight of dark stairs, from the brain

to the base; the pavement of the base, below all,
lay in the trees and seas of Broceliande.
But in the visionary sleep, at the height of the flight,
where the brain of Logres opened in the main of space,
grew a golden throne, of two dragons twined,
where a king sat crowned, around him figures
of great lords; Taliessin saw himself
stand on the king's left hand among the lords.
His own voice had just sung and ceased.
All were gazing, and he, near the king's chair,
down the stair; they waited and watched for a coming,
for the sea-coming of the Trinity through Broceliande.
So full were they fixed that his sleeping eyes pricked
to see and feel their gaze; at once, with the pricking
he swung to the waves on the deck of a moving ship,
drawing to the watchers: but whether the king's poet's style
and desire for verse palpitated in the young Taliessin
to more than his function, and rated himself in sleep
higher than any crude folly, waking, could;
or whether Brisen and the operation of the rite
wrought in his brain to an emanation of Nimue,
the mother of all operation; or whether some true
foreboding grew of Dindrane the sister of Percivale,
she who was called Blanchefleur in religion, and to be
farther from and closer to the king's poet
than any, the eidolon of his beatitude, his blood's bounty;
or whether Merlin among all the phantasmagoria
showed him the final term and the firm purpose
of heaven, and the errand of Helayne the daughter of Pelles
—there, on the deck above the flood, stood
the daughter of a king, holding an unseen thing
between her hands, but over her hands a veil,
the saffron veil of the sun itself, covered
all; her face was pale with stress of passion
as the ship ran—and even in a sleep within a sleep
Taliessin trembled; terrible was the form of the princess,
the covered shape terrible; as the stupor loosed
he saw himself below himself asleep

deep within the protective pentagram, where burned
the four fires, and Brisen self-fiery,
at the five angles, and the tree-tangles beyond
in the first beginning, in the spinning of Merlin's spells
when the wise twins came from the wood: but all that stood
at the height of the brain faded into the space
again of a starry night; through the reach of Logres
the stones of the waste glimmered like summer stars,
as if the king's poet's household of stars
shone, in a visible glory, on the dreaming Taliessin.
The spells of Merlin worked in each episode of time,
each code of initiation, each vocation and rule,
each school of power, the foundation of Camelot, the bond
of the two kings in Carbonek, Caerleon, and Camelot,
of the Holder of the Hallows and the new-designed house
of the Hallows in the Empire. Taliessin's brain lost
again the vision of Imagination at the full;
he heard the final voice of Merlin lull
once more his body and mind to deep sleep:
'Son of the bards, go; go, Taliessin;
take the track of the Empire; go to Byzantium.
Thereafter you shall buy souls in many markets,
low be the purchase or high—all's low,
so the show of summer stars be thereby heightened.
If in the end anything fail of all
purposed by our mother and the Emperor, if the term
be held less firm in Camelot than in Carbonek,
as well my sister and I may guess now
and prepare the ambiguous rite for either chance
in the kingdom of Arthur; if cease the coming from the seas
at the evil luck of a blow dolorously struck,
it may be that this gathering of souls, that the king's poet's
household
shall follow in Logres and Britain the spiritual roads
that the son of Helayne shall trace westward through the
trees
of Broceliande; they who shall be called and thralled
by Taliessin's purchase and their own will

from many a suburb, many a waste; say
that they are a wonder whose origin is not known,
they are strown with a high habit, with the doctrine of
largesse,
who in his house shall be more than the king's poet
because of the vows they take; but now haste
all we three on the roads—Brisen to Carbonek,
I to Camelot, and Taliessin to Byzantium.'

In the morning, they rose, ate, blessed each other,
bade farewell, and parted—Brisen to Carbonek,
Merlin to Camelot, and Taliessin to Byzantium.

Taliessin in the Rose-Garden

THE king's poet walked among the queen's roses
(all kinds all minds taking),
making verse, putting distance into verse,
cutting and trimming verse as the gardeners the roses.
He turned, at a path's end, between two bushes
of cabbage-roses, scions of Caucasia, *centifoliæ*,
hearts folded strong in a hundred meanings.
Along the level spinal path Taliessin,
his eyes abused by the crimson, confused saw
for a moment in the middle distance a rush of the crimson
shaping at the garden's entrance to a triple form,
to three implicit figures of the mind; his eyes
cleared; appeared three women of Camelot—
the feminine headship of Logres, the queen Guinevere,
talking to Dindrane, Percivale's sister; beyond,
as the ground-work she was and tended, a single maid
hardened with toil on the well-gardened roses:
what was even Dindrane but an eidolon of the slaves?

The air was clear, as near as earth can
to the third heaven, climax tranquil in Venus.
Only (what lacks there) it breathed the energy

from Broceliande that ever seethed in Logres,
the variable temperature of mastering Nature; Taliessin's
senses under Nimue's influences stirred and trembled
with the infinite and infinitesimal trembling of the roses.
At the entrance to the long rose-path he saw
the sensuous mode, the consummate earth of Logres,
the wife of Arthur, the queen of the kingdom, Guinevere.
Hazel-lithe she stood, in a green gown;
bare against the green, her arm was tinged
with faint rose-veins, and golden-flecked
as the massed fair hair under the gold
circlet of Logres; on one hand was the ring
of the consort of Logres; deep-rose-royal
it drew the rose-alleys to its magical square.
There, in the single central ruby, Taliessin
saw, in the sovereign gem of Logres, the contained
life of Logres-in-the-Empire; till the flush of the roses
let seem that the unrestrained rush of the ruby
loosed a secular war to expand through the land,
and again the shore of Logres—and that soon—
felt the pirate beaks in a moon of blood-letting;
and within, yet encircling, the war, the sacred stone
shook with the infinitesimal trembling of the roses
and melted inwards into the blood of the king
Pelles, belted by the curse of the Dolorous Blow;
so rich was the ring and by Merlin royally runed.
The path of the garden was a verse into the wound,
into the secrets of Carbonek, and the queen's majesty,
in the king's poet's mouth; he heard himself say:
'The Wounded Rose runs with blood at Carbonek.'

Making the poem he made, he heard himself
say in the rose-garden to the queen of Logres—
she ? he spoke low; she talked and laughed;
under her brow she looked for the king's friend
Lancelot. Taliessin heard himself say:
'Tristram and Mark were in love with the Queen Iseult.
Palomides studied her more; so I

everywhere study and sigh for the zodiac in flesh—
scandal to men, folly to women! but we,
Palomides and I, see everywhere the hint,
in a queen's shape or a slave's; we bid for a purchase;
the purchase flies to its aim in the heart of another;
our fame is left us darkling, and our mind to find
a new law; bitter is the brew of exchange.
We buy for others; we make beauty for others;
and the beauty made is not the beauty meant:
shent is pride while the Rose-King bleeds at Carbonek.

'Scandal to the pious Jews, folly to the sly Greeks!
But I was Druid-born and Byzantium-trained.
Beyond Wye, by the cauldron of Ceridwen, I saw
the golden sickle flash in the forest, and heard
the pagans mutter a myth; thence by the ocean
dreaming the matter of Logres I came where the hierarchs
patter the sacred names on the golden floor
under the Throne of Empire; I saw how the City
was based, faced fair to the Emperor as the queen to the king,
slaves to lords, and all Caucasia to Carbonek.
The magnanimous stair rose in the hall of Empire.
The Acts of Identity issued from the Throne; there
twelve images were shown in a mystery, twelve
zodiacal houses; the sun of the operative Emperor
wended through them, attended by the spiritual planets,
attributing to the themes their qualities of cause and permanence:
in each the generation of creation, in each the consummation.
All coalesced in each; that each mind
in the Empire might find its own kind of entry.
Aquarius for me opened the principle of eyes
in the clearness above the firmament; I saw below,
patterned in the stellar clearness, the rosed femininity
particled out of the universe, the articled form
of the Eve in the Adam; the Adam known in the Eve.
To visionary eyes the path of man began
to pass through the themes and the houses; can I recall

all ? shall even the queen be seen in the full
glory now in Camelot outside Byzantium ?
Nay, say only that the Twins ran in the arms
and laired in the hands, in the queen's hands, in Rome
the City of Twins, wolf-twins, cubs
humanized to labour, making muscles and thumbs,
that each might neighbour the other to instruments and
    events.
The Scorpion-contingency, controlled and ensouled in
    Jerusalem,
held its privy place; the Acts of Identity
furnished with danger the anger of the laden tail.
Earth and the queen's body had base in Libra.
Glorious over Logres, let the headship of the queen
be seen, as Caucasia to Carbonek, as Logres to Sarras.

'Within and without the way wove about the image,
about the City and the body; I followed the way
from the eyes; it was swallowed in the sweet dark pit
of the palms—lit how ? lit by the rays
from the golden-growthed, golden-clothed arms,
golden-sheathed and golden-breathed, imperially
shining from above toward instruments and events,
rays shaken out towards the queen's hand stretched
to welcome the king's friend, or a slave's to trim
the rose or pluck a nut from the uncut hazel,
or the princess Dindrane's to the fair conclusion of prayer.
Under the flashes, down a steep stair, I came
to a deep figure; I came to the house of Libra.
Libra in the category of flesh is the theme of Caucasia,
the mesh of the net of the imperially bottomed glory;
and the frame of justice and balance set in the body,
the balance and poise needful to all joys
and all peace. I studied universal justice
between man and man, and (O opposite!) between man and
    woman
by their own skill and the will of the Throne; light
compact in each fitting act of justice in the City,

and support-in-the-flesh of the sitting body of beauty.
Scandal to the Jews, folly to the Greeks! let the hazel
of verse measure the multifold levels of unity.

'Under the rays I studied arch-natural justice.
Suddenly at a moment the rays ranged wild
and the darting light changed. The roseal pattern
ran together, and was botched and blotched, blood
inflaming the holy dark; the way of return
climbed beside the timed and falling blood.

'The zodiac of Christ poorly sufficed the Adam;
they bade the Scorpion sting; they looked wildly
on the crookt curves of identity; venom is hereditary,
and the Adam's children endure the Adam's blood.
Cain, seeking a cure, was driven farther
into the pit; at a blow he split the zodiac.
He called into being earthly without heavenly justice,
supposing without his brother, without the other,
he solely existed: fool! the rosed shape
vanished; instead, the clearness of Aquarius was bloodshot,
the Twins for very nearness tore each other:
the way climbed against timed and falling blood,
by a secular stair of months, deep-rose-royal.
And I there climbing in the night's distance
till the clear light shone on the height's edge:
out of the pit and the split zodiac I came
to the level above the magnanimous stair, and saw
the Empire dark with the incoherence of the houses.
Nay, there, as I looked on the stretched Empire
I heard, as in a throb of stretched verse,
the women everywhere throughout it sob with the curse
and the altars of Christ everywhere offer the grails.
Well are women warned from serving the altar
who, by the nature of their creature, from Caucasia to Carbonek,
share with the Sacrifice the victimization of blood.
Flesh knows what spirit knows,

but spirit knows it knows—categories of identity:
women's flesh lives the quest of the Grail
in the change from Camelot to Carbonek and from Carbonek to Sarras,
puberty to Carbonek, and the stanching, and Carbonek to death.
Blessed is she who gives herself to the journey.

'Flesh tells what spirit tells
(but spirit knows it tells). Women's travel
holds in the natural the image of the supernatural,
the shed metrical of the shed anthropometrical.
Truth speeds from the taunt, and Pelles bleeds
below Jupiter's red-pierced planet; the taunt
yields to the truth, irony to defeated irony.
The phosphor of Percivale's philosophical star
shines down the roads of Logres and Broceliande;
happy the woman who in the light of Percivale
feels Galahad, the companion of Percivale, rise
in her flesh, and her flesh bright in Carbonek with Christ,
in the turn of her body, in the turn of her flesh, in the turn
of the Heart that heals itself for the healing of others,
the only Heart that healed itself without others,
when our Lord recovered the Scorpion and restored the zodiac.
Blessed is she who can know the Dolorous Blow
healed in the flesh of Pelles, the flesh of women;
and hears softly with touched ears in Camelot
Merlin magically prepare for the Rite of Galahad
and the fixing of all fidelity from all infidelity.

'This I saw in a chamber of Byzantium; the princess
Dindrane again opened my eyes in Aquarius.
Let the queen's majesty, the feminine headship of Logres,
deign to exhibit the glory to the women of Logres;
each to one vision, but the queen for all.
Bring to a flash of seeing the women in the world's base.'

Taliessin saw the queen from the Throne, again
from the rose-garden; she talked sideways to Dindrane.
The king's poet came to the entrance; the queen said,
with the little scorn that becomes a queen of Logres:
'Has my lord dallied with poetry among the roses?'

The Prayers of the Pope

EARLY on the feast of Christmas the young Pope
knelt in Lateran—Deodatus, Egyptian-born,
slender, white-haired, incandescent,
seeming in his trance of prayer a third twin
of Merlin and Brisen, masculine touched with the feminine,
except for their black hair strangely bleached
as if time's metre were smitten by sacred grief.
Over the altar a reliquary of glass held
an intinctured Body; the Pope waited to pass
to sing his tri-fold Eucharist; meanwhile he prayed
alone and aloud in the candled shroud of the dark.
Sweet his voice sounded in the new Latin
founded on Virgil but colloquial, capable of rhyme,
fastening in a time of genesis Lupercal and Lateran
and hastening by measure the flood of the soul in the blood.
The young Pontiff's meditation set to *Magnificat*,
to the total Birth intending the total Death,
to the Love that lost Itself, nor only an image
nor only all the images but wholly Itself.
The Pope prayed: 'But each loss of each image
is single and full, a thing unrequited,
plighted in presence to no recompense, no
purchase of paradise; eyes see no future:
when the Son of Man comes, he brings no faith in a future.
Send not, send not, the rich empty away.'

A tale that emerged from Logres surged in Europe
and swelled in the Pope's ears; it held nothing
of fulfilment of prophecy and the sea-coming of the Grail

but only of bleak wars between Arthur and Lancelot,
Gawaine set to seek his heart's vengeance,
the king's son gone whoring with fantasy,
and mobs roaring through Camelot; the Pope's letters
had brought no staying of the slaying nor ceasing of the sin
nor healed the dichotomy of battle. The tale spread,
till the governors of the themes knew it in their own dreams;
forsaking the Emperor, they chose among themselves,
here one and there one, foes
among themselves, puppets of reputation,
void of communicated generation of glory;
clouds covered the Imperial Throne in Byzantium;
and the Acts of the Throne were let by infidels; none
cared how men were shaped in body or mind,
nor pined for the perfect Parousia; all gave
their choice to the primal curse and the grave; their loves
escaped back to the old necromantic gnosis
of separation, were it but from one soul.
Frantic with fear of losing themselves in others,
they denounced and delivered one other to reprobation—
Mordred or the Khan of the Huns or the Khalif of Asia
or any neighbour they envied in labour or love.
They rejected the City; they made substitutes for the City;
mutes or rhetoricians instead of the sacred poets,
cheating for charity, exposition for experience,
braggadocio or burlesque for faith and hope.

The Pope prayed before the Body in Lateran:
'Rich in sorrow, rich in heart's heaviness,
blessed are we, bearing soul's wealth now,
and cannot anyhow part with that wealth, laden
with loss, and the loss always an affirmation,
double affirmation—image and the opposite of image—
which our wit, as courteously thine, O Blessed, carries,
but thine thyself only and the lack of thyself;
send not, send not, the rich empty away.'

The line faltered along the Danube and the Rhine;
pale in London and Lutetia grew the tale of peace,
and bloody the Noel-song; the towns of Logres
felt the sliding planes of the raiders' sails,
and Gaul all the push of the Northern woods,
savage growths, moods infinitely multiplied
across the bleak plains, under rains and snows
of myths bitter to bondage, where in race
by sullen marshes separated from race
virtue is monopolized and grace prized in schism.
The consuls and lords fought for the fords and towns,
but over the Rhine, over the Vistula and Danube
pressed the grand tribes; the land shook
as band after band stamped into darkness cities
whose burning had lamped their path; their wrath grew
with vengeance and victory; they looked to no returning.

The Pope prayed: 'Where is difference between us?
What does the line along the rivers define?
Causes and catapults they have and we have,
and the death of a brave beauty is mutual everywhere.
If there be difference, it must be in thy sense
that we declare—O Blessed, pardon affirmation!—
and they deny—O Blessed, pardon negation!—
that we derive from them and they from us,
and alive are they in us and we in them.
We know how we have sinned; we know not how they.
Intend for us the double wealth of repentance;
send not, send not, the rich empty away.'

Now within the frontiers, the evil wizards,
the seers of the heathen, with thumbs instead of fingers,
marked on the earth the reversed and accursed pentagram;
they lit and fed the flickering spectral flames
of the rituals of necromancy; they poured on the fires
mastic and gum-aromatic; they uttered invocation
of smouldering deities whose very names were lost,
but the half-broken and half-spoken syllables

wrought resurrection in the Pit; yet even those wizards
hid their eyes where some few, their chief,
the beastliest and chillest in blasphemy, called farther
on the powers of P'o-l'u, on the antipodean octopods,
on the slime that had been before the time of Merlin
and below the trees and seas of Broceliande.
Then, in that power, they called and enthralled the dead,
the poor, long-dead, long-buried, decomposing
shapes of humanity; the earthy shapes stirred,
all whom the governors of the themes had once slain,
the uneyed images of old blockade and barricade,
children starved in sieges, prostituted women,
men made slaves or crucified; before the Parousia,
before the Redemption made manifest, the poor bodies
were drawn again slowly up through the earth,
and, held steady on their feet, stood and answered.
With rods of desecrated hazel the sorcerers
touched them and bade them walk; bloodless, automatized,
precursors of the tribes in a necromancy of justice,
those mechanized bodies stalked across the fords,
and the hordes of the heathen followed the corpses to battle.
Consuls and lords felt the cold coming
and the drumming of the earth under the tribes, but they
shrank
only before the ghosts of the past—from graves
drawn by maleficent spells, but too-veritable ghosts
before those hosts moving in a terrible twilight.

The Pope saw himself—he sighed and prayed—
as a ruin of the Empire; he died in a foreboding.
He felt within him the themes divide, each
dreadfully autonomous in its own corporal place,
its virtue monopolized, its grace prized, in schism,
and the little insane brain whimpering of pain
and its past; before the Parousia, before the Redemption,
all his unredeemed deeds and words
rose as once they had been, fire in his body,
chill in his mind, and everywhere in mind and body

the terrible schism of identity into the categories
and the miserable conquest of the categories over identity
split all, and fatally separated the themes
which in the beginning were mated with identical glory.
Such is death's outrage; so the Pope
died in a foretasting; only, hasting
still to the salvaged and re-engaged Body,
he prayed: 'And for me, in that new day, O Blessed,
send not, send not, the rich empty away.'

Against the rule of the Emperor the indivisible
Empire was divided; therefore the Parousia suspended
its coming, and abode still in the land of the Trinity.
Logres was void of Grail and Crown, but well
had Mordred spelled his lesson from his father King Arthur.
The prince had hungered; he had waited to-morrow and to-
    morrow
till the sorrow of his waiting, satiating his blood,
drove him to change the double wealth of loss
for the single having; his craving refused itself.
He sought his vision by mere derision of the vision.
He drew into the ordained place of the Table
the unstable pagan chiefs; all personal
griefs in Logres burst and curst the impersonal
formulæ of glory; he assuaged his own image
with the image of the Throne, setting both against the
    Empire,
and begetting by the succubus of his longing, in a world of
    pagans,
the falsity of all images and their incoherence.

The Pope prayed: 'O Blessed, confirm
nor thee in thine images only but thine images in thee.
Bestow now the double inseparable wonder,
the irrevocable union: set in each thy term.
The formulæ of glory are the food of intellectual love,
from the rose-gardens to the wardens of the divine science,
and so to the sacred Heart; the Flesh-taker

with the God-bearer, each the off-springing of other,
the Maker a sharer only and the making as much.
Let the chief of the images touch the Unimaged, and free
the Love that recovered Itself, nor only an image,
nor only all the images, but wholly Itself;
free It that we, solely the rich, may pray
send not, send not, the rich empty away.'

Taliessin gathered his people before the battle.
'Peers of the household,' the king's poet said,
'dead now, save Lancelot, are the great lords
and the Table may end to-morrow; if it live,
it shall have new names in a new report.
Short is Our time, though that time prove eternal.
Therefore'—he lifted his hands to the level of his brow,
the hands that had written and harped the king's music;
there the ageing began ere the hair was grey,
or the tongue tired of song, or the brain fey;
O but the Bright Forehead was once young!
'Therefore now We dissolve the former bonds—'
the voice sounded, the hands descended—'We dissolve
the outer bonds; We declare the Company still
fixed in the will of all who serve the Company,
but the ends are on Us, peers and friends; We restore
again to God the once-permitted lieutenancy;
blessed be Dinadan by whom the lieutenancy began
when he called Us on the day of fools, on his own day.
We restore it to God in each singly and in all.
Receive it in God.' One of the household said,
shining through grief, the king's poet's steward,
a strong star: 'This is the last largesse;
give we freely, companions; but first, lord,
let us live again the moment of ratification,
a superfluous necessity; let us lay our hands again
between my lord's, and swear that the household endures
for ever, and we yours in it.' Taliessin
answered: 'What skill have We had but to be the will
of the whole Company?—We a needful superfluity,

the air in which the summer stars shine,
nay, less—the mode only of their placing and gracing.
It is a command; swear.' While it was done,
lightly each in turn and each with the other,
and each with the king's poet, the least of his household,
all the household exchanged the kiss of peace.

The Pope prayed: 'Keep thy own for thyself.
When the Thrones vanish—the imperial Throne hidden,
the vassal thrones changed—and forbidden lives
floating about the headless Emperor in P'o-l'u—
keep thy word in thine unknown elect:
no wise their supernatural parts sundered
from their natural hearts; little shall those hearts suffer—
so much shall the healing metaphysic have power upon
them—
from evil and mischief and the crafty assaults of the devil.
Purely their souls shall go and their bodies securely,
whether in body or soul they drink deadly,
or handle malice and slander as they handle serpents,
by the magnificence in modesty, the modesty in magnificence
that the doctrine of largesse teaches; what recovers
lovers in lovers is love; let them then
go into every den of magic and mutiny,
touch the sick and the sick be healed, take
the trick of the weak devils with peace, and speak
at last on the coast of the land of the Trinity the tongue
of the Holy Ghost. O Blessed, for ever bring
thine own to thyself and for ever thyself to thine own.'

Jupiter rode over Carbonek; beyond Jupiter,
beyond the summer stars, deep heaven
centrally opened within the land of the Trinity;
planetary light was absorbed there, and emerged
again in its blissful journeys; there the three
lords of the quest landed from the vessel of the quest,
Bors, Percivale, and Galahad the High Prince—
the chief of the images, and the contemplation of the images,

and the work of the images in all degrees of the world.
They lay for a year and a day imprisoned in a trance,
waiting among moving rocks and granite voices
the dawn-hour of the trine-toned light
and they in fine drawn to the canon of the Grail.
Whereof afterwards Bors should bear to Logres
the tale in his heart and the last largesse of Galahad.
He should follow the sun; which now behind the lords
rose from the saffron veil that, on the deck,
covered the body of Dindrane, Percivale's sister,
Taliessin's love, Galahad's foster-warden.
The sun outward ran a year's journey;
the earth span around the sun for a year;
for a year and a day the lords lay entranced.
The sun ran; it saw, and shuddered as it ran,
the bounds of the Empire breaking; beyond P'o-l'u
it saw the giant octopods moving; their tentacles
waving, stretching, stealing souls from the shores,
feeling along Burma, nearing India,
appearing above ocean, or sinking and slinking
and spreading everywhere along the bottom of ocean,
and heading inward. But there they touched and clutched,
somewhere in the deep seas, something that invited
holding—and they held, enfolding—and the tentacles folded
round long, stretched limbs, like somewhat of themselves
but harder and huger; the tentacles were touched and
clutched,
flung and were clung to, clung and were not flung off,
brainlessly hastened and brainfully were hastened to.
The roots of Broceliande fastened on them
length lying along length and gripping length;
in the ocean where near and far are infinite and equal
the hollow suckers of the vast slimy tentacles
were tautened to Nimue's trees through the seas of P'o-l'u,
and fixed to a regimen; held so for ever
to know for ever nothing but their own hypnotic
sucking at the harsh roots; the giant octopods
hung helpless; the wizards and gods of the heathen

far along the Northern line, beyond Rhine and Danube,
helpless dwindled; helpless, the headless Emperor
was loosened, and sank and dissolved in the uncoped seas,
a crimson tincture, a formless colour, the foul
image of the rose-gardens of Caucasia now
losing itself, drifting in the waters, and none
to know what was real and what unreal
or what of sense stayed in the vagrant phosphorescence
save the deep impassable Trinity in the land of the Trinity,
uttering unsearchable bliss. The lords stirred
as the triple-toned light broke upon them
and they heard in their mode the primal canon of the Grail.
The roses of the world bloomed from Burma to Logres;
pure and secure from the lost tentacles of P'o-l'u,
the women of Burma walked with the women of Caerleon.

The Pope prayed: 'Thou hast harried hell, O Blessed,
and carried thence the least token of thyself.
Thou hast spoken a word of power in the midst of hell,
and well are thine Acts everywhere qualified with eternity.
That Thou only canst be, Thou only
everywhere art; let hell also confess thee,
bless thee, praise thee, and magnify thee for ever.'

The Pope passed to sing the Christmas Eucharist.
He invoked peace on the bodies and souls of the dead,
yoked fast to him and he to them,
co-inherent all in Adam and all in Christ.
The magical march of the dead by Rhine and Danube
and the tread of the necromancers who affirm only
vengeance and value of victory he lonely
received; he sheaved there the corn of his prayer.
The gnosis of separation in the Pope's soul
had become a promulgation of sacred union,
and he his function only; at the junction of communion
he offered his soul's health for the living corpses,
his guilt, his richness of repentance, wealth for woe.
This was the Pope's prayer; prayer is substance;

quick the crowd, the thick souls of the dead,
moved in the Pope's substance to the invoked Body,
the Body of the Eucharist, the Body of the total loss,
the unimaged loss; the Body salvaged the bodies
in the fair, sweet strength of the Pope's prayer.
The easement of exchange led into Christ's appeasement
under the heart-breaking manual acts of the Pope.
Before the host on the rivers, the automatized corpses
stopped, dropped, disintegrated to dust;
and the lust of the evil magicians hung in the air
helpless; consuls and lords within the Empire,
for all the darkening of the Empire and the loss of Logres
and the hiding of the High Prince, felt the Empire
revive in a live hope of the Sacred City.

Kneeling after the Eucharist, the Pope said,
for the riches of loss, *Magnificat*; prostrate, he prayed:
'Send not, send not, the rich empty away.'

PRINTED IN GREAT BRITAIN
AT THE UNIVERSITY PRESS, OXFORD
BY VIVIAN RIDLER
PRINTER TO THE UNIVERSITY